Community Music

Community Music

In Theory and In Practice

Lee Higgins

OXFORD
UNIVERSITY PRESS

Oxford University Press, Inc., publishes works that further
Oxford University's objective of excellence
in research, scholarship, and education.

Oxford   New York
Auckland   Cape Town   Dar es Salaam   Hong Kong   Karachi
Kuala Lumpur   Madrid   Melbourne   Mexico City   Nairobi
New Delhi   Shanghai   Taipei   Toronto

With offices in
Argentina   Austria   Brazil   Chile   Czech Republic   France   Greece
Guatemala   Hungary   Italy   Japan   Poland   Portugal   Singapore
South Korea   Switzerland   Thailand   Turkey   Ukraine   Vietnam

Published by Oxford University Press, Inc.
198 Madison Avenue, New York, New York 10016
www.oup.com

Oxford is a registered trademark of Oxford University Press

Library of Congress Cataloging-in-Publication Data

Higgins, Lee, 1964-
   Community music : in theory and in practice / Lee Higgins.
      p. cm.
   Includes bibliographical references and index.
   ISBN 978-0-19-977783-9 (hardcover : alk. paper)—ISBN 978-0-19-977784-6 (pbk. : alk. paper)
1. Community music—History and criticism. 2. Music—Social aspects. I. Title.
   ML3916.H56 2012
   780.71—dc23
                                                                                2011041759

Printed in the United States of America
on acid-free paper

Patricia Shehan Campbell

For your hospitality and friendship

ACKNOWLEDGMENTS

Like any journey, you rarely complete it on your own. This book is no exception. I want to acknowledge the music education faculty from Boston University, Massachusetts, and from the Westminster Choir College, Princeton, New Jersey, for their support and encouragement during this project. I would particularly like to thank Roger Mantie for his insightful critique during the latter stages of my writing.

I would like to thank Sarah Houghton for her work in the coordination of the illustrations that appear in chapter 6. Thanks to Aaron Brantly, Graciela Sandbank, Jane Bentley, Matt Smith, Joel Barbosa, Alexandra Balandina, Steve Dillon, Don DeVito, Andre de Quadros, Valentina Iadeluca, Pete Moser, Gillian Howell, Mary Kennedy, Jane Southcott, and Andrea Sangiorgio for sharing their projects and approaches to practice.

Thanks to Joel Barbosa, Aaron Brantly, Pat Campbell, Thomas Chalmers, Matthew Daniels, Steve Dillon, Maurice Gunning, Brock DeHaven, Gillian Howell, Pete Moser and Rachel Pantin for permission to use their photography.

Thanks also to the research collaborators who gave "voice" to chapters 4 and 10.

Suzanne Burton, Adam Cohen, and Erica Woods Tucker of OUP; my copy editor Mary Anne Shahidi; and to all the anonymous reviewers who helped propel the ideas forward during the development stages: thanks to all of you for your work and investment in this project.

I want to send my love to Michelle, Holly, Esme, and George, without whom things would have significantly less meaning.

Finally, to Patricia Shehan Campbell, for whom this book is dedicated: thanks again for your friendship, belief, and generosity.

CONTENTS

DETAILED CONTENTS

PHOTO LIST

1. Soundshifter
2. Yakama Musicians
3. Girl, Guitar, and Music Leader
4. Don DeVito and the Sidney Lanier Center
5. Ukrainian youth rock band
6. West end festival
7. What Cheer at HonkFest!
8. Sound It Out Music Project
9. Music Making in Fitzgerald Park
10. Gamalen Project
11. Buddy Beat
12. Jam2Jam
13. Defile Logo
14. Playing with sticks
15. Stages band
16. Adult drummers
17. Quiet moments of discovery
18. Filarmônica Ufberê
19. Westminster Bucket Drumming

Community Music

CHAPTER 1

Opening

Although the term *community music* has recently gained in popularity, I suspect that there is still confusion as to what it means. This is understandable because many have been resistant to defining it, believing that such a statement would not do justice to the endeavor of community music. The claim has long been that activities named community music are just too diverse, complex, multifaceted, and contextual to be captured in one universal statement of meaning.

Many supporters and advocates of community music have viewed the act of defining the term as a violation of the very project of community music, choosing instead to describe its dispositions and thus leaving the concept open to individual interpretation. I want community music, in the broadest sense, to influence what I have to say, but I also want to be specific about my particular use of the term. From the outset then, I suggest three broad perspectives of community music: (1) music of a community, (2) communal music making, and (3) an active intervention between a music leader or facilitator and participants.

It is with the third perspective of community music that I am chiefly concerned. In short, my focus is on the music-making interactions outside of "formal" music institutions, as well as on partnerships between the formal, nonformal, and the informal music education settings. The specificity of *my* definition will, I hope, make my argument focused and enable the reader to follow its unfolding. It may be that my determination of community music is a little different from your own. Although it is my intention to find connections with a broad understanding of community music, the sheer size and scope of an open concept makes the territory hard, if not impossible, to traverse successfully. You can, though, be sure that the ideas found in this book have been drawn from a wide understanding and experience of community music practice. In short, although my argument and perspective takes a particular form, it is embedded within the many ways of community music. To further clarify my position, I will elaborate my three "definitions" listed above.

Perspectives 1 and 2 describe music that is made by any community at any time. Both of them point toward an expression, through music, of a community's local identities, traditions, aspirations, and social interactions. From this perspective, "music in the community" and "communal music making" are ways of describing and understanding music in culture with a particular emphasis on the impact it has on those who participate. For instance, perspective 1 uses the term *community music* as a descriptor for a musical identity beholden to a particular group of people. Consider, for example, samba reggae, a style of music that reflects particular Afro-Brazilian communities of Salvador, Bahia, in Brazil, or Drum Damba, an annual New Year's festival celebrated by the Dagbamba people of Ghana, West Africa. Both of these instances could be described as the "music of the community."

Perspective 2, community music as "communal music making," is closely aligned to the first perspective but has its emphasis in a different place. Whereas perspective 1 identifies and labels a type of music, perspective 2 describes being part of, or exposed to, that music. Two examples are the Irish music session in Dolans Pub, Limerick, Ireland, or RiverSing, a public singing event on the banks of the Charles River, Boston, Massachusetts, United States. Both of these examples involve musicians and participants drawn from the communities where the music is being made. They are "communal music-making" events because they strive to bind people together through performance and participation. In the musical contexts described above, it has been my experience that musicians will mostly describe themselves as "musicians" rather than "community musicians." They will, however, have a very strong sense of place and a deep rootedness to the people they perform with and for.

The third perspective suggests that community music may be understood as an approach to active music making and musical knowing *outside* of formal teaching and learning situations. By *formal*, I mean music that is delivered by professionals in schools, colleges, and other statutory organizations through formalized curricula. From this third perspective, community music is an intentional intervention, involving skilled music leaders, who facilitate group music-making experiences in environments that do not have set curricula. Here, there is an emphasis on people, participation, context, equality of opportunity, and diversity. Musicians who work in this way seek to create relevant and accessible music-making experiences that integrate activities such as listening, improvising, musical invention, and performing. There are many musicians and music educators throughout the world that do work in this way. I have found that musicians will actively identify themselves as "community musicians" if they have had connection to local, national, and international organizations that support, advocate, and name *community music*. If there has been no organizational experience of this type, musicians and music educators will most often identify themselves in other ways: for example, music educator, music teacher, cultural development worker, musician in residence, and music outreach worker.

In order to consolidate the trajectory I intend to take, I am providing a list of distinctive traits that capture the significant principles that constitute the community music practitioners. These attributes will of course vary from musician to musician and offer "ideals" rather than guarantees.

Community musicians

- are committed to the idea that everybody has the right and ability to make, create, and enjoy their own music;
- seek to enable accessible music-making opportunities for members of the community;
- consciously encourage and develop active musical knowing and doing with participants;
- seek to foster confidence in participants' creativity;
- acknowledge both individual and group ownership of musics and are committed to celebrate the participants' work;
- work within flexible facilitation modes and are committed to multiple participant/facilitator relationships and processes;
- strive for excellence in both the processes and products of music making relative to individual goals of participants;
- recognize that participants' social and personal growths are as important as their musical growth;
- are committed to lifelong musical learning;
- work in such a way to show respect for the cultural property of a given locality and/or community;
- put emphasis on the variety and diversity of musics that reflect and enrich the cultural life of the community, the locality, and of the individual participants;
- are particularly aware of the need to include disenfranchised and disadvantaged individuals or groups;
- recognize the value and use of music to foster intercultural acceptance and understanding;
- participate in an ongoing commitment to accountability through regular, diverse, and relevant assessment and evaluation procedures.

Using the approach to music making that is named here *community music* (an active intervention between a music leader or facilitator and participants), musicians owe a great debt to the *attitudes* exerted by those active in *communal music making*. In other words, although I have made forceful distinctions in creating three "definitions," I do so in order to add focus to my discussions and provide a clear pathway for what follows. As a caveat to this, the borders I have created through this process are not meant to be rigid and fixed. There is, and always has been, a certain bleed between them, and I would encourage the reader to be mindful of this throughout.

PURPOSE

My purpose for writing this book is fourfold: first, to construct a historic perspective describing the development of community music from the late 1960s to the present day; second, to develop a theoretical framework supporting claims that community music is a distinctive field of musical discourse; third, to develop conceptual approaches through which community music practices can be described, analyzed, and understood; and fourth, to consider community music as an international field of inquiry and practice. The following four questions have helped guide my purpose:

1. What is community music?
2. What are the histories of community music, and what can we learn from them?
3. Where are the illustrations of practice?
4. Can a theoretical framework be developed that would help describe and promote understanding of community music practices?

Illustrations of practice pepper the text and have been chosen because they display key characteristics of community music as articulated by my guiding themes. Each illustration provides a different perspective of community music within the broader landscape of music and music education. It is through these examples that my "imaginative" conceptualization of community music is tested as an approach for analyzing and describing the practice.

The phrase *boundary-walkers* captures the spirit of this work. Kushner, Walker, and Tarr (2001), in their introduction to *Case Studies and Issues in Community Music*, explain: "Community musicians are boundary-walkers. Uncertain as to their own professional status they inhabit territories that lie between other professions" (p. 4). The implications of uncertainty, in this instance, are seen as negative. However, I wish to reload the phrase *boundary-walkers* with positive connotations. Boundary-walkers inhabit margins, borders, limitations, and edges. The parameters point toward the center of a structure but with a sense of going beyond. Their limits offer an affirmation of the transcending abilities of margins. So although one of my purposes is to stress the importance of community music and challenge the music makers, the music education profession, funding agencies, and governments to take notice, I am not suggesting that community musicians move toward a center and thus replace their boundary-walker status. In fact, I would go further and suggest that it is the margins that provide a position of strength for community musicians. The edges of the metaphoric circle afford community musicians the space to question and challenge dominant forms of practice. This is a vital position to protect if those who work in community music wish to remain connected to its history and continue to challenge through innovation and resistance.

SIGNIFICANCE

Community music is an expression of cultural democracy, and musicians who work within it are focused on the concerns of making and creating musical opportunities for a wide range of people from many cultural groups. Whether working in the United Kingdom, Australia, Scandinavia, or the United States, community musicians have been reliant on the erratic world of grant aid, project funding, and volunteering. This economic platform has created a landscape of professional insecurity and resulted in the majority of community musicians assuming a freelance employment status. Although fixed-term job contracts can periodically relieve this situation, the imperative to generate funding and employment has never been far away. Community music's initial venture also offered an active resistance toward institutionalized structures and was particularly evident in the critiques toward the various gatekeepers of cultural monies and the education establishment, both seen as custodians of "high" art and therefore continuing the oppression of working-class musical vernaculars. As a political position, this ensured a sharp critique toward the establishment but also reduced the chances of securing permanent resources. The community musician as boundary-walker therefore manifested instability in terms of resources, training, education, advocacy, and political influence. Due to the economic limitations of self-employment, community musicians needed to secure dependable income and jobs in order to pursue their objectives. Dictated by the capitalist imperative, practitioners developed a rich tapestry of practical projects but found it difficult to find time and space to critically reflect.

The inheritance of this "tradition" has meant a dearth of scholarly and academic writings pertaining to community music, community musicians, and the worlds that they inhabit. However, there are some interesting offerings in published reports and journal articles, book chapters, and practitioner handbooks.

Published reports that specifically explored community music practice include the following: Saville Kushner, Barbara Walker, and Jane Tarr's (2001) *Case Studies and Issues in Community Music*, Anthony Everitt's (1997) Gulbenkian report *Joining In*, Tim Joss's (1993) "A Short History of Community Music," my own *Community Music and New Technology: Conference Report and Reflections* (Higgins, 2000), the Sound Links report from Australia (Bartleet et al., 2009), and George Mckay and Ben Higham's (2011) *Community Music: History and Current Practice, Its Construction of "Community," Digital Turns and Future Soundings*. The quarterly journal *Sounding Board*, a publication of Sound Sense, the national development agency for participatory music making in the United Kingdom, provides a regular forum for discussion and debate.[1] Seminar proceedings collated by the Commission for Community Music Activity (CMA) and published by the International Society of Music Education (ISME) provide a record of projects, thoughts, and research dating back to the late 1980s (Drummond, 1991; Leglar, 1996; ISME, 2002; Coffman and Higgins, 2006; Coffman, 2008b, 2010).[2]

From a traditional scholarly perspective, articles included in the *International Journal of Community Music* provide the greatest density of writings specifically surrounding community music practice and theory.[3] Other important texts significant to the development of community music include Bruce Cole's (1999) article "Community Music and Higher Education: A Marriage of Convenience,"[4] Bengt Olsson and Kari Veblen's (2002) chapter "Community Music: Towards an International Overview," Bryan Burton's (2003) entry in the *Encyclopedia of Community*, Kari Veblen's (2005) "Community Music and Praxialism: Narratives and Reflection," Constantijn Koopman's (2007) article "Community Music as Music Education: On the Educational Potential of Community Music," a number of my own articles (Higgins, 2007a, 2007b, 2008), and *Community Music Today*, an edited book that features twenty projects from across the globe (Veblen et al., 2012).

Finally, there are a growing number of practitioner handbooks offering ideas and directions in the organization and running of community music workshops, such as *Community Music: A Handbook*, edited by Pete Moser and George McKay (2005). Other handbooks, such as Rod Paton's (2000) *Living Music*, John Stevens's *Search and Reflect* (1985, 2007), Philip Dadson and Don McGlashan's (1990) *The From Scratch Rhythm Workbook*, and Anne Cahill's (1998) *The Community Music Handbook: A Practical Guide to Developing Music Projects and Organisations*, vary in content and usefulness.

I think it is clear that there is a limited collection of writing on community music. This need not have been a problem. However, because of education providers' growing interest in community music, there has been a steady increase in demand for scholarly writing from both students and those guiding their learning. The limited research literature has been further amplified by a growing number of specifically tailored undergraduate and more particularly postgraduate courses and programs in the United Kingdom, United States, Ireland, Australia, and South Africa. As a scholarly endeavor, my aim is to address, at least in part, some of the areas that have had little exposition.

Three strategies of research provide the framework of my analysis of community music: (1) historical (re)construction of community music through documentation and autobiographical foreknowledge; (2) illustrations and exemplars of community music in action; and (3) a theoretical framework that supports community music's key characteristics expressed through the themes of hospitality, the creative workshop, friendship, and cultural democracy.

HISTORICAL (RE)CONSTRUCTION

In order to present a conceptualization of community music, it is important to outline a historical perspective. Tim Joss (1993), Anthony Everitt (1997) and George McKay (2005) have all sketched a history of community music in the

United Kingdom. Although useful and informative, I felt that none of their accounts were substantial enough for my purposes here. I have therefore utilized a wider range of documents: most noticeably *Sounding Board,* the work of the CMA, and personal contacts. This has enabled the articulation of a historical perspective that embraces a number of significant moments from around the world.

In support of the above documentation, I have employed autoethnographic memory, a form of critical recollection of my professional activity as well as a consciousness toward the traces of my past (Ellis and Bochner, 2000; Reed-Danahay, 2001; Spry, 2001; Jones, 2005; Chang, 2008; Davis and Ellis, 2008). To quote Andy Medhurst (1999), from his article "What Did I Get? Punk, Memory and Autobiography," it is "because I was there" (p. 219). This is a nod toward my own experience of growing through, and being at, some of the significant developments of community music over the last two decades. On this autobiographical note, I have worked in many sectors that currently employ community musicians, including: health and well-being, criminal justice, special education, primary, secondary and tertiary education, youth and community, and orchestral outreach. I have also run projects in the United Kingdom, Ireland, United States, New Zealand, Europe, Norway, and South Africa. Experiences such as these, plus my work with ISME have brought me into close contact with many community musicians, cultural workers and policy makers and have shaped my historical account.

ILLUSTRATIONS AND EXEMPLARS

Illustrations of community music practice are used throughout to either simply showcase the practice or to provide examples of the concepts in question. These instances of practical activity are crucial to the overall thrust of the book because community music's growth through "grassroots" music making cannot be abandoned for philosophical musings. It is important that the theoretical framework is just that: a scaffold that supports and aids theoretical construction, rather than saturating and drowning a practice that is vibrant and live. The illustrations of practice have been gathered in the following three ways: (1) ethnographic fieldwork, with its emphasis on participant observation and extensive periods on site; (2) case study research, utilizing methods of observation, interview, and documentation; (3) autoethnographic memory with support from historical documentation.

Examples of practice are sometimes brief, isolated cases that enable the reader to understand more clearly the many dimensions community music can take. These instances have been chosen because they represent both exemplars and diversity of practice. Sometimes the illustrations enable the theoretical language to be woven within examples of practice. The intention is that the reader accumulates an unfolding lexicon of ideas that are united with the practice. As such, community music practices can be discussed and examined using a "new" language that has been derived from the practice itself.

THEORETICAL FRAMEWORK

This book is not a philosophy of community music. It does not set out to investigate the nature, causes, and principles of community music reality, knowledge, or values, based on logical reasoning rather than empirical methods. The illustrations of practice, as discussed above, are paramount, serving to ground any theoretical ideas I might have through its approaches, methods, and models. However, I do present a theoretical framework through which one might describe and understand community music. Although the development of this theory has emerged from the practice of community music, its conceptual underpinning draws heavily upon continental philosophical positions, particularly those of Jacques Derrida, Emmanuel Levinas, Simon Critchley, and John Caputo.[5]

Schooled in the history of philosophy, Derrida, Levinas, Critchley, and Caputo, like many of their contemporaries, wrestle with, and respond to, a vast array of thinkers from ancient Greece to the present day. Critchley and Caputo metaphorically move in and between both Derrida and Levinas, critically responding to them both and providing a fulcrum between the two. It must be noted, however, that they have both developed personal philosophic statements that have also influenced the development of my ideas. It is well beyond the scope and necessity of a book dedicated to community music to attempt a thorough exploration of the vast oeuvre of four philosophers, but it does seem important, if not essential, to contextualize their work, and it seems appropriate to do so here rather than clog up the text further down the line. What follows is an overview, albeit brief and inadequate, of the key theoretical contributors Jacques Derrida, Emmanuel Levinas, Simon Critchley, and John Caputo.

Jacques Derrida, Algerian born and of Jewish decent, developed a reputation for his gesture of deconstruction, an activity that calls into question some of the basic ideas and beliefs that legitimize institutional forms of knowledge.[6] It is interesting to note that although Derrida's work is most frequently associated with the term *deconstruction*, it is a term with which he himself has never been satisfied, describing it as a problematic and difficult word (Derrida, 1991b). Broadly, Derrida follows Friedrich Nietzsche and Martin Heidegger in elaborating a critique of Western metaphysics, not just as a philosophical tradition but also as an operation within everyday thought and language. Derrida argues that particular philosophers have been able to impose their various systems of thought by ignoring and suppressing the destructive effects of language. This claim has given rise to much controversy, leading to accusations of the corruption of all intellectual values and of being a direct threat to Western philosophy.

Derrida, on the other hand, has seen deconstruction as a mode of responding affirmatively to Western philosophical traditions.[7]

Simplistically, deconstruction might be explained through three gestures: first, establish the stable field and note its "construction"; second, destabilize the field by inversion—"deconstruction"; third, reinstate the field with an awareness of the continuing possibility of destabilization—"reconstruction." Using previously articulated concepts and ideas as sites of dislocation, Derrida (1981b) foregrounds the incompleteness, blind spots, and fault lines always already at work in any given text, insisting that "[deconstruction] is not *neutral*. It *intervenes*" (p. 93). Derrida's (1997b) preoccupation with disjunction leads him to insist on heterogeneity, on "what prevents unity from closing upon itself, from being closed up" (p. 13). This has been an important idea in my analysis because community music sets out to encourage musical access through intervention and a resistance to closure.

As a response to structuralism, an academic fashion that flourished most widely from the 1950s through to the 1970s, poststructuralism had offered a critique of the human subject, historicism, meaning, and philosophy and supported the idea that "reality" is purely a discursive phenomenon, a product of codes, conventions, languages, and signifying systems. Derrida was a preeminent poststructural thinker (although Derrida probably would not align himself to such a term), and his (1997a) much-quoted saying "There is nothing outside of the text" helped propel poststructural ideas (p. 158).[8] However, as a discourse, deconstruction does not celebrate an infinity of "freeplay," nor does it hold a position that supports clear separations from the constraints of truth reference or valid demonstrative argument.[9] Deconstruction demonstrates and sustains the impulse of the enlightenment critique while subjecting the tradition to a radical reassessment of its grounding concepts and categories, a strategy I use when considering community music as a historical field of practice. Through a keen sense of the ethical, Derrida advocates a democracy that has yet to arrive while critiquing the barricades that stand in its way. While wary of deconstruction's resistance to the reduction of a concept, "Deconstruction is not a method or some tool that you apply to something from the outside. Deconstruction is something which happens and which happens inside" (Derrida, 1997b, p. 9), my theoretical ideas, which have flowed from community music practice, are therefore tied to active music making.

Emmanuel Levinas was born in Lithuania to a Jewish family but spent most of his adult life in France. His work has two discrete strands: phenomenology and religious texts. Although Levinas (1984) stated that both aspects of his work "may ultimately have a common source of inspiration," he nevertheless always made a clear distinction between them (p. 54). Building on the revolutionary implications of the phenomenological enterprise of Edmund Husserl and Martin Heidegger, Levinas sought to consider life as it is lived. Shaped by philosophical debates of his time and place, Levinas's "humanism" presents man as vulnerable and open to the suffering of others.

As a philosophic enterprise, and often in synergy with Derrida, Levinas's (1996) thought reprimands the Western philosophy tradition for its emphases of the "same" at the expense of the "other." This perspective is important for the ideas in this book because community music has an orientation toward the distinctive features of individuals and what each person might achieve rather than a universal method or approach. In a challenge to thinking that searches for foundations, certainty presence-to-self, and unity, Levinas suggests that the relentless pursuit for absolute truth has subsumed "difference" into the black hole of the same. In an effort to expose this, Levinas interrogates notions of "alterity"[10] and concludes that traditional accounts of ethics have been grounded in *egoism*: my relation to myself is the primary relation par excellence. Reflected in the identification that knowledge is control, Levinas suggests that ethics has been reduced to the sphere of the ego and thus become a grand project of totalization. Espousing a pluralistic program of thought, Levinas tries to coerce alterity back from the spell of monolithic thinking while advocating that our basic understanding of ourselves as human beings presupposes an ethical relation with other human beings. This is an enterprise that is synonymous with the questions that community musicians have asked, and continue to ask, from those who perpetuate the dominant culture.

As a response to the horrors of Nazi Germany, his immediate postwar writings demonstrate a determination to think through a nonmastering community (Levinas, 2001). From the claim that ethics is first philosophy, Levinas's work challenges Heideggerian phenomenology as self-centered: "I see others 'like me' in some respects and 'unlike me' in others, but both are ways of seeing are in terms of 'me'" (Treanor, 2006, p. 16). From this vantage point, otherness dominates through an assignment of meaning both in relation to who I am and the context I operate in: for instance, through the act of naming "my" students, "my" jazz band, "my" choir, and so on. Rather than eliminating otherness, through an act of naming it or analyzing it (in order to reduce it to a known quantity), Levinas seeks to preserve the otherness of the other and to respect the difference that distinguishes the other from the self. In the same way, community music seeks to celebrate difference both at the level of the individual and through our distinctive localities and contexts.[11] Finally, Levinas (1985) summed up his own philosophy as *Après vous Monsieur*, that is, "After you, sir!" (p. 89). Levinas's philosophy is a system of thought that is before an open door, a promise toward responsibility in which acts of hospitality and a welcoming to the other are described with the adjective "ethical."[12]

Simon Critchley (2010), an English philosopher based in New York, argues that philosophy commences in disappointment, either religious or political. Alongside Critchley, I also believe that there is an essential connection between biography and philosophy, a resistance toward a modernist perspective that understands objectivity and truth as being available separately from those who were investigating it. His first book, *The Ethics of Deconstruction: Derrida and Levinas*, became an acclaimed source on deconstruction and was one of the first to argue for an ethical dimension to deconstruction (Critchley, 1999). Critchley's reading of Derrida through Levinas is important here because I emphasize the one-to-one encounter between the music facilitator and the participant explored extensively in chapter 10.

John Caputo (1993), describes himself as a hybrid philosopher/theologian treating "sacred" texts as a poetics of the human condition, or as a "theo-poetics," a poetics of the event harbored in the name of God. Caputo's work attempts to persuade us that Derrida is a thinker to be reckoned within theological discourse. His book *The Prayers and Tears of Jacques Derrida* (1997) and the subsequent postmodernism and theology seminars, hosted at Villanova University,[13] sparked considerable interest in deconstruction within theology and religious studies. Pushing the notion of what Caputo (2006) calls "the weakness of God," a position that suggests that theology is best served by getting over its love affair with power and authority, he amplifies Derrida's notion of "*the* impossible," an important notion to my final claim in chapter 12 that community musicians are at heart "dreamers" who exercise a passion for *the* impossible.

OUTLINE OF CHAPTERS

The book is divided into two parts. Part I, "Inheritances and Pathways," presents three main themes: (1) a historic perspective through which to understand the emergence of an international field; (2) a consideration of what makes community music a distinctive enterprise; and (3) illustrations of practice from around the world. Part II, "Interventions and Counterpaths," utilizes the practice of community music to reveal philosophical strategies that enables an approach to analysis, discussion, and understanding.

Beginning with the question "What is community music, and what are the conditions that have enabled it to flourish?" chapter 2 describes the background through which community music can be known. Taking a wide view that embraces all three of the perspectives stated in the opening of this chapter, I initially discuss a range of possible histories I could have pursued but chose not to because of my specific line of argument and use of the term *community music*. In order to locate community music as an active intervention between a music leader or facilitator and participants, I rationalize why I settled for an examination of the community arts scene in the United Kingdom and community cultural development from the United States. As an initially Western enterprise, community arts grew from the development of new artistic expressions that offered a challenge to the dominant culture, cumulating in the counterrevolution of the 1960s and 1970s. Using this as a starting point for the growth and development of community music as an active intervention, I plot the ideology, context, and definitions that shaped the United Kingdom's community arts movement. This becomes the primary case study through which I present the wider development of community music as an approach to music making outside of "formal" music institutions. International manifestations of socially responsibly art are considered alongside this case, demonstrating that community arts as a movement was a product of its time, a cultural expression that emerged from cultural upheaval and professional community development practices initiated after World War II. As a direct response to those who polarized notions of art making into "high" and "low," "serious" and "vernacular" community arts is finally understood as a collaborative arts activity that seeks to articulate, engage, and address the needs, experiences, and aspirations of the participants and as such is defined by its method of work and aims, rather than by any art form itself. This leads into a discussion of community cultural development, a lens through which contemporary international practice can now be seen. This broadens the historic perspective to include developments particularly representative in the United States and Australia.

Using the United Kingdom as the site for exploration, chapter 3 makes a shift toward describing community music as a distinct musical practice that emerges as a substrand of the community arts and the community cultural development movement. In order to situate and untangle this complex history, I choose five themes that reflect significant milestones in the growth and development of community music: musicians in residence, music animateur, music collectives and punk rock, the formation of a national development agency, and definitions. As a form of activism located within the politics of the New Left, community music can be initially seen as a protest against the dominant culture's articulation of music's nature and purpose. Both chapters 2 and 3 serve to describe the cultural, economic, and political backgrounds that supported the reinstatement of community-based art and music as an important human endeavor. By explicating the United Kingdom's community arts and community music movement as reflective of these developments, I provide a foundation through which the full extent of the international community music scene can be explored.

Chapter 4 affirms both the roots and distinctive traits of community music through an extensive ethnographic account of one project. The Peterborough Community Samba Band provides a case study of community music through which significant traits of practice, identity, context, community, participation, and pedagogy can be examined. Through observation and interviews, participant testimonies are woven together as a multilayered patchwork, which reveals the characteristics and intentions of what constitutes a community music project.

As community musicians in the United Kingdom began to network, coordinate, and debate, the International Society of Music Education's (ISME) Commission for Community Music Activity (CMA) was in the process of being formed. The CMA serves to link and nurture a growing international network of practitioners, and chapter 5 considers the CMA as a prism through which one can view global expressions of community music practice. Through an examination of its work and the parallel growth of community music education, training, and professional preparation, I suggest that the development of the *International Journal of Community Music* heralds the emergence of a scholarly field.

To underline this proposition, chapter 6 offers both a portrait and celebration of community music projects worldwide. Fourteen projects from nine countries are presented as pithy illustrations describing background, intent, practice, and future challenges.

To invigorate future conversations, chapter 7 concludes part I by considering other fields of inquiry that intersect with the characteristics of community music. To begin, I acknowledge the importance of ISME within the growth of the international field of community music and point out that its institutional orientation has had significant effect in its growth. To this end, I initially reflect on two areas of school-music education that have had an impact in recent discussions: democracy and lifelong learning. Community music therapy, cultural diversity in music education, and applied ethnomusicology are then considered individually through a review of the literature and an exampling of the types of projects that most closely reflect the practice. Seeking to situate community music within the social, economic, political, and cultural world of participatory arts, the first seven chapters make a claim that community music can be known as a distinctive field of practice identified by its history and commitment to cultural democracy. As an active intervention, its distinctive attributes are exampled through illustrations of practice representative from projects from around the world.

The next four chapters work together to develop concepts and conceptualizations that connect practice with theory. This is best explained through the following four steps: (1) conducting a broad-based inquiry that considers the distinctive dispositions of community musicians through an examination of the name "community music"; (2) narrowing of the task to reveal the approaches of practice; (3) tightening of the focus through questions surrounding the one-to-one relationships between music facilitator and participant; and (4) folding back through the historic traces to resituate community music within its inheritances articulated in part I.

To begin part II, chapter 8 puts forward an explanation of the concept *community* as it relates to the larger concept of *community music*. After an etymologic analysis of the concept, I suggest that the *community* within *community music* is best understood as "hospitality," as initially articulated by Derrida. Using the proposition that hospitality encompasses the central characteristics of community music practice, I propose that community, conceived actively as "an act of hospitality," runs deeply through the practice of community music, and that an acute awareness of hospitality will expose the distinctiveness of community music within the field of music more generally.

Chapter 9 focuses on the strategies used by community musicians when working with participants. In other words, what are the processes that typify community music intervention? Approaches to music making are discussed through the concept of the creative workshop considered to be the most significant pedagogic practice employed by community musicians. Building upon the conceptual scaffolding of hospitality, outlined previously, the creative workshop is described as an *event*, a temporal and spatial domain that enables authentic musical doing. Following this, an approach to working with people, *facilitation*, is explored as the key intervention tactic used by community musicians in their efforts to enable music interactions. The *welcome*, the *gift*, and *safety without safety* are presented as concepts that become an approach for thinking and initiating creative music making. From this perspective, community music is articulated within a framework that promotes cultural diversity and equality of opportunity, key ideas that have shaped the definition of community music.

Although collaborative group music making is community music's most significant pedagogic characteristic, chapter 10, turns toward the individuals that make up groups of musical participants and asks, "How can we understand the relationship between community musicians and the participants they work with?" Using data drawn from interviews and observations from three countries, four themes emerge to guide the discussion: (1) individual participant, (2) working together, (3) trust, respect, and responsibility, and (4) friendship. As the chapter progresses, the relationship between the community music facilitator and the participant emerges as a friendship: an honest, committed, and respectful relationship of fluctuating inequality, a togetherness of one face toward another.

Chapter 11 returns to the inherencies of community music and asks, "How can community music's political force manifest itself within a claim that locates community music as an act of hospitality?" Through a resituation of the idea of "cultural democracy," the political imperative of community music inherited through a history that includes community arts and cultural community development, I explain that its impetus can be understood through (1) the "negotiation" between those that take part in community musicking and those who just might, and (2) a challenge to individuals, organizations, and institutions that have a hand in arbitrating funding for music, music teaching, and musical resources. The final section makes the claim that cultural democracy is made from the stuff of dreams and as an interstitial practice that questions the status quo, community music exerts both a passion and a faith for *the* impossible.

In my concluding chapter, "Another Opening," I summarize my main findings through the headings, history, practice, and theory, teasing out the significant contribution of this study. This chapter also explores future implications and directions for community music teaching and learning, employment, and practice. Avenues of thought unearthed but not fully explored constitute the section on implications and future directions, while the afterword recalls the journey beyond those moments emphasized in the opening. This becomes the final node before the book's lines of flight are set free.

PART ONE

Inheritances and Pathways

CHAPTER 2

Community Arts and Community Cultural Development

W hat is community music, and what are the conditions that have enabled it to flourish? This is an important question because the character of community music is formed in its past as well as the present and the future. Future community music contexts are therefore transformations of past community music contexts. Any attempt to situate a set of practices is at first daunting; there are many possible ways to account for what might be considered community music. As with all historical accounts, I have made a number of significant choices that shape my articulation: where to start, who to include, what resources to highlight, and so on. Through my use of the term *community music*, a musical practice that is an active intervention between a music leader or facilitator and participants, my basic thesis asserts that community music, as both a contemporary and an international practice, can be most lucidly grasped through an excavation of the British experience. Evidence for this assertion is twofold. First, I have had experience with the International Society of Music Education's (ISME) Commission of Community Music Activity (CMA). As a participant, a board member, and past chair, I have witnessed the influence that the U.K. and Irish delegates have had on the general shaping of the discussions both theoretically and practically. Second, those currently exploring community cultural development suggest that community arts hail from the sociopolitical activism of the United Kingdom (Adams and Goldbard 2001). Writing from an American perspective, Arlene Goldbard (2006) notes that during the 1960s through the mid-1980s, community arts work in Britain was particularly innovative and influential in adapting vernacular cultural forms to the purpose of democratic cultural development. Norwegian community music therapist Brynjulf Stige (2004) states, "To my knowledge, community music—as a semi-professional sociomusical tradition and movement—is rather unique to the British and Irish context" (p. 101). Christopher Fox (1999), an English composer, rather crudely suggests, "'Community music,' . . . or however else one chooses to name the phenomenon . . . is a great British invention" (p. 136), and American arts activist Beverly Naidus (2009) notes that socially engaged arts education has had a longer and more engaged tradition in England.

Before I begin my historical narrative, a perspective that reflects my overall purpose, I would like to acknowledge the vibrant discussions surrounding community music that took place in the United States during the 1920s and 1930s. During that time, there were a number of people vehemently advocating for something they called "community music." Decidedly different from the field I am predominantly exploring, this strain of community music promoted both a narrow vision of music and a restricted view of what equality of opportunity might mean and is the reason that it is not a significant feature in my account. The general approach advocated during that time is summed up by the following: "We refer to enterprises which affect an entire community, and which are open to those *qualified* [emphasis added] to participate in the activity program" (Eilert, 1940, p. 17). Indeed, community involvement in music was seen as a duty that unless carried out, "will not yield the finest [musical] fruit" (Normann, 1939, p. 33). The Brahms scholar and avid community music supporter John Lawrence Erb (1926) underlined this popular perspective by announcing that "the increasing importance of Community Music becomes apparent; not what is commonly understood by the term, but music which serves its new Master, the Community, in its various relations and activities" (p. 442). In the same text, "Music for a Better Community," Erb offers an early definition: "Community Music properly includes all forms and phases of music which serve the Community and grow out of it" (p. 442).

Foreshadowing the current concern in the United States for music and life-long learning, the Music Teacher National Association's 1931 appointment of a Committee on Community Music, or "socialized music" as it was also called, formally recognized public school's obligation to further the types of musical activities that were most likely to carry over into adult life (Norton, 1931; Dykema, 1934; Normann, 1939; Sault, 1944; Manor, 1945). The National Music Study, appointed by the Playground and Recreation Association of America, sought to increase the value of amateur music, describing it as "an unexplored area of human wealth" (Zanzig, 1930, 1932). Advocating the delights and necessity of this pastime, Augustus Zanzig (1930), the then director of the National Music Study, describes community music as a "social harmonizer or a physiological let-off," confirming that "there will always be an important place for the sort of general spontaneous singing that we usually mean by community music" (p. 29). Zanzig builds his argument in support of amateur music through a clear distinction between the committed amateur musician and those music-making occurrences that just happen: namely, community music.

Other manifestations of community music in the United States include an example of musical outreach provided by the Extension Division of the Louisiana State University, which assigned a music specialist to the local community for the purpose of organizing and directing musical groups (Funchess, 1939). This was part of a broader arts extension initiative throughout universities in the United States. Resonant in the approach to many community musicians working today, music projects under the Inter-American Music Day celebrations (part of National Music Week) worked within the Good Neighbor Policy to foster closer collaborations with peoples from different cultures (Hetrick, 1941). The National Music Study, the university extension programs, the Inter-American Good Neighbor Policy, and the Federal Music Project, which employed around 16,000 musicians and provided music classes in rural areas and urban neighborhoods, all contributed to an active "community" musical landscape.[1]

This time of American history appears to be a fertile period for the promotion and support of amateur music making. Individuals such as Max Kaplan (1958, 1956, 1954) dedicated themselves to community music service projects (Krikun, 2010). Although marginalized by the music education profession at the time, Kaplan remained an avid amateur musician, chaired the 1958 Music in American Life Commission for the Music Educators National Conference, and was pivotal in the development of the Greater Boston Youth Symphony Orchestra.[2] Other noticeable individuals include Emma Azalia Hackley, who dedicated much of her career to the promotion of music activities in black communities (Karpf, 2011, 1999), and John Langstaff, who was committed to using music to find pathways between schools and society (Bartolome and Campbell, 2009).

From an American perspective, community music as a strategy for human development, democracy, and change was eluded to from the 1920s until around the 1950s but lost visibility and momentum soon after. With the chill of the Cold War, the McCarthy period had profound effects on civil rights, critical thinking, progressive movements, and culture (Cockcroft, 1974; Naidus, 2009). The onslaught of McCarthyism gave way to the heralding of abstract expressionism as a symbol of America's belief in individual freedom and experimentation. The values of abstract expressionism, "art for art's sake," prompted by the work of artists such as Jackson Pollock, Willem De Kooning, Barnett Newman, and Mark Rothko, were dubbed by the "high" art world as the new American style and displaced funding support for community music activities. With a more sinister twist, Frances Saunders (2000) details how the CIA committed vast resources to a secret program of cultural propaganda in Western Europe and how American abstract expressionist painters were funded as part of this campaign for cultural imperialism via the Congress for Cultural Freedom, run by the CIA from 1950 to 1967. In these nervous times, the style, content, and approach of much of the art created through schemes such as the Federal Music Project, an offshoot of the New Deal and the Works Progress Administration, were seen as "hotbeds of Marxist ideology and Communist subversion" (Naidus, 2009, p. 19). Funding for these musical activities soon dried up, and the dominant capitalist culture of consumerism soon began to overshadow socially engaged participatory work.[3]

Alongside this American example, there are two other noticeable community music "histories" that I am aware of: the development of community music schools in Scandinavia (Bergethon, 1961; Olsson and Veblen, 2002) and the contextualization of Australian community music (Hawkins, 1993; Cahill, 1998; Bartleet et al., 2009; Harrison, 2010). Conscious that other historic narratives exist, I decided to drive *my* historic perspective through a U.K. perspective because there is compelling evidence to suggest that mining the British experience will provide the strongest context through which the current international field can be situated. My purpose in this chapter is not therefore to write or construct *the* history of community music, or to claim that the work in the United Kingdom is unique or any better than work anywhere else, but simply to provide a workable springboard that will enable an articulation of community music as an active intervention between a music leader or facilitator and participants. With this in mind, this chapter takes the following form: to present the growth and development of the community arts movement in the United Kingdom, a Western enterprise growing from the ferments of the counterculture in the late 1960s. I initially outline the growth of community arts as a resistance to institutionalized arts teaching and learning. This provides the context and framework from which the discrete discipline "community music" flows. Through a consideration of those who shaped it, community arts is understood as a collaborative arts activity that seeks to articulate, engage, and address the needs, experiences, and aspirations of the participants and as such is defined by its method of work and aims, rather than by any art form itself. This transitions into a discussion of community cultural development, a lens through which contemporary international community music practice can now be seen.

BACKGROUND

The Second World War had destroyed long-established working-class communities, consequently generating a new mobile employment trend as people moved from destroyed cities to new towns. These movements created new communities, and the comfort of "knowing your neighbor," was now not a given. In order to try to overcome problems caused by this mobility, a new profession of the community worker arose toward the end of the 1940s. Against the broader impetus of community development, these initiatives were concerned with social and economic development, the fostering and capacity of local cooperation, self-help, and the use of expertise and methods drawn from outside the local community.

The necessity of these initiatives also led to the development of community education in the 1950s. Already established in the working men's institutes in the nineteenth century, community education was not a new idea, but its requirements were new in postwar Britain. The practical purpose of community education now revolved around assisting individuals with new social and economic concerns, including the interpretation of government forms, private employment laws, benefits, rebates, and pensions, and aiding those who spoke English as a second language. Through new government legislation, civil rights issues such as voting rights, civil liberties, and social responsibilities also began to grow. Those working within this broad sphere of community education recognized the lack of cultural activities within their remit and began to add a cultural element to its practical purposes. Benefactors of the new cultural impetus began to ask for arts activities as part of the service, and consequential requests for arts activities rose throughout the 1950s and the decade to follow. As these developments collided with the cultural radicalism synonymous with the late 1960s, it is possible to locate the emergence of the community arts movement and, therefore, community music also.

Community arts was loosely based on the retrospective recognition of the similarities of aims and methods of its founders' work. According to Owen Kelly (1984), community arts began as one strand of activism among many during the late 1960s. As a watershed for cultural radicalism, the late 1960s became synonymous with those attempting to reform social conditions and to change "the human condition" or to escape from it (Chalmers, 1991). The latter came to be called the *counterculture* and had its values in antimaterialism and nonconformity, and its emphasis on personal growth. Throughout the world, many industrialized nations began to acclimatize to the changes brought about by the cultural and political shifts symptomatic of the 1960s (Teodori, 1969; Levy, 1994; Lyons, 1996; Hamilton, 1997; Marwick, 1998; Green, 1998; Giles and Oergel, 2003; De Groot, 2008). Britain was no exception, and it appeared to follow suit with an impression of material prosperity, cultural innovation, and youthful rebellion. As notions of community development became associated with shifts toward more radical approaches in education, this inevitably involved a turn from community education toward social action. Those working in community arts gained energy from this and other political and social stands, such as black consciousness, the feminist movement, the gay and lesbian movement, and student uprisings protesting against the Vietnam War and the H-bomb. In short, community arts can be seen as a product of the cultural upheaval that took place during the late 1960s.

After the long period of boom in Britain during the 1950s, a prosperous capitalist economy governed by the Conservative Party began to show frailty. For the first time since the general election of 1959, the Labour Party began to move ahead in the polls, and the Conservatives' close association with national greatness, the Church, the Queen, and the Empire, began to look outdated. In the general election of 1964, Harold Wilson's Labour Party narrowly defeated the Tory Party and took office for the following six years. Against the background of an emerging counter culture the newly elected Labour government had inherited what many conceived to be a relatively affluent society. This perceived prosperity had focused people's attention on private needs rather than social and public needs. With its new facilities and comforts, private ownership was becoming more important than traditional social activities such as the pub, the cinema, or the fish-and-chip shop. Housing patterns were changing and under-mining traditional neighborhood solidarities, while car ownership opened up new horizons for private leisure, far beyond the local community. For some, such as sociologist Anthony Crosland (1963, 1974), the affluences were no more than a social fiction. Real social needs had been neglected, while the middle classes were benefiting more from the welfare state than the working classes; to all intents and purposes, there was a growing shift toward politicizing the personal.

Growing ever more concerned with the promise of the liberal individual and his or her relation to society, those involved with community arts turned politi-cally toward socialism, in which the idea of community was central to the think-ing. Here, as a retort to capitalism community, artists found solace in social affirmations, including the Marxist position that saw the opposition between the individual and society as false. Alliance to Marxist thought appeared snug for a time, but in a changing world the Marxist perspective had fallen under theoretical and pragmatic strain. As a "development" of Marxist thinking, an alternative group calling themselves the New Left had formed. They believed that the forces of capitalism had triumphed over those of the traditional left (Long, 1969; Teodori, 1969; Friedman, 1972; Vickers, 1975; Isserman, 1987; Katsiaficas, 1987; Archer, 1989; Levy, 1994; Gann and Duignan, 1995; Mattson, 2002; Gosse, 2005).

Characterized by a sense of personal responsibility, perhaps most significantly seen in the Campaign for Nuclear Disarmament (CND), the New Left's social constituency predominantly included students, schoolteachers and academics, social workers, and those working within the arts. The New Left initiated socially active demonstrations that created pathways toward the ideology of those who began an artistic journey within community arts. Thus, culture had become the site for conflict rather than contentment, and community artists found resonance within this politic. With its emphasis on agency, culture, class-consciousness, and the centrality of the social experience, the New Left had reworked Marxism into an open, critical, and humanist project, a position reflected in the work of critical theorists working in the twentieth century (Althusser, 1972; Gramsci, 1988; Marcuse, 1991; Adorno, 2001). One of its significant features was the *New Left Review*, a journal founded in 1960 with an emphasis on political intervention. Redesigned and relaunched in 2000, it continues to feature major analyses of the global economy and anticapitalist resistance as well as discussions of world litera-ture and world cinema, cultural criticism, and the avant-garde.

GROWTH

In the early 1970s, the Association for Community Artists (ACA) was initiated. According to Malcolm Dickson (1995), the ACA was "the single most important element in forging the community arts movement" (p. 17). The ACA enabled practitioners to discuss issues surrounding policy and practice, arguing and campaigning for adequate funding on behalf of the movement. The initial discourse appears to have been somewhat stifled: Kelly (1984) noted practitioners' reluctance to engage in any serious theoretical debate, resulting in a lack of development of any political framework and practical strategy. Deficiency in consensus resonates throughout community arts documentation of this period.

The formation of the ACA was as a direct result of a seminar initiated by the Arts Council of Great Britain. With a collection of like-minded artists, the Arts Council set up a working party to ascertain whether it should fund community arts in any way. The report of the Community Arts Working Party, under the chairmanship of Professor Harold Baldry (1974), concluded that a community arts panel should be established and a dedicated officer should be appointed. Baldry's report had described community arts so broadly that it made opposition almost impossible, and thus the Arts Council could find no real reason not to release funds.[4] In establishing government funding, activities initiated by community artists were now being understood and identified in their own right. One of the common problems at this stage of its growth was an overreliance on limited funds. During this period, Kelly (1984) describes an epidemic of applications for money as "grant addiction" (p. 26). Preceding the initial Arts Council funding stream, community artists faced allegations that the practice had been led by whatever funding was currently available. This accusation was critical because community arts projects focused on providing communities with the tools to sustain their own cultural enterprises. Reliance on grant aid, which would inevitably carry strings or implications, distorted the work and was contrary to the ideas of sustained independence.

A question leveled at the practice of community arts probes the notion that funding agencies had dictated the development of practice. Dickson (1995) cites this as a common tension. The reluctance of community arts to engage in the development of a theoretical framework resulted in short-term scrambles to obtain money and resources. Writing in 1997, Mark Webster reflected on funding, concluding that community arts have not had a great deal of influence on the funding system and that "the possibility of supporting long-term sustained change is becoming more remote" (p. 70). Within a funding pragmatism, the community arts movement moved into almost total dependence on revenue funding from limited sources. Developmental work is reliant on adequate time, but it was in the funder's interest to organize revenue into short-term payouts. This is contrary to initial community arts projections that insisted that the work follow long-term commitment. One might suggest that it was the failure of practitioners to define their activities that generated the feeling of slavery to the funding bodies. Kelly (1984) affirms this position by describing community arts as "a movement of naive, but energetic, activism which, bereft of analysis, drifted into the arms of those groups it set out to oppose" (p. 97). The "addiction" to funding or the realities of any economic situation resulted in a complex web of idealism and pragmatism. Kelly is dogmatic when he notes that community arts were "ceasing to be a movement of activists and beginning to become a profession" (p. 31). This point is more generally articulated by saying that there was an apparent ease and speed with which the decade's cultural radicals were being absorbed into the establishment they so vociferously opposed (Gilbert and Seed, 1992). The initial conceptualization of community arts as social activism meant that professionalization was viewed by many in the movement as an antithesis of its actions (Brooks, 1988). In other words, working with educational institutes to produce "training" and/or "education" programs might create a situation of exclusivity: those "certified" to do the work and those who are not. This debate is still current for community musicians today and is a theme I will elaborate on in chapter 5.

The growth of the arts center as a focus for local activity helped stimulate arts projects and community recognition of the value of community arts activity (Lane, 1978; Nicholls, 1985; Bellekom, 1988). The first art centers opened in the 1940s, but growth did not significantly accelerate until the end of the 1960s. In 1984 the National Association of Arts Centres reported over 300 centers throughout the British Isles (Neumark, 1989). From the perspective of the arts center, arts activity gained an elevated status that sought to undermine previous notions that the arts were no more than a minority interest. The arts center became a forum for communication and proved paramount in its role in the development of the social and cultural life of the community. According to Victoria Neumark (1989), art centers employing artists with the right collection of skills "provided a jolt of aesthetic experience which can transform the recipients' experience of the Arts and enable them to grasp techniques and forms for their own expressive needs" (p. 11).

Between 1984 and 1988, the Calouste Gulbenkian Foundation set up an apprenticeship program to train would-be community artists. Rod Brooks (1988) considers the methods used by community artists, and notes that not only were good art skills required but also "the confidence and sensitivity to work in and with communities" (p. 3). Attributes described by Su Braden (1978) as a blend of "'community development' techniques and artistic skills" began to find a place in the later 1970s within the employment sector. Job titles such as *arts development worker* or *community arts development worker* became more common across the United Kingdom (p. 108). Arts workers of this type occupied a number of statuses, including animateur, institutional outreach worker, community arts officer, and freelance worker. François Matarasso's (1994) book *Use or Ornament? The Social Impact of Participation* represents an attempt to provide a comprehensive overview of the skills, issues, and context that underpin community arts work, while Ian Henry (1993) offers a detailed analysis of political ideologies for both cultural and leisure policy, citing the role that community arts had in stimulating political action across London. Henry stated that community arts could potentially help develop the "working-class consciousness" by placing community arts within the promotion of the "New Urban Left." As an example of this, when the Labour administration took control of London's County Hall in May 1981, there was a determination to initiate "cultural democracy" (a sharing of values among the many cultural groups) and "radicalism" within the Greater London Council (GLC). In short, the committee tried to redefine the whole notion of cultural politics, challenging the dominant concept of arts as "high culture" and increasing general participation across all art forms (Pitt, 1986).[5] Three main threads drove the community art initiative. First, there was a passion for creating new and liberating forms of expression. Second, there was a move, by mainly fine artists, out of the institutionalized galleries and onto the street. Third, there was an emergence of a new kind of political activist, one who believed that creativity was an essential tool in any kind of radical struggle.

ATTITUDES TO ART

Community arts found a way into the cultural critique of the New Left, positioning itself alongside attempts to upset "enlightened" categories of art and culture. Those working in community arts resonated with the avant-garde's attempt to destroy the polarity that had appeared to separate art making and culture. There was a call to erode the status of the individual artist as genius, instead committing to the idea of collaborations and the obliteration of the distinction between performer and the audience. Practitioners insisted on a redefinition of the role of the artist and attempted to demystify the artistic-doing and undermine discriminatory distinctions between "high" and "low" art. Alongside this political positioning, it was not long before community musicians were actively challenging the unquestionable state support for orchestras and opera companies at the expense of vernacular musics.

Braden (1978) suggests that those working within the community arts movement had gradually begun to understand the underlying forces that controlled culture and access to self-expression. There was also recognition that people in every type of community had been making art for as long as communities had been documented. It therefore became apparent that those who had been making art, rather than only the elite, privileged, and specially trained artists, were often marginalized peoples. In the early 1970s, community artists identified the work made by the working class, women, or the non-European as being on the fringe, suffering from an oppression of the dominant hegemony of contemporary capitalist society. In this way, community artists differed from artists in the community by acting as conscious facilitators or art leaders for people in communities to express themselves artistically.

Reminiscent of the challenge to dominant historical perspectives, articulated by a growing wave of poststructural and postmodern viewpoints, community artists sought to redress the balance between polarities such as "high" and "popular" art.[6] Community arts' earlier manifestations were therefore associated with the working class and working-class values, placing the work in opposition to the so-called elitist art worlds of classical theater, art galleries, and opera. In short, the general notion of community arts initiated a time of reevaluation. Braden (1978) underlines community arts commitment to the working-class ethic: "'High Art' is associated with the middle class and its values and Community Art is associated with the working class and its values" (p. 179). Braden's report was a comment on the Gulbenkian Foundation's artist-in-schools project, which was a program to encourage links between professional artists and schools. It was an attempt to break away from traditional concepts of the artist-in-residence in order to try new things in new environments. Central to Braden's conclusions was the polarity between artistic product and artistic process. Indeed, her research was principally concerned with the context for art, the generation of a "new" relationship between artist and the work in specific communities.

In practice, issues of participation were brought to the fore because, as Baldry notes, the attitude of the community artist differs from practitioners of the more established arts in that they are "chiefly concerned with a process rather than with a finished product" (Kelly, 1984, p. 16). Bruce Cole (1999) clarifies the community arts position by explaining that community artists rejected the traditional notion of the artist as "inspired" professional and "sought to develop a more participatory approach to art in which the *process*, the interaction between people, was given more emphasis than the *product*" (p. 141). Community arts projects served the interest of communities in which they were located, and in this way the work was *with* the people rather than *on* the people. The community arts enterprise reflected a broader emphasis throughout the performing and fine art world on the context of the artwork rather than just the content. For example, there was a growing emphasis on site-specific work (Kaye, 2000; Kwon, 2002), "happenings" instigated by performance artists such as Allan Kaprow (Hamilton, 1997), the work of Robert Whitman, Carolee Schneemann, and Claes Oldenburg (Kirby, 1965; Sandford, 1995), the Fluxus experimental art group created by George Maciunas (Nannucci, 1995; Hendricks and Danto, 2002), the international political and artistic movement Situationist International (Viénet, 1992; Ford, 2005), environmental art from artists such as Richard Long (1997) and Christo (1985), and the philosophical writings of Guy Debord (2009, 1995). It is interesting to note that Günter Berghaus (1995) suggests that there was a particularly close connection between happenings and music scenes in Britain. Writing in the mid-sixties, Al Hansen (1965) states, "I think of happenings as an art of our time. . . . Schooling is so old fashioned that individuals get crammed into a compartmentalized egg crate approach to life. The goals of this education aspire to high ideas, but the results are poor. The happening is about man's displacement from order" (p. 1). The sentiments of Hansen's theme are explored more extensively five years later by Ivan Illich's (1983) critical discourse on education in his radical book *Deschooling Society*.

From the community artist perspective, there was an initiative to put art and artist back into social contexts. With a trajectory that advocates the necessity for the artist to produce conditions in which artwork will have greater relevance, community art practitioners resonated with the ideas of Walter Benjamin (1992) by suggesting the destruction of an elitist "aura" in order to emancipate artist doing and generate greater opportunities for active participation. Using dicta that describe art as not merely socially desirable but socially necessary, community artists attempted to create spaces and opportunities that enabled active arts participation and reconciled both context and ideology. The primary concern for the community artist was the impact upon the community and the relationships the artist had with it. As agents of change, the community arts practitioners developed skills beyond just aesthetic considerations, encroaching across the psychological, social, and political divides. Formalistic understandings of art were rejected for a belief in arts capabilities to incite affirmation. Brooks (1988) describes community arts as "a living practice" and one "which happens with people in their daily lives" (p. 15), whereas Roger Hill (1993) stresses the importance of self-education through a breadth of arts activity that includes making clothes to one's personal design, magic/conjuring, photography, and gardening.

Figure 2.1 illustrates the polarity community artists of this time sought to overturn. On the left-hand side is a *modern* vision of art and art making. On the right-hand side is a *postmodern* position, advocating an emphasis on people, process, community, participation, and informal/nonformal education.[7]

Community artists have understood that aspects of their work cannot be easily replanted from one context to another; the meaning of the work is situated within the locality and through the development of community relationships

Modern	Postmodern
Artist	People
Purpose	Play
Form (closed)	Antiform (open)
Product	Process
Individual	Community
Aesthetic	Extra-aesthetic
Consumption	Participation
Cultural idealism	Cultural democracy
Authorship	Coauthorship
Formal education	Informal/nonformal education

Figure 2.1:
Comparison between modern and postmodern perspectives

seeks to draw upon local skills and local sites. Projects of this nature can be illustrated through the following examples: Red Ladder theater group,[8] the mural and print projects of Telford Community Arts (1984), the Theatre Workshop,[9] Needleworks,[10] the political theater of John McGrath's 7:84,[11] Beechdale Arts Forum,[12] Action Space Mobile,[13] Cardboard Citizens,[14] the celebratory performance of Welfare State International,[15] and the Lewisham Academy of Music.[16] Projects supported by the Rowntree Foundation, such as those explored within the video presentation *Culture Makes Community,* indicate the emphasis community artists give to context and meaning (Wolheim, 1998). Concentrating on how community cultural activities contribute to programs of regeneration, the six projects highlighted in this documentary video examines the empowering effect of arts on individuals in the light of local community. This document is a testament to partnerships with local councils, artists, and funding agency and demonstrates the potential of cultural content within regeneration programs. Projects like those initiated by the Rowntree Foundation have their roots within the work of the GLC outlined above.

CULTURAL DEMOCRACY

Through actions of intervention, "community artists" differed from "artists in the community" because they acted as conscious facilitators for people to express themselves through artistic means. This cultural and political ambition oscillated around the emergence of empowerment through participation and strongly resonated with Paulo Freire's (1985, 2002; Freire and Faundez, 1989) approach to libratory education. Those working as community artists shared a dislike of cultural hierarchies and believed in coauthorship of work and in the creative potential of all sections of the community. Community artists sought to promote leadership over authority, understanding that to make progress upon the pressing issues affecting society—such as poor arts education, environmental hazards, poverty, homophobia, and so on—one must demand not authority from on high but changes in attitudes, behavior, and values (Heifetz, 1994). For some practitioners, their belief went further, suggesting that community arts could provide a powerful medium for social and political change akin to other sorts of social and political groupings such as the underground press, organized squatting, free festivals, the yippies, and the Black Panthers. Webster (1997) suggests that "the Arts have the power to transform communities and to change the lives of people," stressing that this is "the single most important feature about community arts activity" (p. 69). Braden's (1978) report on the artist-in-residence programs funded by the Gulbenkian Foundation supports the view that practitioners were intent on influencing a cultural change that reevaluated the relationship between artists and society.

In order for community artists to achieve any sense of political democracy and change, it was widely considered that the instigation of cultural democracy was of utmost importance. Cultural democracy in its extreme form condemned the cultural heritage of Europe as bourgeois and stood against the Arts Council's attempts at the "democratization of culture." Herbert Marcuse (1991) noted that "such assimilation [democratization of culture] is historically premature; it establishes cultural equality while preserving domination" (p. 64). From the perspective of cultural democracy, the Arts Council, in its attempt to reach a wider audience by opening the doors of its galleries, theaters, concert halls, and opera houses, had failed to understand that the debate centered around active arts participation, not just arts consumerism. The Arts Council's concern over the notion of cultural democracy appeared to lie in its challenge to the concepts of "excellence" and "quality." Misunderstandings implied that "high" art was the custodian of standards, whereas through its argument for democracy, community arts somehow advocated a reduction in artistic standards. As far as community arts had any common philosophy, it did argue that a cultural democracy—in which creative arts opportunities, enjoyment, and celebration would be available to all—was paramount to its cause. In a project titled "Your Town, Your Life, Your Future," the Council of Europe commissioned twenty-one community arts projects throughout Europe. In its conclusions it states, "At least from the outset of the 1980s, the principle of cultural democracy has been accepted as a basic value of cultural policy. . . . It means acceptance at least in theory of the internationally held view on cultural policies that it is not enough to take cultural services from the centre to the periphery" (Eskola and Hammerton, 1983, p. 27).

As a concept, *cultural democracy* became a key phrase in European politics and an important guide for action (Duelund, 2007). During the 1976 Oslo Conference of the European ministers of cultural affairs, they issued a statement that read, "The theory of cultural democracy assumes that there is not only one culture, but many cultures in a society" (Graves, 2005, p. 11). One of the prime movers of this popular strategy was the French cultural entrepreneur August Girard (1972), who coined the term "cultural animation," or *animateur*, a phrase that became synonymous with a particular type of paid cultural worker. This echoed the work of Rachel Davis DuBois in the United States, who is seen as paramount in the development of the concept (Graves, 2005). Counter to the philosophy of the time that promoted ethnic assimilation, DuBois was among the few educators preaching that differences should be celebrated (Lambert, 1993). DuBois founded the Service Bureau for Education in Human Relations, later identified as the Service Bureau for Intercultural Education, and in 1941 she began the Intercultural Education Workshop in New York, later called the Workshop for Cultural Democracy. Those who worked under the cultural democracy banner attempted to offer "a system of support for cultures of our diverse communities that is respectful and celebratory, that gives voice to the many who have been historically excluded from the public domain, and that make no claim of superiority or special status" (Graves, 2005, p. 17).

By the beginning of the 1980s, the British government began mandating that organizations applying for money declare charitable status. This had the effort of neutralizing the community arts enterprise in terms of its community activism. Frustrated by the rules of charitable status, the ACA attempted to circumvent them by becoming a charity itself. Through this switch, it lost its campaigning capacity but gained the Shelton Trust, which in 1980 took forward the national debate after the ACA disbanded. The Shelton Trust (1986) aimed to continue those ideas outlined by the ACA: to create an "egalitarian and plural society, by the extension of democratic practice to all social relationships" (p. 64). With the backdrop of *Thatcherism*, an era defined by the economic and social policies pursued by Margaret Thatcher, British prime minister from 1979 to 1990, the Shelton Trust's rhetoric fought against the dominant culture's ideological stranglehold. The Shelton Trust's political stance was rooted in Marxism, overtly describing its concerns as the radicalization of the "Arts" against a background of "a dominant hierarchical culture that causes and sustains oppression in society" (p. 6). This manifesto sets out its objectives with clarity, introducing the politicized term *cultural democracy*. The manifesto states, "Cultural democracy offers an analysis of the cultural, political and economic systems that dominate in Britain. More importantly, it offers a tool for action" (p. 9).

Elaborating on the notion of cultural democracy, the manifesto notes that any genuine democracy must allow its people to create culture rather than having culture made for them. Kelly (1984) provides us with an analogy—"the compliant purchaser who has been taught that democracy is being allowed to choose between the different packets on the supermarket shelves, and that the choice of what should be put on the shelves in the first place is a job for experts" (p. 25). Braden (1978) connects cultural democracy to the broad aims articulated in the Universal Declaration of Human Rights, citing the "right to culture" (p. 14). The Council of Europe's response to its own directive implemented the creation of the "socio-cultural animateur," described by Braden as "part priest, part artist, who breathes life into a community" (p. 178). These types of employment opportunities flourished in the United Kingdom in the 1980s, emphasizing local cultural expression and making available the appropriate media of expression, such as visual arts, drama, dance, or music. With ideas grounded in socialism and a desire for new social contexts in which to practice, community artists believed in a new classless politics. Community artists recognized that there was a weakening of social structures and a growth of individualism coupled with an increase in consumerism. One of the key directives sought to enable communities to take control of their own lives, to resist dominant ideology, and to forge out the most appropriate path for its growth. Somewhat simplistically but with reference to street art as a popular medium that could address the inequality of those art forms that had become inaccessible for the majority, Kelly (1984) paints the image of community artists "giving it back to the people," a sort of Robin Hood character fighting against injustice and tyranny. Essentially, cultural democracy was a doctrine of empowerment, a polemical call for practical action and political intervention. As a touchstone, it is still an important idea for contemporary community music analysis, and I will revisit it in chapter 11.

With the concept of cultural democracy as a guide, community artists aligned themselves with an idea of art making that emphasizes group collaborations and the obliteration of the distinction between performer and the audience. In short, community arts challenged the status of the individual artist, actively eroding the dominant notion of artist as genius. It was not too long before community musicians were plowing this pathway, challenging the state support for orchestras and opera companies at the expense of vernacular music: "Community Arts is, if nothing else, about change, and about using the Arts to achieve change" (Webster, 1997, p. 69).

DEFINITIONS

The early work of the ACA created no manifestos or official proclamations. There was no conscious attempt to create a membership, just a fluctuating group of mainly young artists working in an unorthodox manner. Through meetings and discussions, the artists involved developed common ideological motives as noted above, leading to a general understanding as to the characteristics of the practice. The Baldry report (1974) had stated that although it was offered many definitions of community arts, it found none of them completely satisfactory. The report concluded that the search for definition is probably futile. Baldry summarized with the following: "*Community artists* are distinguishable not by the techniques they use . . . but by their attitude towards the place of their activities in the life of society" (Kelly, 1984, p. 16). Braden (1978) qualifies this statement, noting, "Community Arts is not a specific form of art, but a specific attitude to art" (p. 107). This is a powerful idea that forces us to consider our own attitudes toward art and art making.

The Shelton Trust's (1986) bimonthly magazine *Another Standard* described seven varieties of community arts and offered a five-point checklist of what constituted community arts practice.[17] Described as a manifesto that "identifies an emerging movement that proceeds from people's personal experiences and communal knowledge," *Another Standard* is powerful in its commitment to radical arts practice (back page). The checklist, which reflects a growing confidence in the aims of community arts and represents the formation of a working definition, reads as follows:

- Community arts is a way of working, not a particular art form.
- Community arts workers use the whole range of media from folklore to video, from fire shows to puppetry.

- Community arts does not aim to build up audience for traditional art forms like theater, although this may be a spin-off.
- Community arts encourages active participation by ordinary people rejecting the trend towards passive consumption in all other areas.
- Community arts aims at being closely relevant to the communities in which it happens, enabling people to express local feeling or experience. (Dickson, 1995, p. 22)[18]

Both Kelly (1984) and Brooks (1988) cite the policy paper written by the Greater London Arts Association (GLAA) as their terms of reference in defining community arts during the mid-1980s. GLAA's pivotal statement acted as a framework for the refinement of a community arts definition:

> Community Arts is … an Arts activity defined by its method of work and aims, rather than by its art form. It is an Arts practice in which artists and communities work in creative partnership in order to articulate, engage and address the needs, experience and aspirations of those communities, and which has as its final aim the creation of a culture of equality. (Brooks, 1988, p. 7)

GLAA's statement managed to embrace the key ideas of the time, emphasizing method, partnership, context, and equality. Although it appears that a working definition was in place, Kelly (1984) insists that community artists failed to reach any agreed definitions. This "failure" meant that community artists could no longer be certain that they shared each other's motivations and understandings. This echoed Braden's (1978) perception that community arts practitioners had no unified philosophy. It appears that the inability to affirm anything but the vaguest of aims became a major obstacle in the growth of community arts.

Issues of definition have continued to provoke discussion and argument. During the 1990s, the Community Development Foundation released its report, *Arts and Communities* (Brinson, 1992). Within the report, community arts were defined as a movement that aimed primarily to "stimulate involvement in the Arts among people in disadvantaged conditions" (p. 85). The definition stated, "It [community arts] sought to empower individuals and communities to participate more effectively in running their own lives" (p. 85). Among the debates surrounding the definition of community arts was an attempt to disentangle the term from *amateur arts*. The *Arts and Communities* report suggested that the simplest definition of amateur arts was "all Arts activity which is self-motivated and unpaid"[19] (Brinson, 1992, p. 88). Anthony Everitt (1997) was later to use these findings to affirm that community-orientated arts are arts with additional social purpose. These purposes included personal development and social cohesion; expressing or reinterpreting cultural, religious, or ethnic affiliations; articulating feelings about social issues or local problems; and stimulating or contributing to local action, democracy, and change. Webster (1997) uses three directives to untangle community arts from amateur arts and the commercial sector: (1) participation is promoted regardless of skill or "talent," (2) the work is undertaken by a group of people who have the same or collective identity, and (3) the work is developed primarily to provide opportunities for people who, through social or economic circumstances, have little opportunity to participate in the arts. In the context of local council arts policy, Webster finally offers five bullets to pinpoint community arts activity: empowerment, participation, access, quality, and partnership. To bring the discussion up to date, the next section takes a brief look at community cultural development.

COMMUNITY CULTURAL DEVELOPMENT

Predominantly used in the United States and Australia, the phrase *community cultural development* replaces the term *community arts* because *community arts* is often used to describe conventional arts activity that is based in a municipality, including the many amateur theaters, drama, dance, and music societies ubiquitously found throughout these countries (Adams and Goldbard, 2001). As a description for musical activities, *community music* is often used in this context also, a signifier for amateur music making, a recreational activity that does not necessarily have an emphasis on social transformation. In chapter 1, I took time to unthread differing perspectives of the term *community music* while loading my use of the term as an active intervention between music leaders and participants. In order to circumvent any such confusion, community artists emanating from the creativity and culture division of the Rockefeller Foundation in America have chosen not to employ the collective name *community arts*, although the term *community artists* is used to describe the individual practitioners. Housed under a general concern for participatory arts projects, *community cultural development* is preferred because "it encapsulates the salient characteristics of the work" (Goldbard, 2006, p. 21). Each word is unraveled in the following ways: *community* acknowledges the work's participatory nature, emphasizing collaborations between artist and other community members; *cultural* indicates a breadth of activity beyond just art and includes the elements of activism and community organization typically seen as part of non–arts social-change campaigns; and *development* suggests the dynamic nature of cultural action, with its ambition of conscientization and empowerment.[20]

Hatched from motivations similar to those in the development of community arts in the United Kingdom, community cultural development bears traces of nostalgia for a human-scale past and Romanticist images of societies prevalent before the onslaught of the Industrial Revolution. Following figures such as

William Morris (1962), some artists believed that they should have a more meaningful social role rather than the nineteenth-century conception of the artist as
a tortured genius set apart from society and those "ordinary" people who inhabit
it. With a history flowing from the Settlement House Movement (Ramsey and
Ramsey, 1933; Elrod, 2001), the Popular Front (Blaazer, 1992; Mullen, 1999),
progressive education (Arthur, 1993; Reese, 2001), and the New Deal (McKinzie,
1973; Berger, 1981; Saal, 2007), community cultural development has its
political roots in the civil rights movement and identity politics, and, like its
United Kingdom counterpart, fosters a healthy dislike of colonization. As a
touchstone, cultural democracy, "the major postwar innovation in international
cultural-policy thinking," has guided this socially engaged work (Goldbard,
2006, p. 127).

As a term, *community cultural development* describes the work of artist, orga-
nizers, and other community members collaborating to express identity, concerns, and aspirations through arts and communications media. Arlene Goldbard
(2006), a leader in the field, describes it as "a process that simultaneously builds
individual mastery and collective cultural capacity while contributing to positive
social change" (p. 20). Examples include projects such as ActALIVE (Arts for
Creative Transformation: Activism, Lifeline, Inspiration, Vision, Education),[21]
AMAL,[22] and Blossom Trust.[23] With chapters in Kenya, Nigeria, Gambia, and
Zimbabwe, ActALIVE is an arts coalition that uses the arts and media to address
HIV/AIDS and other human development challenges. AMAL, meaning "action"
in Urdu, is a youth-focused HIV/AIDS action group and is one of the most visible
advocates for prevention, treatment, and awareness in Pakistan. Its mission is to
empower and strengthen individuals, communities, and organizations through
advocacy, capacity building, and the provision of knowledge, skills, and services
toward the creation of a society that is gender-sensitive, supports young people,
and addresses the needs and threats associated with HIV and AIDS. In Tamil
Nadu, southern India, the Blossom Trust is a nongovernmental organization
(NGO) that focuses on women's rights, gender equality, and empowerment.
Utilizing community participation, the Edu-Clowns are a theater group connected to Blossom Trust. With painted red noses that symbolize their fury upon
seeing certain unacceptable situations and lifestyles in the community, they
campaign for child health and sexual education.

Other examples of community cultural development include the Albany Park
Theater Project (APTP) in Chicago, an ensemble-based theater company consisting of teens and young adults.[24] APTP's work is primarily based on telling the
real-life stories of immigrant and working-class Americans through original performance. Providing a forum for exploring issues important to the local community, APTP attempts to enhance the vitality of the neighborhoods and create a
place where youth recognize and pursue their ability to lead ambitious, engaged
lives. Beatz to da Streetz, Toronto's first nonprofit arts program, also aims to
empower and provide a safe supportive space for young people.[25] The program

seeks to leverage the powerful connection between young people and music in order to promote opportunities for creative expression and self-discovery. With an orientation toward long-term sustainable social change, the Beatz to da Streetz projects aim to build life skills and open access to professional mentorship, education, and income generation. Using a broader array of expressive opportunities, Carclew Youth Arts in South Australia provides an active youth arts arena designed specifically for the cultural needs of young Indigenous South Australians.[26] In an effort to advertise and showcase its activities, Carclew distributes the monthly e-based newsletter *Handprints*.

Building upon the work of Augusto Boal (2002, 2000), the Cardboard Citizens, a homeless people's professional theater company based in London, specializes in forum theater (an interactive form of theater that explores options for dealing with problems or issues).[27] The company seeks to impact and change the lives of those living on the street through performance arts. In a similar vein, Performing Life helps youth who are working and/or living on the streets of Cochabamba, Bolivia,[28] while in Guatemala, Iqui Balam, a company composed of mostly of ex-gang members, create theater and videos based on their personal experiences with violence. Like the Cardboard Citizens and Performing Life, their work attempts to support, inform, and encourage change.[29]

Although there are many different and diverse projects, the field has adopted seven key principles to guide the work:

- Active participation in cultural life is an essential goal of community cultural development.
- Diversity is a social asset, part of the cultural commonwealth, requiring protection and nourishment.
- All cultures are essentially equal and society should not promote any one as superior to others.
- Culture is an effective crucible for social transformation, one that can be less polarizing and create deeper connections than other social-change arenas.
- Cultural expression is a means of emancipation, not the primary end in itself; the process is as important as the product.
- Culture is a dynamic, protean whole, and there is no value in creating artificial boundaries within it.
- Artists have roles as agents of transformation that are more socially valuable than mainstream art world roles—and certainly equal in legitimacy. (Goldbard, 2006, p. 43)

As these examples demonstrate, the global field of community cultural development is a powerful, ground-level approach that seeks to give voice to those who are struggling for visibility. Socially engaged, the field is grounded in social critique while attempting to connect people to their feelings, their pasts, their dreams, and each other (Naidus, 2009). The practice is a response to the current social conditions, a direct comment on globalization, and a meaningful way to assist communities struggling to cope with the forces of modernization.

SUMMARY

Community music's history is located within the endeavors of the community artists of the 1970s. As a critique of Western capitalism, the community arts movement was part of the fabric of the counterculture prevalent throughout the Western industrialized nations during the late 1960s. Politically charged, community arts offered a resistance to the perceived "high" art domination of the ruling classes. Philosophically, community arts is indebted to classical Marxist theory and its variants, such as those proposed by Althusser, Adorno, Marcuse, and Gramsci. As a trace of community arts, community music followed ideological suit with the notion of redressing the balance between musicians/ nonmusicians, product/process, individual/community, formal music education/informal music education, and consumption/participation. With the concept of cultural democracy as a guiding light, community arts had extended the gamut of activity employed by the professional community workers. As Britain began to develop strategies to deal with the societal changes brought about by World War II, those working with communities in the late 1940s and 1950s were beginning to realize that a cultural element to their work was vital. Beneficiaries of this community service began to demand cultural stimuli, anticipating the work of the community artist a decade or so later. As an attitude to art making, the community arts movement profiled its socialist alliances by taking defiant and oppositional positions toward Arts Council policy. Frustratingly, community arts' attempt to rupture dominant ideology often left it being judged by those it opposed, particularly when it involved issues of funding.

Projects run under the umbrella term *community cultural development* embrace many of the key ideas housed within the United Kingdom's model of community arts. These include active participation in cultural life, cultural equality (democracy), diversity, social transformation (change), and cultural expression as a means of emancipation (process over product). Artist, writer, and teacher Suzi Gablik (1992) understands this process as the *reenchantment* of art, a kind of art that "speaks to the power of connectedness and establishes bonds, art that calls us into relationships" (p. 114). Analogous to arguments of supportive commentators in the United Kingdom, the community artist is understood as an agent of transformation and needs to be seen as equal in legitimacy to those who occupy the mainstream art world: "Once relationship is given greater priority, art embodies more aliveness and collaboration, a dimension excluded from the solitary, essentially logocentric discourses of modernity" (p. 106).[30] As a field of practice, community arts and community cultural development becomes the umbrella that cloaks specific disciplinary fields such as community dance, community video, community drama, applied drama, community theater, applied theater, and community music. Using the United Kingdom as the site for exploration, the next chapter makes a shift toward describing community music as a distinct musical practice that emerges as a substrand of the community arts and the community cultural development movement.

CHAPTER 3

The Growth of Community Music in the United Kingdom

Alongside community dance,[1] community video,[2] community drama,[3] and community theater,[4] community music in the United Kingdom emerges as a substrand of the community arts movement and has close connections to the unifying principles of the field of community cultural development. As a form of activism located within the politics of the New Left, community music can be initially seen as a protest against the dominant culture's articulation of music's nature and purpose. This position maintained that social engineering, through social and cultural hegemony, enabled the bourgeoisie to identify themselves with art music and thus confirmed their higher social status (Maróthy, 1974; Spruce, 2002). This type of cultural construction and social stratification gave rise to the perception of art music's inherent superiority over other musical vernaculars and was hence reflected and reinforced in the music curriculum.

Reflective of the Weberian (Weber, 1978) concept of traditional authority, notions of music as an autonomous, nonutilitarian construct propelled a music curriculum that advocated refined taste and sensibilities ensuring a pursuit toward the music "object" that was codified in a restriction of access and musical "ownership." Music performance had been relocated into the concert hall away from public and community venues. The concert hall became accessible only to those that could afford it and provided a powerful control mechanism for the ruling class. However, with the decline and collapse of the traditional European empires in the twentieth century, there was an emergence of indigenous musics and amateur music making (Russell, 1987; Stokes, 1994; Gerstin, 1998; Guy, 1999; Heath, 1994; Sugarman, 1999; Gonzalves, 2010). In some cases, these musics found their way onto the international scene, and in other instances, musics from past-colonized territories were reintroduced into the countries of origin through peoples returning to their homeland.

At the same time, the development and commercial exploitation of new music in Western culture, such as those associated with youth subculture since the

1960s, created other music phenomena (Hebdige, 1981; Gelder and Thorntone, 1997). The community music movement developed in the 1970s as a way to acknowledge and support a whole range of musical activities that reflected both music for youth subcultures and the musics of immigrant cultures. In order to situate and untangle this complex history, I have chosen five themes that reflect significant milestones in the growth and development of community music in the United Kingdom: (1) musicians-in-residence, (2) music animateur, (3) music collectives and punk rock, (4) the formation of a national development agency, and (5) definitions. It is not my intention to deny other traces important to the notion of community music, such as the brass band tradition,[5] choral societies,[6] folk clubs,[7] and amateur music making,[8] but I consider these expressions of musical doing marginal in terms of my overall thrust.

MUSICIANS-IN-RESIDENCE

The influence of the composer-teacher had been developing throughout the twentieth century, with Igor Stravinsky, Arnold Schoenberg, and Paul Hindemith, all of whom shared musical ideas and techniques with students. In England, Gustav Holst taught evening classes at Morley College for Working Men and Woman and later was appointed YMCA music organizer, Michael Tippett worked with amateur choirs, Benjamin Britten was a composer-in-residence, and the composer Peter Maxwell Davies provided a high-profile example of an approach to teaching music within an avant-garde frame during his residency at Cirencester in 1959 (Pitts, 2000; Laycock, 2005).[9] Some years later, Cornelius Cardew founded (with Howard Skempton and Michael Parsons) the Scratch Orchestra. Designed to get a wide variety of people playing music together, the Scratch Orchestra was described by Cardew (1974): "A large number of enthusiasts pooling their resources (not primarily material resources) and assembling for action (music-making, performance, edification)" (p. 11). "The Great Learning" was the Scratch Orchestra's most influential piece reflecting experiments in harmony and structure synonymous of the time. This particular piece is highlighted because it provided accessible music-making opportunities for people with no particular musical training. The compositional approach involving improvisation was reflected in many early community music projects such as the Tale of the Tiger, a project directed by Ben Higham (1994) in 1992. Placing jazz musicians alongside people with disabilities, this project has its focus firmly on the "Process" rather that the "product," and it provided an open space for shared music–making experiences in the way Cardew had envisaged.

Community music can also be traced to the experimental music vocabulary of composers and educators such as John Paynter (1982, 1992), Peter Ashton (Aston and Paynter, 1970), George Self (1976), and R. Murray Schafer (1975, 1976, 1992). All of these composer/educators contributed to the development of "new" classroom practices and the musician-in-residence programs popular throughout the 1970s and 1980s. Both Bruce Cole (1999) and Christopher Fox (1999) agree that community music's beginnings stem from the experimental music education ideas of the 1960s. During this time, there were changes in the approach to classroom teaching; significantly these included an emphasis on creative group work. R. Murray Schafer (1975) for example, invites participants to take risks and to approach music making with a spirit of adventure. He encourages music educators to "teach on the edge of peril," to remember that "failures are more important than successes," and to be mindful that "there are no more teachers. There is just a community of learners" (pp. 132–133). In short, the likes of Paynter, Ashton, Self, and Schafer had a desire to transform the classroom into a workshop space. As a space for experimentation, the workshop provided an environment more conducive for young people to explore music and music making, instigating shifts that were significant through the adoption of creative group work. As approaches to music education began to emphasize creativity and self-expression, the teacher's role began to change from a possessor of predetermined knowledge to somebody who facilitated creative exploration. This radical approach to teaching placed emphasis on creativity, expression, spontaneity, and cooperation—attributes synonymous to what I think of as community music.

From the current trends in music education during the 1960s and the early 1970s, the increased attention given to popular and world music forms and styles were also significant in terms of the development of community music (Falck, Rice, and Kolinski, 1982; Vulliamy and Lee, 1982; May, 1983; Titon, 1984). Anthony Everitt (1997) notes a parallel between the birth of community arts and the growth of rock and pop, citing its key instigators as hailing from the working classes. There is also the growing economic strength of young people brought about by increased job opportunities and increasing earning potential, new forms of music making that challenged conventional relationships between active performing and passive audiences, and the onset of affordable instruments, namely guitars and drums, that provided a wider base through which to encourage an atmosphere of music participation. Projects such as those run by Core Arts,[10] for people recovering from, or suffering with, mental health problems (Peggie, 1998), the band project in Moorland prison (Spafford, 1997), and those recording projects that blurred the boundaries between community music and the music industry, such as the "Readipop" project (Lombos, 1998), all serve to reinforce this. One professional band, Asian Dub Foundation, was so convinced about the benefits these types of projects can have on youth that they set up their own music education organization (they also named their 2000 recording "Community Music").[11]

While music education was incorporating techniques of the prevailing avant-garde, a number of people working in ethnomusicology (another significant intersection for community music that will be explored in chapter 7) turned toward *cultural anthropology* and began emphasizing the inseparable relationship between music and culture (Merriam, 1964). Developing the notion that music is in fact a cultural phenomenon, John Blacking's classic work *How Musical Is Man?* (1973) influenced many community musicians working in the United Kingdom. Blacking's conviction that "music cannot be transmitted or have meaning without associations between people" (p. vi) and that no musical style has its own terms—"Its terms are the terms of its society and culture, and the bodies of the human beings who listen to it, create and perform it"[12] (p. 25)—was deeply influential on Christopher Small, a seminal figure for those working in community music during the 1980s.

First published in 1977, Christopher Small's *Music, Society, Education* (1996) provides a theoretical base that helped advocates of community music to argue for alternative orientations in music making and music education. Small's text cracks open aspects of music as a social force, analyzing the "ritual" of concertgoing and traditional notions of music and music education. Small's emphasizes the importance of the art process rather than "the relative unimportance of the art-object" (p. 4). Through discussions about music making in other cultures, Small (1998) stresses the social imperatives, later stating, "Music is not a thing at all but an activity, something that people do," and further comments that "to take part in a music act is of central importance to our very humanness" (pp. 2–8). Early community music practices certainly resonated with Small's celebration of the art process rather than the art object. This is evident in projects such as the Tale of the Tiger, but also in the work of Core Arts, the band project in Moorland prison, and even projects that had a product-oriented outcome, such as Generate (see figure 3.1) and the Underdogs (figure 3.3). *Music, Society, Education* projected a communal activity of "musicking," bringing together a pluralist vision of music making with a critique of formal music education. Small (1996) understood that some musicians were attempting to "restore lost communality" in Western music, aiming for a restoration of the creative process over that glossy finished product (p. 152). Cole (1999), who had started the first master's degree in community music at the University of York, echoed Small's attack upon Western European concertgoing and the loss of participation to consumerism: "The effect of groupwork in music education was profound, opening a new world of artistic communality which many commentators felt to have been missing in European culture" (p. 142).

Stemming from the shifts in music education and ethnomusicology, the introduction of the musician and composer-in-residency programs became fashionable within both primary and secondary level education (K–12). Recognizing needs within music education, these programs served as an addition to the new wave of creative group work pioneered by the likes of Paynter. David Cain, a jazz and medieval music specialist with seven years experience in BBC Radiophonic Workshop, worked in the Cleator Moor area of Cumbria, United Kingdom, between 1973 and 1975. Cain's experience provides an example of these early music residencies (Braden, 1978; Joss, 1993). Interviews with Cain reveal the

Generate

An intergenerational songwriting project initiated by singer-songwriter Sally Goldsmith and writer–visual artist Jan Flamank, Generate provided opportunities for six groups of children and older people from Sheffield to write, perform, and record new songs. Using oral testimony, creative writing, and music games, each group created new compositions drawn from their life histories and their future hopes. For example, eight elders aged between 80 and 90 met up with ten 9-year-olds to create a song about working lives and working together. Unlike a lot of intergenerational work, the sessions did not always take place in residential homes: their working environment included the outside. For example, a group of ten 6-year-olds joined heath walkers and the Ranger Service in a local park. During their time together, they created a new song, "A Walk in the Park." In order to commemorate and celebrate the achievements, they recorded a CD that featured a couple of songs from each group. Goldsmith notes that these types of interactions can break down prejudice about age and promote tolerance and understanding while learning about younger and older peoples' differences and common experiences (Deane, 2002).

Figure 3.1:
Generate: An intergenerational songwriting project

lack of clarity in the construction of the early residencies, highlighting confusion between musician, school, and funding agencies. Expectations of partnerships within community arts initially failed to realize that attempts to bridge gaps between professional and amateur music making required more than just good musicianship. The implications for the education, training, and professional development of community musician will be addressed in chapter 5, but for now it suffices to say that the musical presence of Cain within a specified geographic area typified the nature of these initiatives, setting a precedence that was to influence the music animateur posts of the mid-1980s.

MUSIC ANIMATEUR

Described by Joss (1993) as a "key year" for the development of community music, the year 1984 witnessed several influential happenings. First, the first orchestral education manager was appointed to the London Sinfonietta. This appointment initiated the first full-scale community residency by a British orchestra. Second, the seventh International Society of Music Education's (ISME) commission, the Commission for Community Music Activity (CMA), was created. Third, the Music Education Working Party (MEWP), organized and managed by the Arts Council of Great Britain, was created. As a significant policy decision, the MEWP's mission was to forge a connection between the worlds of education, community development, and music.

The development of these projects and commissions helped generate a new breed of music professionals and opened a significant space through which to actively enable and support music participation beyond the school classroom walls. The MEWP's recommendations were a turning point in the growth of community music because they led to the creation of a specific job type, the music animateur. The word *animateur* derives from the French *animation socio-culturelle*, and although it was consciously chosen to reflect the "animation of people," for many practitioners the term was problematic. Common misconceptions often led to mistakes of identity, including music "amateur" and a belief that the musician worked with "animation."[13] What these employment opportunities did, however, was establish a prominence in local communities during the mid-1980s, encouraging active musical doing in a variety of contexts. The animateur posts were most often attached to art centers or educational institutions, or they were designated as particular positions such as music outreach or music development workers for orchestras or opera companies (see figure 3.2). The locations of these posts were often the results of initiatives of individual practice and partnerships with arts organizations and local authorities.

In practice, the music animateur demanded a flexible approach to music making. David Price suggests the analogy of a Swiss army knife to describe the array of skills needed to fulfill this type of job (Cole, 1999, p. 143). Joss (1993) thought of the music animateur as "a new kind of [music] professional" (p. 6). He pinpoints the combination of musical, facilitatory, administrative, and communication skills as keys to the knowledge domains needed to execute the practice. Musically, many community musicians had adopted what George McKay (2005) calls "the spirit of improvisation," a phrase that affirms community music's link to the free jazz styles developed at the time of the 1960s counterculture (p. 62). Prominent in establishing wider participation through improvised music making was John Stevens, a founding member of Community Music Ltd. that described itself as a comprehensive music resource offering a wide range of music services to the community as a whole, and particularly those disadvantaged groups that would not normally get the chance to receive professional musical guidance. Formally known as the National Jazz Centre Outreach Team, their base was in Islington, London, and was managed by Dave O'Donnell.[14] According to Stevens, improvisation is the basis of learning to play a musical instrument. Although Stevens understands the usual routes of formal study, he pinpoints the limits of the one-to-one approach and advocates group workshops. Described as the "the first musician to run an improvising class," Stevens's developing pedagogy is

In Search of Angels

 In Search of Angels was a commissioned community opera produced by Glyndebourne Education in March 1995. It aimed to take people on a journey, to experience
something that was enriching, and life changing, because such events can "stay in
your memory, and those memories are the things that you can actually build on for
your everyday life" (Deane, 1995, p. 14). Established in 1986, the education wing of
Glyndebourne delivers work under three headings: (1) Youth and Community, which
includes youth opera, performances for schools, work-related learning, and opera
experience workshops; (2) Talks and Events, including study events and preperfor-
mance talks during the festival and tour; and (3) New Work, including working with a
composer-in-residence on a commissioned opera on all scales for young people and
the community. Building from their first community opera involving over 300 people
on Hastings Pier and the second *Dream Dragons* in Ashgate in 1993, Jonathan
Dove (composer) and Alistair Campbell (writer) created a "community opera
mega-project" that featured between 500 and 1000 participants. Using local
knowledge to source existing arts group and potential participants, the project began
with "taster" workshops to get various schools involved exploring local stories from
which the narrative and libretto followed.

 Although the final performance was quite spectacular, with action in the
cathedral, causeway, guildhall, and shopping center, there was a feeling amongst
some that the project had been "produced" on the people of Peterborough rather
than being created alongside them. This was evidenced by a lack of participation
from the local opera group, the large Italian and Asian populations, and those
involved in the youth rock music scene.

Figure 3.2:
In Search of Angels: A community opera

outlined through his conversation with Derek Bailey (1993), another pioneer in
free jazz (pp. 118–123). Stevens's approach to improvised music making is
presented in *Search and Reflect* (1985), a music workshop handbook that had a
tremendous influence on music animateurs during the 1980s and early 1990s.[15]
It is interesting to note that Christopher Small writes the foreword to Stevens's
book and begins by asking a question that affirms the position of community
musicians at that time:

> What is it that makes a musician important? Is it in the creation of compositions for
> performance in concert halls and opera houses for the delectation of those who like,
> and can afford, to frequent such places? Is it in holding halls full of such people
> enthralled with performances of past masterpieces? Or is it in using his or her gifts,

---

The Underdogs

Founded in 1996 by Cardiff-born Darren Ford, also known as 4Dee, the Underdogs, a voluntary youth music group, worked with young people on St Mellons housing estate, teaching them how to rap and create hip-hop music as a creative outlet. In the summer of 2001, Ford and six other young musicians and DJs traveled to Ghana to visit a traditional music organization that works with disadvantaged youngsters. Steve Garrett organized the trip through his Welsh-based company Cultural Concerns. As an organization that interacts with music and arts projects from around the world, Cultural Concerns focuses its energies on culture and the arts as a means of empowering individuals and communities. Hosted in Ghana by Africa Bezalel, an organization that promotes traditional Ghanaian cultural practices such as producing handcrafted drums and percussion instruments, the young people from Wales were exposed to some of the realties, life, and culture in West Africa. According to Garrett, the collaboration proved to be "a great bridge builder which created instant friendship between people from different sides of the world" (Garrett, 2001). As well as attending drumming and dance workshops on the beach, the group's members were able to spend a day in a local recording studio recording music alongside their newfound friends. The final recording incorporated elements of both musical cultures. On their return to Cardiff, a series of workshops took place in community venues around the locality. Songs and music inspired by their Ghanaian adventure were incorporated into visual projections, and the group engaged in a question-and-answer session to educate other young people from Cardiff about life in West Africa and the experience of collaboration.

Figure 3.3:
The Underdogs: A voluntary youth music group

skills and experiences to awaken and to guide the dormant musicality of those whose music has been taken from them? (p. iv).

Participation in active musical doing grew alongside the music animateur network throughout the 1980s and early 1990s. Through this process of growth and development, there were shifts from a generic community music worker to a worker with a remit that specifically reflected an aspect of the communities in which the work took place: for example, both the Jazz Animateur in the town of Wigan and the Gamelan Animateur in the county of Lincolnshire reflected a commitment to particular types of music and music making. Toward the beginning of the 1990s, inadequate administrative support and a squeeze on local authority funding saw a decline in the animateur posts.

MUSIC COLLECTIVES AND PUNK ROCK

Punk rock, best characterized as part youth rebellion and part artistic statement, serves as another key site through which to consider the development of community music. With the social and economic problems of the 1970s, Britain had inadvertently provided a catalyst and timing for the development of a punk subculture. Against a background of young people's frustration concerning Britain's social and economic problems and as a reaction against the era's rock superstars, punk aligned itself with the Anti-Nazi League and with Rock against Racism. Like those working in community arts and consequently community music, punk rock musicians emphasized class politics, creating a potent fusion between music and political statements (Savage, 1991; Sabin, 1999). Jacques Attali's (1985) thesis on the political economy of music describes sound (noise) and music as instruments of sociopolitical power, "a tool for marking territorial boundaries" (p. 6). Many punk and community musicians understood that music was inscribed within the panoply of power; its primary function was not to be sought in aesthetics, but in the effectiveness of social participation. As Wayne Bowman (1998) notes, music's unrivaled capacities for affecting separation and integration makes it an ideal vehicle for the articulation, identification, reinforcement, and subversion of social structures.

For many, the punk *Zeitgeist* created an atmosphere of dread and antisocial behavior, but for (mainly) young people, the punk scene created an environment of participation. The visible potency of participatory music making of this period began to galvanize those working in community music, and attitudes resonated with what Attali (1985) describes as "the creation or consolidation of a community, of totality. It is what links a power center to its subjects" (p. 6). Both punk and community musicians rebelled against the focus on consumerism perpetrated by the self-styled "music industry." The business world of the music industry had generated a vacuum that had polarized participation and product. Small (1996) had commented on the notion of the "experts" as dictators of the vogue, suggesting that experts "tell us which of the products of the composing or performing experts we should be listening to" (p. 90). As the result of an onslaught of the capitalist music industry and the loss of creative opportunities, the music cooperative or music collectives grew throughout towns and cities during the 1970s and early 1980s. Punk rockers disregarded the sophistication and virtuosity of many rock bands, such as Genesis, Yes, and Led Zeppelin, replacing notions of virtuosity and staging with performances of raw energy and passion. Dispelling the feeling of musical elitism created by iconic worship and unattainable technique, punk musicians explored, celebrated, and affirmed the identity of those who participated. The initial punk performances were not bound in traditional musical expectations. Performances were stripped back, fudging the barriers between performer and audience, thus propelling them toward an ethos that might be described as postmodern. Mastering instrumental technique was not a prerequisite to performing. The act of participation was the barometer by which to evaluate an event.

The punk embodiment of participation evolved a "have-a-go" attitude that promoted the message that anyone could take part in music making. *Sniffin' Glue*,[16] a punk fanzine, published three chords with a rallying participatory cry: "This is a chord. This is another. This is a third. Now form a band." In resonance with community musicians working during this time, those involved in the punk scene took an oppositional stance to the dominant culture and challenged traditional views of professionalism, ensemble, and audience. As chief instigators in the creation of music cooperatives, both punk and community musicians were brought together in a short-lived ideological allegiance. Music cooperatives encouraged a communal spirit that often resulted in musicians pooling money. Consequently, bands were sharing larger and better equipped rehearsal spaces with increased resources, such as PA systems and recording facilities. Through these endeavors, the music collectives recorded compilation albums, showcasing local acts and offering opportunities for exposure beyond the rehearsal garage. The Greater London Council (GLC) had been of great importance to the development and support of the participatory arts in general; its abolition in 1986 led to the demise of many of the capital's music cooperatives. By this time, the punk scene had faded, but it left an indelible mark on many aspects of British cultural life. Contemporary assessments of punk overlook its impact on those radical musicians who turn toward the broader scope of music education under the banner of community music.

THE FORMATION OF A NATIONAL DEVELOPMENT AGENCY

The momentum of the musician-in-residence programs, the music animateur networks, and the music collectives culminated in 1989 with Making Connections, Britain's first nationally focused community music event. Held over the weekend of April 15–16, 1989, at the Abraham Moss Centre in North Manchester, it was organized by the regional arts council, North West Arts. It attracted 130 delegates from a wide range of backgrounds, including music animateurs, orchestra and opera outreach workers, community artists, and local arts officers. The event sought to boost the national profile of community music, celebrate and share the variety and diversity of the practice, and explore and discuss some of the emerging difficulties inherent in the practice of community music at this time. Echoing issues previously highlighted at the first national community arts seminar (as reported by Harold Baldry), community musicians across the country discussed definitions, values, and key principles. One of the most important aspects of this meeting was the suggestion that a national association representing community music activity would be advantageous to those who were currently involved in its practice. The organization that was generated from this idea, eventually named Sound Sense, proceeded to hold its inaugural meeting in December that same year (Deane, 1999). Sound Sense's emphasis was on representing the interests of people working in community music, describing itself as the national community music association.

One of the key issues for those working as community musicians was their identity and professional mission. To help address these concerns, those who attended Making Connections committed themselves to seven basic principles:

- By valuing everyone's participation, community music asserts music making as a human right.
- Music can be an integral part of social life but is under pressure to occupy a separate enclosed world.
- Community music emphasizes participation, planning, organizing, and composing, as well as singing and playing.
- Community music creates opportunities for skill exchange and as a consequence values group activities.
- Community music embraces and respects a diverse world of musical styles and contexts.
- In community music, the professional worker is a resource offering skills, ideas, and support.
- Community music needs a new kind of professional, and so training is vital. (Drummond, 1991)

The introduction of Sound Sense and *Sounding Board*, the quarterly published journal (or bulletin, as it was originally called), established a mechanism for ongoing networking and dialogue among those interested in community music work. Consolidating its national status with a second conference in 1991, "Community Music—The Official Version?" the members of Sound Sense moved toward establishing an agenda for community music. This second national event took place in the northeast city of Middlesborough in November 1991, and those attending attempted to address issues on three distinct fronts: the creation of radical alternatives for music making by emphasizing new contexts, empowering participants to develop a musical agenda, and committing resources to those socially and economically disadvantaged. However, there was not a unified sense of what constituted community music practice. Joss (1993) notes that "a problem of direction has to be faced: a common definition of Community Music has so far eluded us" (p. 3).

Building upon the ideas and energy generated from the first meeting in Manchester, what eventually emerged was a new confidence in community music practice. This is reflected in Joss's remark that "only in 1991, at the second national community music conference, did Britain's community music practitioners dare to call themselves a movement" (1993, p. 3). The conference's concluding statement affirms this sentiment, presenting five criteria that represented contributions from those who had attended. First, community music aims to provide access to music for people who are not usually able to participate in musical activity. Second, community music aims to offer opportunities for active participation in making and creating music. Third, community music is based on partnerships in which any "professional" input is biased toward "enabling" rather than "leading." Fourth, community musicians are concerned with additional social purposes rather than "music for music's sake." Finally, community music projects offer physical resources to outside individuals or groups (Joss, 1993, p. 3). As community musicians across the United Kingdom began to find their voice, subsequent articles appearing in *Sounding Board* began to adopt a defiant mood: "Get Organised!" says Pauline Muir (1992); "Get Connected!" says Duncan Chapman (1992). Both Muir and Chapman echoed a call from Sound Sense, asking for community musicians to unify in recognition that greater momentum and effect would be generated under a united critical mass.

DEFINITIONS

Although a set of principles had been constructed, issues surrounding the definition of community music still sparked heated discussion. Dave Price warns against the definition trap, suggesting that it would be "an act of collective kamikaze" (Swingler, 1993, p. 32). On a similar note, Tim Swingler suggests that issues of identity and purpose are important but getting absorbed in an introspection that has less and less to do with the real world is a dangerous occupation (p. 32). In an effort to resist a polarization between practice and theory, Irene Macdonald (1994) expresses a need for community music to become "more of a consciously exercised, defined, recognized and known activity" and that although "navel-gazing" debates are not necessary, there is a need to draw lessons, define issues, and clarify practices out of the actual experiences of community music making (p. 24).

By January 1995, community musicians working in the United Kingdom finally had a set of statements that clarified their working practices. The members of Sound Sense had recognized that if the development of community music was to progress, then *they* were best placed to address the issue of what community music does. Macdonald (1995), then chair of the organization, explained that there were two important reasons that the organization needed to attempt an answer to the vexed question of what community music is: first, to establish an agreement of shared values so that the organization had a common foundation on which to build, and second, to have a clear view about what it was that Sound Sense was trying to promote. The statement read as follows:

• Community music involves musicians from any musical discipline working with groups of people to enable them to develop active and creative participation in music.

- Community music is concerned with putting equal opportunities into practice.
- Community music can happen in all types of community, whether based on place, institution, interest, age or gender group, and reflects the context in which it takes place. (Macdonald, 1995, p. 29)

Described by Kathryn Deane (1999, n.p.), as "not so much a formal definition, but a three-part 'test,'" the composite declaration has been a stable backbone to Sound Sense's work from 1995 to the present. In 1998, Sound Sense published a promotional leaflet confronting the question, "What is community music?" With a response statement that began "Music with everyone, everyone with music and much more besides," the leaflet underscored the work of community musicians using five discrete categories: people, participation, places, equality of opportunity, and diversity (Sound Sense, 1998). These sentiments are consequently found in Sound Sense's dictionary of training opportunities *Which Training?* and the student pack *Making a Difference with Music* (Deane, 1998; Sound Sense, 2000). As a conduit for "solving" the issues surrounding the definition of community music in the United Kingdom, Sound Sense has been successful in brokering the debate and finding a collection of statements that satisfy the majority of its members.

SUMMARY

Throughout the 1970s and into the 1980s, community arts laid the pathway for the independent development of specific arts practices, such as community dance, community theater, and community music. During the mid-1980s, community musicians organized themselves and began to articulate what they stood for. This provided the foundation for a political voice that found momentum during the 1990s and ensured involvement in such developments as the Music Manifesto,[17] a collaborative campaign between government agencies and organizations invested in music, and Youth Music,[18] a U.K. charity set up in 1999 that aims to transform the lives of disadvantaged children and young people through music. From within the historical perspective of community musician work articulated here, I have identified five key themes of practice: identity, context, community, participation, and pedagogy. These five themes aid the organization of the next chapter, which affirms the characteristics of community music practice through an ethnographic account of one exemplar project.

CHAPTER 4

The Peterborough Community Samba Band

Situated some seventy miles from London, United Kingdom, Peterborough is an example of an English new town. Built on the cusp of the meadowlands of east Northamptonshire and the flat fenlands, Peterborough has developed into a significant site within the east of England. Its geographic location places it within easy reach of some of England's largest towns and cities. Birmingham, Northampton, Cambridge, Nottingham, Leicester, Norwich, and London are all within a 100-mile radius. As a city within the county of Cambridgeshire, Peterborough is a commercial and retail center for a subregional area of half a million people, an area designated within the counties of Lincolnshire, Northamptonshire, Rutland, and Cambridgeshire. Over the last forty years, Peterborough's population has grown to around 175,000 people living in 71,000 households. In population terms, the city is one of the largest in the region.

Between 1993 and 1996, I undertook the role of music animateur for the City of Peterborough and its greater constituency within the county of Cambridgeshire. The Peterborough Arts Council had responded to previous research that suggested that its arts development strategy would benefit from the implementation of a full-time music animateur. The first few months of employment involved circumnavigating the area for which I was responsible, and the construction of a short-, medium- and long-term plan of music development. My initial reaction to the city suggested that there was a lack of cultural activities for adults and a seeming lack of "community" hustle and bustle throughout the neighborhoods and city center.

Although easily accessible from its surrounding areas, many people access Peterborough from the A1 dual carriageway (highway). As one of Britain's busiest roads, the A1 runs from London to Edinburgh and provides a main route from the northeast to the southeast. As one approaches Peterborough from the A1, Junction 17 provides the slip road (ramp) toward the city center. From this entrance, it is initially difficult to detect that you have entered the outskirts of a large city. Peterborough's roadways radiate from its center and are lined with trees and shrubs dividing Peterborough's interior and acting as a disguise for its everyday communal activities. As a key feature of Peterborough's "garden" design, its roads and roundabouts cut through the flat horizon of the fenland landscape, offering only glimpses of the community at large through the broken foliage. From this perspective, it is possible to think that you have entered a topography where vehicles flow but people do not live.

Heading from the A1 on the A1139, it takes around five minutes before you notice the huge sturdiness of Peterborough's Norman cathedral on the left. The massiveness of the building is uninterrupted by landscape, its many steeples puncturing the sky in a celebration of Christendom. Peterborough Cathedral denotes one's arrival into the city. With a history dating back to 655, Peterborough Cathedral is a dominant force in the city's history, both past and present. As a reflection of faceless town planning and a failed attempt of creating community, Peterborough's landscape is a metaphor for its lack of vibrancy. Within the boundaries of eastern England, Peterborough's tourist information and its cultural strategy attempt to describe Peterborough as "the place to be." This is a hollow suggestion underlined at the time by its local nickname: the cultural desert.

It was first impressions such as these that led to the decision to initiate an adult-oriented music activity that could wake up the "sleepy city." During previous professional activity, I had experienced the effectiveness of community drumming, and decided that this should be my starting point in Peterborough. It was here, during the first percussion classes that I ran, that the Peterborough Community Samba Band (PCSB) emerged. The original goals for the percussion classes were to create a space for adults, regardless of musical experience, to come together through music and for this to spill out into their social worlds.

Initiated against the background of a sleepy city, the PCSB developed into a thriving cultural activity that has been able to transcend the city's "sleepy" limits. In a similar vein to those musical treasures exposed by Ruth Finnegan (1989) in *The Hidden Musician*, those participating in the PCSB found cultural refuge in an activity that initially seems quite a paradox to the persona of the city. Drawing from documents,[1] testimony,[2] participant-observation, and experiential memory,[3] this ethnographic account describes the PCSB and its traits of practice, and attempts to place the reader "inside" of the project. Much of the material used for this chapter is the result of a weekend reunion, organized in conjunction with the current incarnation of the PCSB. Constructed as a chance to meet old friends, enjoy a weekend of drumming, and contribute to the development of community music, the reunion arrangements took place six months before the designated meeting on May 29, 2004, in Peterborough. The reunion also served a purpose in the process of participatory development, providing an opportunity for participants both current and past to meet and spend a day drumming and socializing. Around thirty people were able to attend that day, and they were representative of the band's twelve-year history. Participants' backgrounds were typically wide and echoed the historic diversity of the PCSB. Their occupations included administration officer, teacher's assistant, peripatetic drum teacher, chartered building surveyor, students, teacher, BBC radio program maker, rural environmental worker, civil servant, musician, and those who were currently unemployed. My account begins by mapping the group's identity through five foundational milestones: constitution, recording, gigs and instruments, rehearsal spaces, and Samba Sizzlers.

IDENTITY

Emily's Story

Advertisements for samba drumming classes at the Peterborough Arts Center (PAC) appeared in local newspapers in May 1993. Just before 7:30 P.M. on a Thursday night, I sat nervously, not knowing whether anyone at all would attend. Emily entered the building first, and I greeted her. Short in stature, heavy in weight, and dressed in baggy clothes, she walked in awkwardly. As she walked toward where I was standing, she was apologetic of her musical incompetence, and appeared as nervous as I was.

Emily has made an incredible life journey since our first meeting in 1993 and she remains a positive symbol for my professional work during my time in Peterborough. She considers the PCSB as a catalyst for a deeper understanding of her current identity. Throughout my research, Emily's story has been outstanding in terms of personal identity and personal growth: twelve years after her initiation into samba, she stated, "By God, I am so glad that I went to this first Samba session, oh yeah." On reflection, Emily noted, "It [the PCSB] made the biggest impact of anything I've done I think. I can't imagine me not doing it now. It's such an intrinsic part of who I am. It's not just something that I do."[4]

During our interview, Emily got visibly tearful as she recounted the process of change. She described herself as a "shadow-little-person" prior to involvement with the PSCB, and expressed feelings about her transformation: "All the experiences that I've gained have made me what I am now and I don't wanna be *not* what I am now. If there wasn't music in my life then . . ., I can't imagine who I'd've been now." Before involvement with the PCSB, Emily had been unhappy with her self-identity, describing herself as "trying to make ends meet" and "mumsy," a derogatory description usually indicating dowdy-looking and worn-out. Emily notes her "phenomenal change": the way she now carries herself, her hairstyle, her attitude, and her lifestyle have all undergone dramatic alteration. The PCSB and its broader intersections have become an intrinsic part of who Emily is. "I am Emily Samba," she noted. This statement is qualified further when she reveals that she has recently started a new relationship and is beginning to now strike a balance between her love for samba and all its community intersections and the commitment of the new relationship. Striking this balance has not been easy, and it is in stark contrast to previous times, when "the only thing that kept me sanely in that period was the fact that I was working with music." Emily admits that samba is "still very, very important, but it's not the *only* thing; now there is something else."

Constitution

PSCB's identity is constructed both through those who take part and through its infrastructure. The structural organization of the group has enabled its purpose and philosophical ethos to flow from generation to generation. The creation of the group's constitution, written by its members in January 1996, is a good example of this. The constitution was drawn up for two broad reasons: independence and funding. Independence was sought from the Peterborough Arts Council. This move was important because, although the Peterborough Arts Council had been a keen supporter of the PCSB, overreliance on agencies that fund projects might hamper growth. Those in the PCSB understood these imperatives and ensured that during the inception of the group there was a drive toward an entity that was self-sustaining. As a group with a clearly documented constitution, the PCSB could open pathways for funding beyond those offered by the Peterborough Arts Council: for example, lottery funding, Eastern Arts Board, and private sponsorship. The PCSB's constitution consisted of four key aims: (1) to provide regular opportunities to explore, and experiment with, music from varied cultures; (2) to provide regular opportunities for improving these skills to performance level; (3) to create a framework for the performance of live music by members of the community; and (4) to encourage community membership of the PCSB.

Recording

The recording of its demo tape, *Desfile*, in May 1996 came about through an initiative to add an extra focus to the band's activities. The group faced a range of new challenges, such as the matter of a recording venue, acoustic considerations, sleeve design, marketing, the hiring of recording equipment and operator, editing, and funding. One of the PCSB's ex-members had been a recording engineer, so the group enlisted his help and eventually hired him to produce the recording. As a set of individuals and as a group, the PCSB sourced a variety of income streams in order to pay for the projected recording cost. Income came from a variety of sources, including the Peterborough Arts Council, the Peterborough City Council, Eastern Arts Board, and *Max Power*. One of the partners of a band member worked for *Max Power*, a magazine associated with fast cars and bold graphics that they kindly provided the resources to produce the artwork for the tape jacket.

During the buildup toward the recording, the band increased its rehearsal time and steadily increased its membership. Because the recording would be permanent, many members consolidated their commitment both to the band and to the particular instruments they played. This period of rehearsal marked a decisive shift in the running of, and participation in, the music workshops. The levels of concentration increased dramatically, as did the musical expectations. Participants would get lost in the cyclic rhythms, closing their eyes in an effort to "nail" their part. On a number of occasions, participants brought in tape recorders and recorded the sessions. In one sense, this was helpful in furthering the participants' understanding of the differences between live performance and recording. In another way, the happy-go-lucky "spirit" began to dissolve.

The final artifact, a run of 1,000 compact tapes, established a tangible product that boosted the confidence and the status of the group while also creating a much needed income stream. Desfile's jacket inlay sleeve neatly summarized the band's ideology and reinforced its constitutional commitment:

> We've come from our houses, offices, shops, factories, workshops, warehouses, studios, community centers and classrooms to parade in carnivals, play in and around the city (even in the cathedral!) and perform with other musicians from rappers to Glyndebourne Opera to other sambistas from all over the country... Catch the spirit of samba. Catch Desfile.

Gigs and Instruments

As a performance art, playing to an audience is the stable diet of many bands. The complex network of relationships within such a band helps bind the participants and their music goals. As a pedagogic strategy, performing had always constituted the finale of the sessions that I had run at the PAC. Performing opportunities became more frequent as the members' confidence and pride in their achievements grew. Throughout its history, the PCSB gigged regularly, and have since notched up a varied and diverse list of performance types and performance locations, including carnivals, festivals, special events such as Lord Mayor's parades, charity events, sporting occasions, pub gigs, and workshops.

The PCSB's eclectic mix of people and its philosophical approach embedded in its constitution enabled a welcoming to anyone who wished to take part. This attitude toward others led to performances alongside DJs, rappers, opera companies, symphony orchestras, rock and pop acts, and other world music ensembles, such as West and East African drumming ensembles. In order to fulfill many of these diverse performance obligations, the PCSB needed ownership of instruments. This was particularly necessary as those in the band looked toward running music workshops of their own, an initiative that flourished successfully in later years and continues today. During the initial period of the band's growth, I had spent around £1,000 of my project funds on the purchase of samba instruments. Although these instruments were for the community's use, the music animateur would often be working with them in other sites across the city. Consequently, the instruments would be unavailable for PCSB participants who wished to run their own samba workshops. Through the Peterborough Arts Council's small grant initiative, the PCSB obtained some funds to buy its own instruments, and this enabled some of its members to run percussion projects within their respective places of work. Later initiatives were more ambitious, and included the purchase of a trailer and the creation of a mobile samba workshop titled "Samba Grooves."

Rehearsal Spaces

A large percussion unit generates a lot of sound, and finding venues in which to rehearse can present difficulties. The PCSB began its residency within the Peterborough Arts Center, but after complaints from its neighbors, the Arts Center regrettably had to ask the band to find an alternative place to rehearse. This moment was recorded in a newspaper article, "Shhhh . . . No More Samba— Band drummed out of art center for being too noisy" (Bartram, 1994). Within a week, the chairman of the Peterborough Pirates, the local ice hockey team, offered a venue for the band to rehearse, stating, "Our fans make quite a lot of noise and the Samba musicians say it fits in well with their kind of music. I look forward to having them down here" (Bartram, 1994).

This first venue shift is significant, because the band's infrastructure became strengthened through the group members' ability to deal with challenges and forge new rapports with others. The relationship between the PAC and the PCSB provided the first of many such affiliations between band and property owner. During the band's history, it moved venues on approximately nine occasions, and with each transition, a new dynamic was initiated through a change of relationship. This may be in the form of performance opportunities, sponsorship possibilities, membership changes, or individual relationships. The ability for the group to maintain its identity and retain flexibility toward its hosts has been important for its survival.

Samba Sizzlers

Initially led by two of the PCSB's participants, Emily Dewhurst and Lindsey McFarland, the "Samba Sizzlers" developed in response to demand from the children of adult band participants and from those who saw the group in public performance. It was common during the PCSB's performances that audience members would ask whether there were opportunities for young people to get involved in the drumming. The PCSB had been set up as an adult band, and this aspect was still important for those in attendance. As music animateur, I had regular workshops within schools, and it was becoming clear that a structured format outside school time could be successful. One member of the PCSB recalls that her young daughter was keen to play drums after my visit to her school: "Samantha thought it was absolutely fantastic. As soon as she heard about the Junior group starting up, that was it, she was there."

The request that the music animateur should support youth samba came from both Emily and Lindsey, who were keen to run the class. Emily recalls, "Well you [Lee Higgins] said once, 'I'd really love to do this, and I know I haven't got time to do it, you see,' and I thought, well, I have, but I haven't got the knowledge to do it, but I've got the time." During the initial publicity, Emily stated, "This is all part of a master plan that will see samba take over the region" (Beating out the Samba Message, 1995).

What soon became known as the Samba Sizzlers began in September 1995 at the Central Library in the Peterborough City Center. Because of the excessive noise, the classes suffered the same fate as the adult band and had to be relocated to another venue. The Samba Sizzlers quickly established themselves as an independently thinking group, organizing a half-term "Thrill of Brazil" week. This initiative attracted a National Lottery grant that enabled guest Brazilian artists to teach and perform. A spokesperson for the PCSB explains: "The idea is to get people excited about Brazilian culture and music, and above all to have fun" (Galton, 1997).

The Samba Sizzlers are an important part of the PCSB's identity for two main reasons. First, due in part to leadership changes between 1996 and 1997, membership had steadily dropped from the adult band. During this period, the Samba Sizzlers had gone from strength to strength: "the Sizzlers were so big and were doing so many gigs and doing so well that we were even getting dads involved." For pragmatic and financial reasons, it was eventually decided to amalgamate the two groups. Operating as a supplement, the Samba Sizzlers enriched the PCSB. This was not without its difficulties, as one commentator recalls:

> There were all sorts of little reasons why that started to get difficult, because the adult band were perceived as an "expert band." They produced a tape and they were very strong characters who felt quite rightly very accomplished. But then so did the Sizzlers. So it was quite a clash. And they haven't done any recording or anything, you know, there was a real feeling of, well, they are coming into our band so they should be gelling in with what we are doing.

Second, the amalgamation signaled a change in the PCSB's adult-only identity. Internal mechanisms and behaviors needed adjustment in order to establish hospitality between the adults and the young people. This happened over a period of time, and the Samba Sizzlers influenced a rebirth of the PCSB that now identifies with a greater cross-section of the community.

The U.K. Samba Scene

The PCSB's operation sits comfortably within a group of activities and practices broadly described as the "U.K. samba scene." In 1998, my research suggested that there were seventy-nine active samba groups in the United Kingdom (Higgins, 1998). Four years later, Daniel Bernstein (2002) estimated that there were approximately 300 active samba bands in the United Kingdom, and calculates around 7,500 *sambistas*, or people who play samba. The number of bands fluctuates from year to year, so for the most current information, visit the U.K. and Irish samba association.[5] Although the growth of U.K. samba bands appears to have plateaued, what is remarkable is that the constituent members are predominantly people who would not have necessarily called themselves musicians before their involvement with this activity. Usually, participants have little or no previous music experience prior to involvement with their samba band, although some bands, including the PCSB, do attract professional musicians. An outstanding feature is that such interest exists for Brazilian music, especially within a country that does not have a large immigrant Brazilian population. This issue is more startling when one considers that samba is so strongly associated with particular cultural traits, as Antonio Adolfo (1996) suggested: "The Brazilian phrasing is linked to the Brazilian culture—the nature, the sun, the way we talk, play football, dance, etc." (p. 33).

Professional workers within cultural sectors promoting participatory development, such as the community music animateur and local community arts officers, were all partly responsible for the growth of samba in the United Kingdom.[6] Fueled by local, national, and international samba aficionados, plus touring percussion ensembles such as Inner Sense Percussion Orchestra active in the mid-1980s and the 1990s, carnival street drumming took root within the United Kingdom. In short, professional cultural workers recognized that the drum ensemble provided opportunities for participatory music development.

Samba's infectious dance rhythms and unmistakable energy demands the attention of passing audiences. The aural (and in many cases visual) assault of the senses has often drawn people toward the activity with a resultant desire to participate. A large number of the samba groups maintain a participatory ethos and regularly welcome new members into their folds. In line with community music practice, the activity often has a strong social element, and this hospitality is extended through the music, in which a communal atmosphere is often encouraged. In this way, a drink with fellow *sambistas* becomes as important as the playing itself. One participant of the London School of Samba explains: "Samba schools are as much about socializing and having fun, as they are about the business of dancing and playing music. Our Sunday workshops are a great way of meeting people who have a shared interest in music and performance." This idea is an adaptation of the Brazilian *escola de samba* (school of samba) model, and it reflects the attributes of a community arts worker described by Su Braden (1978) as a blend of community development techniques and artistic skills.

A large proportion of the U.K. samba groups can be understood as community music projects. However, as you might expect, band leaders have employed a variety of approaches to run their bands and some of these approaches would not align themselves to the characteristics of community music as described here. Ex-members of the PCSB who had moved from the immediate location and attempted to take part in other bands highlighted examples of approaches that felt foreign to them. One of the *sambistas* said, "I couldn't go to the band in Glasgow because I had to go through an audition." This is decisively different from those in the PCSB who actively resisted any such barrier.

The spectrum of people playing in community drumming bands is surprisingly diverse. My visit to the Suffolk School of Samba enabled me to meet a taxi driver, a teacher, a potter, a full-time mother, and a telephone engineer. As these multi-occupational groups extend their membership, the internal range of skills increases creating an effective infrastructure that supports the music activity as well as organizes social events, fund-raising promotions, and outreach music workshops. This is certainly the case within the PCSB. Run sensitively and skillfully, diverse mixtures of people can form strong relationships, bonding together to create a formidable, hard-working team. They can provide a safe, supportive situation for all current members and offer a hospitable welcome to potential participants. During the initial growth of the U.K. samba scene, the majority of people taking part had not previously been exposed to street drumming music of this kind. This may help explain why such mixes of musical abilities are found effectively learning and performing together. In a situation such as this, musical baggage is reduced, creating a level playing field. Everyone is now a beginner, whether or not one chooses to call oneself a musician.

Carnival Encounter: National Samba Meeting

Brighton's Carnival Collective organized a carnival encounter to coincide with the locally coordinated Brighton Festival, which celebrates a wide variety of local, national, and international arts activities. Described as a weekend event that includes workshops, performances, and parades that celebrated carnival arts from all over the world, the encounter was the finale to the annual Brighton Festival that runs the entire month of May. This event is becoming increasingly important for the U.K. samba scene, and members of the PCSB take part in its activities. By participating, they gain new skills and network with other organized samba bands and individual *sambistas*.

The carnival encounter, held May 22–23, 2004, represented the third event of its kind and had an additional aim in establishing an annual focus to the flourishing U.K. samba scene. Samba bands and those interested in samba constituted the majority of participants, and they appeared to enjoy a range of drumming and dance styles. Although the majority of participants regularly drummed in samba bands, the emphasis on the broader aspect of carnival arts ensured representation of musical and artistic styles from Africa, India, the Caribbean, and England.

Saturday's parade revealed the enormity of the U.K. samba scene, providing a showcase for bands from the four corners of the United Kingdom. Over twenty bands paraded, and each group established its identity through visual images such as dedicated colors on T-shirts or costumes, and by offering interpretations and arrangements of standard samba repertoire and/or new hybrid composition reflecting the group's participants. A week later, members of the PCSB recalled having an overwhelming feeling that, although there may be typical band characteristics as expressed in Bernstein's report, there was no typical person involved in samba and no typical band that could be heralded as representative.

The PCSB represents an activity within the larger umbrella of the U.K. samba scene, and thus its identity may be understood against and within this cultural milieu. The samba scene is also vibrant in many other parts of the world, most noticeably Austria, Australia, Denmark, Finland, France, Germany, Holland, Italy, Japan, Poland, Switzerland, the United States, and Brazil.[7] It would be no surprise to cite Brazil as the obvious blueprint for samba activity; it is, after all, the country that people immediately think of when the word *samba* is mentioned. Although the U.K. samba scene is very different from its counterpart in Brazil, the music's traces are identifiable within Brazilian culture and are therefore identifiable within this tradition. The next section considers the band's contextual parameters, locating the PCSB in its immediate locality, Peterborough, and within its initiating agent, the Peterborough Arts Council.

CONTEXT

The City

Peterborough's recorded history begins in the mid-seventh century with the founding of a Saxon monastery around which grew a settlement called Medeshamstede.[8] Danish raiders destroyed both monastery and town, but eventually a new abbey was built, which in 1541 became a cathedral, and the town became a city. Peterborough remained a small cathedral and market city until the nineteenth century, when it changed dramatically into a railway and industrial center with a reputation for excellence in engineering.

In 1967 Peterborough was designated a *new town* (i.e., planned community), and a year later the Peterborough Development Corporation (PDC) was created. The PDC had two main objectives: first, to help relieve London's housing problem by providing jobs and homes in the city; and second, to improve amenities for current residents. A fair proportion of those who have participated in the PCSB moved into the area from London. In attempting to marry an ancient cathedral city and a planned new town, Peterborough was considered a "bold experiment in town planning" (Brandon and Knight, 2001, p. 124). Peterborough's garden design linked its housing estates, so-called townships, to its center through a network of roads and bike paths. As one of Britain's fastest growing cities, Peterborough attracted significant numbers of peoples of Italian, East European, and African-Caribbean origin, but its ethnic minority population is dominated by Pakistanis, Bangladeshis and others from the Indian subcontinent. Along with other new towns across the United Kingdom, Peterborough experienced a "baby boom" in the early 1970s, and although Peterborough's population declined from mid-1965 to 1998, its population is back on the increase, standing at 173,400 in 2007 and predicted to reach 191,000 by 2020.

Peterborough Arts Council

The Peterborough Arts Council (PAC) was set up in 1948, with its main objectives the promotion and development of the arts in Peterborough (Greater Peterborough Arts Council, 1978). During the years between 1948 and 1965, the council's objectives focused on enhancing the city's artistic and cultural reputation through concerts, weekend schools, and festivals. In 1965, Peterborough underwent governmental reorganization. Consequential shifts in authority produced a gap of around four to five years during which time there was very little artistic and cultural activity on an organized basis. Although documentation around that time seems enthusiastic toward participatory arts, its reference to arts specifically, or even generally, is slight. This lack of insight and deeper understanding as to the nature of participatory arts strategy meant little progress was made in embedding regularly organized cultural activity into the city: "It has to be accepted that arts development in Peterborough over the last 15 years has been essentially haphazard rather than strategically planned" (Masefield, 1986, p. 5).

Paddy Masefield's development proposal of 1986 paved the way toward filling Peterborough's arts "vacuum." The document offers a detailed analysis of the city's provision, pinpointing current areas of activity and making recommended priorities. Masefield's sensitivity toward community arts, its ideology and its practicality, resonates throughout the report and lays the foundations for an arts strategy that not only promotes participation but also provides a methodology with which to achieve its aims. An important aspect of the Masefield report was the creation of a community arts team and the utilization of its existing arts center, Lady Lodge.

A survey of the Lady Lodge Arts Center's reports between 1981 and 1989 reveals an arts program trying to respond to its community but lacking sufficient arts development insight and strategy. Throughout the early 1980s, "traditional" arts and crafts—weaving, woodwork, needlework, patchwork, and quilting— dominated the arts center's program. Much like the arts and crafts program, the initial music program was limited. In the early years it mostly revolved around classical concerts, monthly folk performances, and recorder and harpsichord workshops. Between the mid- to late 1980s, the arts center's activities began responding to the wider cultural imperatives: the synthesizer workshop of 1987 appeared to be popular, as was the jazz residency in schools during the 1988/1989 season of events.

As a direct response to Masefield's report, the arts center's management committee requested a team of arts animateurs for Peterborough. During this period, the creation of a music animateur post became one of the main thrusts of the arts center's music agenda. In 1993, the management of the arts center transferred to the newly formed company, the PAC. It was during this period that I joined the Arts Council as the music animateur. The PAC was now providing full-time arts workers in video, community arts, dance, and music. As the city's music animateur, I initiated and ran projects such as music residencies in schools, special education centers, prison and probation service, family centers, rock schools, large-scale community arts projects alongside other agents such as Puppetworks, Glyndebourne Opera, and orchestral outreach with the Britten Sinfonia. Although the work was varied and responsive to community requests, it was the PCSB that defined my work during this period.

The next section opens with an illustrative account of the PCSB's interior supportive system, described as the "aunties." Focusing on the friendship networks developed by participants, I explore the effect it had on the Hutchens and Ellis families.

COMMUNITY

Aunty

The initial "kids" samba band workshops of 1995 generated enthusiasm from both the participants and their parents. During the first term of workshops, the leadership shifted from both Emily and Lindsey to just Emily. Throughout this process of change, parents became aware that for all Emily's enthusiasm, she was finding the group difficult. With limited teaching experience, Emily became a little anxious and began to ask parents whether they would be willing to lend a hand. Helen Hutchens and Beth Ellis offered to help. Both had had teaching experience. As the Samba Sizzlers grew both in numbers and in terms of a performing band, a couple of other "mums" also began helping out in managing them. As Helen confirms, it was "in a proper sense of managing the band, you know, organizing it, being secretary and treasurer and sorting out the gigs and organizing the coaches and this sort of thing, because it really did grow into a successful junior band. And we got invited all over the place." Because Helen and Beth attended the Samba Sizzlers' rehearsals, they began to absorb the skills required to playing the samba instruments. In turn, they formed a "sticking-plaster-attitude" of playing anything that was needed in times of low attendance: "Beth or I would jump in, you know, just to keep it going." From this perspective, the amalgamation of the Samba Sizzlers and the adult band can be understood as organically grown through necessity.

As a mother of two daughters involved initially with the Samba Sizzlers and later with the PCSB, Helen reflected over the dramatic impact the band has had on her family:

> Our two girls have met and experienced a much broader diversity of people than they might otherwise. We joke about it but in all seriousness . . . They have good interpersonal skills, are not quick to judge, and are very worldly wise. Of course, it is not possible to quantify what, if any of that is a direct consequence, but my opinion is that it will have had an impact.

Helen's children Mirriam and Samantha began playing with the Samba Sizzlers at ages eight and ten, respectively. They both left some ten years later to study at university. Mirriam says, "It was a social thing from quite early on and I gained lots of friends, then my parents got involved in the organization and families started socializing out of the group." As a hobby to begin with, samba for Mirriam was a distraction from school but soon became "something which allowed me to express myself." She noted, "The people that I played with became my family and as a consequence of samba I visited places and got involved with activities that I would never have been a part in otherwise."

For Mirriam, samba ignited her interest in other cultures and was an influential factor in her decision to study social anthropology. Although Mirriam came to know samba on British soil, it was always being contextualized in terms of Brazilian culture. This fascinated Mirriam to the extent that it cultivated a desire to study people and culture. Karen, one of her contemporaries in the Samba Sizzlers, also attended university and has fond samba memories: "We always refer to it [the PCSB] as our extended family and I still feel that way." Karen understands the band as paramount to her history and reflects on her adolescent years: "I've grown up with the PCSB. Some of us went through those troublesome teenage years [while we were with the] PCSB."

With a group of twenty or so performers, the parents became aware of the manner in which the children were speaking to the adults. Reminiscent of her mother, Helen remembers thinking, "We really shouldn't be allowing them to speak to other adults like that." On the other hand, Helen supported the development of the children's individual and collective voices encouraged through an activity that gave ownership and responsibility. She recollects an alternative position to her initial reaction, stating, "Yeah, you've got a point of view and it's valid and you've got a right to say what you think and I'm pleased and proud that you are actually standing up for yourselves."

The young participants of the Samba Sizzlers were encouraged to develop their voice, but this was not without its difficulties. Creating tensions between some children and some adults, the positive nature of this action was not initially understood by all involved. Helen states,

> I wanted the girls to be seen as individuals standing up for their own. . . . [I]f they've done the wrong thing, fine, you tell them, they are out of line, you know, they're out of order. . . . Don't come to me as a parent expecting me to shut them up, because actually they have got a valid point of view.

Nurturing the voice of the participants had a profound effect on Leyla Halabi. Leyla joined the Samba Sizzlers after performing in her school's samba band, a group formed because of workshops I had completed while music animateur. Of Iranian descent, Leyla notes that performing never seemed particularly "in sync" with her father's beliefs: "Going to samba meant I was able to do something which he approved of, while I was also able to socialize and incorporate other less-conforming aspects of my personality, e.g. dancing, wearing bright clothes for carnival, etc." Leyla pinpoints the PCSB as "the first group of adults, that I had ever been told to address by their first names!"

Responding to the moments of tension between the children and the adults, both Helen and Beth recognized the need to "look after each other" and cultivate communication channels. Through a nurturing support network, the Samba Sizzlers developed a cross-parenting textuality that allowed the children decision-making abilities within a responsible, creative, and functional structure. With their extended community responsibility, the adults became known as "aunties."[9]

For the Hutchens family, samba was something "we could enjoy as a family." Paul Hutchens remarked that his main motivation for involvement with the PCSB "was a desire to have shared experiences with my family." Paul had considered a career in music after early exposure to singing in the Welsh eisteddfods[10] and later earning high grades in both trumpet and piano. His performance anxiety initially prevented him from joining the PCSB, but as the rest of his family became increasingly committed, he decided to overcome his fear, finally deciding to participate in 1998. Helen explains Paul's dilemma:

> Samba was sort of ruling the lives of those core few families and certainly was dictating what we did half of the summer-time. I think this is how Paul and Jacob

[Beth Ellis's husband] and eventually Victoria and Bryan all ended up, we all ended up playing as families together, because essentially then the kids were saying "Well no, we're not going on holiday then, because we got Strawberry Fair and we got, you know [laughs]."

From the Ellis family, Karen attributes samba as part of the reason she has "a great relationship" with her parents, because they "do this as a family." Both the Hutchens and the Ellis families recognized that to continue the group's commitment to be open and accessible, it needed continued nurturing: "We have responsibilities to this community band and this is what we have to do for it and unfortunately this is gonna have to be considered within our family life."

Samba family outings such as the annual Drum Camp embraced a wide variety of experiences and colored the nature of parenting for both the Hutchens and the Ellis families. Helen explained: "I think, it made us confident as parents to let go of the children." Helen cites an example of this, involving Mirriam's first attendance at the Glastonbury Festival:

She [Mirriam] went with a group of friends and one particular man was virtually neurotic [with worry] and thinking, you know, "how can you [Helen] be so cool?" and I thought, "Well, actually . . . I'm quite happy that she knows where she is and she knows she's safe and she knows how to be safe around those people and at least we can explore the issues and laugh about it together."

The Hutchens and the Ellis families remained members of the PCSB, although the children were occasional participants, performing when they could and attending during vacation time. Helen commented on the positive effect the band has had on their lives: "The PCSB led us as a family along a certain path which has greatly influenced our children's lives."

Friendships

As well as bringing families closer together, band members formed close friendships. Being a member of the PCSB often meant sharing a fish-and-chip supper with your fellow *sambistas* or enjoying a picnic midway through rehearsals. Participants such as Christine, Karen, and Jacob noted the great sense of camaraderie and closeness between the members of the band. Karen is quite particular when she suggests that, "it's this uniqueness of closeness that is so enjoyable and probably the reason why playing with another band is not as good fun." Throughout its existence, the band had a transient population of as many as 400 participants. Although many members came and went, the PCSB managed to maintain its initial philosophical ethos articulated through its constitution.

For a number of participants, the band was initially seen as a way to build new friendship networks. Abigail joined the band in 2002 soon after moving into the area for work. She was looking for ways of social involvement. Miriam had also moved into Peterborough for employment and was struggling to find new friends. As she explained it, "I'd moved to Peterborough, picked up a teaching job and knew nobody here and I've been here two years and this was one of the ways of trying to make friends in Peterborough. So that pretty much these people are my friends in Peterborough." In addition to fostering new friendships, the PCSB has also aided deeper relationships between old acquaintances. Helen notes, "I have gained a whole new friendship group" but makes particular reference to the growth of her friendship with Emily, another regular member of the band. Beth also states that one of her main motivations for attendance is "being with friends, old and new."

Christine suggests that friendships occurred in ways that she had not experienced before. Karen also points toward these relationships, stating, "It's a relationship that [is] hard to define as the only connection really is samba and this is the only time I see them. I don't think I would find a relationship like that in any other situation." Because a band regularly performs in a variety of quite diverse settings, the ability of its members to engage with new experiences is paramount. This may account for participants suggesting that their time with the PCSB has opened new social doors. As Jacob states, "All in all I am glad I joined, it has opened up a whole new outlook on life." From Jacob's perspective, the band operates quite differently from his normal working day. He notes, "I work in a formal structured atmosphere where there isn't much 'fun' or social interaction between staff." In instances such as these, the band becomes an alternative to other social duties and a chance to relax and enjoy people socially.

Other friendships have aided significant changes of lifestyle. As a professional musician, Iain joined the group around six months after its inception and left after the band's performance at the Notting Hill Carnival in 1996. Unlike the majority of the PCSB's participants, Iain had a formal music education, having studied percussion at the Royal College of Music in London. Iain originally joined the PCSB because he wanted to do more playing and wanted to broaden his background in world music. Having joined, he recognized the band's value in expanding his network of friends, and in turn made some lasting friendships that continue today. It is through his meeting with a local musician–instrument builder that Iain began the process of changing jobs. The shift from record producer to music workshop leader and teacher has its roots within this friendship: "Samba band also gave me the opportunity to do workshops with adults, which I hadn't done much before 'cause you [Lee Higgins] were away for a couple of weeks, maybe three weeks, and I did a couple of them." His musical relationship with Colin, another ex-band member, has also flourished, resulting in a number of music collaborations. During our interview, Iain noted, "So, you know, socially it did make a difference as well as musically." Iain's story introduces the next section on participation and is unusual because Iain was a professional musician who opted to perform within a community music project. Following this, participants discuss their musical experiences before involvement with the PCSB.

PARTICIPATION

Iain's Story

Although a number of participants in the PCSB had musical backgrounds, few would have called themselves professional musicians. Iain was a classically trained percussionist and did earn his living through music. His perspective as a participant is therefore seen through a trained musician's eyes, and is consequently different from other accounts. Iain's story has two interesting angles: first, Iain's rapport with the band enabled some valuable musical experiences that enriched his professionalism; and second, although Iain understood what the PCSB was about, his musical background shaped experiences that reveal differences between a professional musical performing band and a community music project.

In 1993, Iain was working as a record producer and a sales executive for Gamut Records. During that period, Iain had not been performing as much as he wanted and was looking for new performing opportunities. The PCSB provided an opportunity that was local and regular. Iain's original motivation for membership was to increase his playing and broaden his background in world music, something that he had wanted to do for some considerable time. Iain's time with the band helped consolidate his desire for world music experiences.

During our interview, Iain stated, "If I'm being brutal, I suppose—when it [the PCSB] stopped being useful to me is when I stopped coming." A perspective that sees the band as having a practical "usefulness" is not one that any other participant divulged. On reflection, Iain now recognizes that a number of musical experiences were probably over and above his initial expectations, and were directly transferable to his work as a professional musician. Performing at the Notting Hill Carnival, for example, provided an experience that Iain had always wanted. During the parade through London, the PCSB performed nonstop for nearly seven hours. The challenge of performing in a large carnival parade presents particular difficulties for musical groups: for example, you are constantly on the move. As a performing musician, Iain had not experienced this type of aural landscaping before. Iain recalls specifically the role of enthusing and encouraging members of the band to continue playing, although at points they showed signs of exhaustion. Coupled with the feedback loop between vast crowds and the performers, Iain's experience on that day has enriched his other percussive pursuits. After the marathon performance, Iain was proud to have been a part of that day and thus was proud to be part of the PCSB.

Iain was asked to produce the PCSB's demo tape because of his previous experience as a record producer. Iain reflects on this venture, stating, "It was interesting, very, very different from anything I've done." Although the musicians were amateurs, Iain's understanding of the band's constitution enabled him to work effectively with the ensemble. Because it was the band's first experience in a recording environment, mistakes were predictably frequent and Iain needed to decide when to rerecord sections and when to move on. The process was at times difficult, and was compounded when neighbors complained about the noise. In Iain's terms, the work environment could not be described as professional, but he does not unnecessarily criticize the recording. An understanding of what the PCSB was about enabled Iain to capture the spirit of the band and thus produce a representative recording. Iain notes, "It was very intense but they did come up trumps. I mean it is probably the most intense thing musically that the non-musicians had done, I guess."

As a professional musician, Iain's frustrations with those performing in the band centered on their lack of discipline and understanding of what constitutes a rehearsal protocol. As Iain recalled,

> They sort of lack standard things or standard codes of behavior that you do in terms of rehearsal technique, you know, you don't play when it's not your turn to play and you listen to what the person running it has got to say, you do whatever is next and you shut up when the person says stop and all that sort of stuff, and that in the end got to me.

Alongside the lack of rehearsal technique and protocol, Iain also notes his difficulties with the band's performance etiquette. He recounts the corporate booking the band had achieved alongside the soul singer Edwin Starr:

> [Edwin Starr] was the main act and he asked people to come up on stage and to take part in the thing and I looked round and all of a sudden there were several members of the samba band up on stage, instead of "Barclay Card" employees, for whom the gig was for, and you know, and it's that type of thing that made me cringe.

Iain recognizes that this "innocent amateurism" was only a small thing, but from his professional perspective, the band had been "employed" and therefore had a job to do. Iain understood that the job involved providing the music and thus helping to give enjoyment to those whose night it was. He reflected that "you're doing a job for 'Barclay Card,' your job is to do the music and not get in the way and while there were four people up there singing with Edwin Starr, it could have been four people from the company, for whom it was designed." Iain's perspective reveals some of the differences between community music projects and professional music projects. His account also illuminates a "professional" musical value within community music projects such as the PCSB. As a practice, community music sets out to reduce the human construction between what is

understood as professional and what is understood as amateur. Iain's story demonstrates that a meaningful two-way learning process can take place when participants of all musical backgrounds decide to welcome each other.

Participants and Prior Music Experiences

In response to questions pertaining to music experiences prior to joining the
PCSB, most of those who replied underlined the importance of music in their
life: "I have always loved music in all forms," "Music was part of my life from an
early age," and "[I was] always a music lover." Responses also articulated a range
of practical musical activities, including "I have taught myself to play the
electronic keyboard," "I started learning the guitar at 15," "I used to write songs
with my sister," and "I always tapped surfaces." From my wider experience
of working with community drumming ensembles, informal music-making
experiences such as those expressed above are common to many participants.
An interest in music is often the connection that leads someone from the initial
"suggestion" whether from advertisement, audience or word of mouth, toward
the first drumming workshop and ultimately toward a role as a committed
performer.

Those participants who engaged in "formal" music education revealed a mixed
reaction to their experiences. Helen, for instance, was "inspired by a great music
teacher" and consequently learned to play the piano and clarinet while also
attending singing classes. This initial flurry of formal music education changed
when the teacher left the school and no replacement was found. She eventually
gave up the piano, gradually stopping any musical involvement until she began
attending the PCSB in 1995, some twenty-seven years later.

Younger participants echoed Helen's experience and included comments that
pinpointed a lack of creative expression and rigidity embedded in a music education system that insisted on a Western classical tradition. Mirriam notes, "I felt
very restricted when it came to expression. . . . I didn't continue to 'A' Level
[advanced level courses normally a prequel to university application]." Abigail
remembers "feelings of obligation and guilt"; she further states, "I don't remember it being a joyful experience." It is particularly interesting to note that Colin's
formal music education stopped at secondary school when his teacher "suggested
I would not be a suitable candidate for 'O' level study [now called GCSE: General
Certificate of Secondary Education]." Colin has since been the local education
authority advisory teacher for music throughout the county of Norfolk. As a
musical development in the United Kingdom, samba began as an informal enterprise, and many of those attracted to the activity had formal music education
experiences like those cited above.[11]

Participants of the PCSB, both past and current, have wide and varied musical
backgrounds. For example, some were professional musicians and teachers, while

others were musical novices. Participants referred to their musical experiences in equally wide terms, ranging from listening to their parents' record collection to engaging in formal piano lessons. The thread between all the responses was a conviction that music had been an important aspect in their life at some time. Beth's response underlines this point: she stated that she had no music experiences before the PCSB except "being a fan of Ska."

As participant-observers during workshops and performances, those involved in performing with the PCSB would often appear in deep thought and appeared to meditate on the aspects of the performance that they faced. Whether they were considering a particular rhythm or a new instrumental technique, the participants contemplated the possible situations that might disclose the meaning and value in the band's music. Occasionally "snapping out" of this zone, participants would often revert to intense levels of concentration. This led to a situation in which the performers seemed somehow separated from the band but paradoxically intrinsically connected.

Through the eyes of a music facilitator, those participating within the PCSB slip in and out of this beautiful expression. The participants' mixture of concentration, enjoyment, escapism, frustration, laughter, fun, and self-achievement swirl together to form a potent blend of unpredictability. Released by moments of musical collapse and timely breaks, the PCSB rides a wave that hovers between amateur and professional. Each musical contributor enters the fray with differing agendas, but all appear to meet within the maelstrom of carnival street drumming. These moments of unity were at first rare, but with time their frequency increased. In the final section, I will discuss the pedagogic approaches utilized within the PCSB. Beginning with Joel's story as an example of someone who successfully negotiated a move from participant to confident music facilitator, I suggest that facilitator techniques have been an intrinsic part in enabling the PCSB to flourish.

PEDAGOGY

Joel's Story

Joel joined the PCSB within its first year of operation and was a regular member for four years. Joel was a practicing drummer in local bands, and his initial motivation was to learn new drum rhythms and techniques. During the course of his membership, Joel embarked on a music facilitator's training course. Unhappy in his job, Joel explored the possibility of earning a full-time wage in music, noting that he "only ever had 'casual' [music] lessons from peers, nothing formal." Joel adds that formal music education convinced him that he was not musical, and proclaims it is "an attitude and belief system I still battle with." Interestingly, Joel now considers the PCSB his first formal music training. In this instance,

Joel understands the conception of "formal" as residing in "somebody else actually organizing and watching somebody else doing something." The pedagogic approach fostered through the weekly music workshops opened an alternative vision for music teaching, one in which Joel could believe. The combination of these experiences and Joel's participation in the band created the situation that enabled him to begin the transition from *bateria* to *mestre*, or from participant to facilitator: "The two experiences linked together enabled me to develop as a musician and educator."

After a period of part-time agricultural work and part-time drum tuition, Joel has finally been able to earn a living from music. He now has a full-time position teaching drum kit in schools. Joel uses this as an opportunity to impart the attitude and spirit he gained while with the PCSB. He states that as a result of the PCSB, he "remains a firm believer that *anyone* can learn drumming [if taught] through a supportive facilitator's style."

The Workshops

The weekly music workshop has been the predominant approach for engaging participants active in the PCSB. Although there have been many styles and approaches throughout the band's history, most of those who had led the band have adhered to a general strategy. Principally, the goal of each workshop focuses on the development of the band's drumming repertoire, while aiming to ensure that the participants reap social and personal fulfillment throughout the duration of the session. This aim has enabled focus and provides a built-in yardstick by which participants consider the session's efficacy.

Because this is a community music project ideologically residing within the notion of participatory development, there is always a tension between an emphasis on the process rather than the product. From my perspective, process and product operate within a play of differences. They are not differing ends of the same pole, as each relies on the other: process haunts product, and product haunts process. Finding a balance between the two has been a continuing issue among the PCSB participants. One participant notes that the "yearn for perfection" can occasionally clash with the band's general ideology, stressing that the fine line between wanting a "tight performance and people just wanting to have fun" is sometimes difficult to achieve. The band's commitment to welcoming new members, enabling the development of a range of instrumental skills, encouraging confidence in leadership, and the striving for high levels of performance has to reside within an appropriate pedagogic approach, something I will explore in detail in chapter 9. One can say, however, that those leading the PCSB have given significant attention to the individuals within the group, the overall health of the group, the social bonding surrounding the workshops, as well as the music making. Each facilitator of the PCSB has found his or her style of facilitation, and those in attendance have adapted to the change of personalities, molding, and remolding around leadership styles.

Facilitation

As a method of delivering music workshops, facilitation has been an effective pedagogic approach. Based on a vision of partnership, shared objectives, and shared achievements, the style of leadership within the PCSB has promoted empowerment and ownership. During the workshops, there was less of a top-down hierarchy and more of a democratic sharing of ideas. Practical applications of this approach encourage individual responsibility for instruments and music and the day-to-day organization and logistics of the band. The play between the facilitator and the group can lead to effective teamwork, and this is strengthened through the encouragement of peer teaching; each instrumental section can accommodate a range of playing abilities, with a leader of each operating a team within a team. As a group of people, the PCSB embraces individual contributions and utilizes them to form a formidable musical and social force.

In a musical sense, the overall sound of samba is reliant on all instruments; no single instrument is considered more important than any other. Participants note that as a mode of guiding learning, facilitation has enabled the group to "deal with people who had no sense of rhythm at all, [but] were incredibly enthusiastic members of the band." Another participant pinpoints the approach to facilitation as a significant contributor to the success of the Samba Sizzlers and suggests that

> someone else leading the band who was a little more authoritarian, someone who said, you know, we're here to play, none of this mucking around. There was . . . a certain dynamic and it was perhaps quite relaxed and perhaps it needed to be like that because there were quite a lot of youngsters in there.

Mindful of the young people in the band, Colin described the pedagogic approach toward the Samba Sizzlers as "nurturing." In the context of working alongside the Samba Sizzlers, Colin's use of the term "mumsy," as in the nurturing nature of the adult women, and "welcoming," as in hospitable and loving, supports a particular perspective of the feminine, and in some sense underlines the structural organization of the "aunties." In relation to the Samba Sizzlers, Helen also applies the term "nurturing," and notes that the pedagogic aims centered on the child's development and emotional learning. She later explained: "We were about educating these kids, not just to be musicians but to be people, to develop their confidence." Many of the children within the Samba Sizzlers have "achieved absolutely their first choice of whatever they wanted to do." Although their observations are based only on speculation, parents describe the pedagogic approaches employed by the PCSB leaders as a catalyst to their child's future achievements.

From *Bateria* to *Mestre*

Within the framework of participatory development, the PCSB has explored notions of the self-sustaining agents through its constitution. The workshop approach has supported this by allowing participants to make the transition from *bateria* (an ensemble of drummers) to *mestre* (master). Colin took over the leadership of the group shortly after the Notting Hill performance in 1996, and consequently replaced me as the lead facilitator. At that time, Colin was best placed to lead the band into its next phase of development because of his understanding of leading music ensembles. Colin's role as the *mestre* of the PCSB was not easy, and he describes it himself as "dreadfully difficult!" Participants recall a workshop style that was quite different from the style to which they had become accustomed. For example, whereas the workshops had always employed a nonformal approach to learning, an emphasis on the experience of playing together without a stress on instrument technique and getting it "right," Colin had the group sit down and hammer out particular phrases and sections until they came close to what he considered to be accurate. This was a marked shift between a focus on nurturing a group dynamic in which participants would enjoy the buzz of playing while learning through an experience of the whole piece, and a more formalized approach of passing on information in small chunks.

In retrospect, the transition from *bateria* to *mestre* was underestimated. Having the music skills was important, but the ability to work with people was required in equal measure. Colin notes that although this was a difficult period, he has used the experience to inform other work: "It gave me the confidence to purchase and lead samba workshops in schools in Norfolk where I was working for the Local Education Authority." Colin continued to use samba as a part of a mixed diet of music activities in both education and community settings.

The transition from participant to able facilitator was a gradual process for Emily that extended over a period of about five years. Like a number of U.K. *mestres*, she enrolled in one of the samba leader's training courses. But because of her past music education, she was not confident in her musical abilities and throughout the process constantly needed reassurance. I asked her, "Are you confident now?" and she replied,

> I'm very confident now, and now I can say to people "Yeah, I can teach you, no problem," and I really feel that I can actually say that but it's taken, what? It's only been in the last three or four years that I've actually been able to stand there and say "Yeah, I actually do, that's what I do. I'm a Musician!"

As well as the musical connotation in a transition between participant and facilitator, there are also personal bridges to build. For many, the *bateria* is the metaphoric "back row." This has a positive image for some, but for others it can continually hide other potentials. A number of respondents relayed the transition as the point that enabled other changes to take place in their social lives. One person said, "If I'd stayed just being a participant, then I don't think things would have changed so much, but going from a participant to being a tutor opened me up to a massive change in my life." Facilitation as a pedagogic tool also enabled movement within the organization of the band. A shift from music participant to treasurer can be just as big a leap as from *bateria* to *mestre*. Beth notes that she has recently become a member of the Eastern Bloco's organizing committee, stating, "Due to the expanding role I now have, it has given me opportunities to meet and work with other bands." This sentiment is echoed by Emily, who adds, "I had to be open to new experiences which meant that I was meeting more people, [and] I was experiencing different sorts of lifestyles."

The pedagogic framework through which the PCSB maneuvers its operation has enabled many personal transitions. Honed from music teaching methods initially introduced by the emergence of the composer-educators, the workshop has become a powerful tool within community music enterprises. The workshop's democratic structure seeks to empower and enable, while calling upon the participants' contributions to form, content, and context. As practice, the PCSB's *mestres* employ this pedagogic approach in order to adhere to the ideological condition of the band's identity. As its stable environment, the workshop has enabled the PCSB to flourish in its particular way and given rise to an identity it can call its own.

SUMMARY

As an ethnographic account, I have attempted to get "inside" the PCSB and to reveal its particular workings. Using the themes of identity, context, community, participation, and pedagogy, I have been able to explore the experience of its *sambistas* that would otherwise be unavailable if one were just observing a musical performance. Individuals such as Emily, Helen, Iain, Joel, Colin, Paul, Beth, Karen, Layla, Mirriam, and Christine have answered questions about their reasoning and motivations, and in doing so have acknowledged aspects of themselves and consequently brought the sound of the PCSB closer to our ears.

As an illustration of practice, the PCSB represents one of many such projects across the United Kingdom and is also representative of many others across the world. In the next chapter, I turn toward the development of community music as an international movement and voice. As British-based community musicians began to network, coordinate, and debate their future practice in the mid- to late 1980s, the International Society of Music Education's Commission for

Community Music Activity (CMA) was in the process of being formed. As a meeting point that serves to link and nurture a growing international network of practitioners and a lens through which I will view international dimensions of community music, the next chapter considers the CMA as a prism through which one can account for the development of an international field.

CHAPTER 5

International Perspectives

D rawing from documents, conversations, and personal experiences, my aim in this chapter is to support Kari Veblen's (2008a) conclusion: "Perhaps the most influential force in [international] community music over the past twenty years has been the Commission for Community Music Activity" (p. 5). For my purposes, the Commission for Community Music Activity (CMA) is a lens through which the U.K. "voice," understood as the context predominantly represented in chapters 2 and 3, is seen in relation to, and as part of, an international field of community music practice.

THE COMMISSION FOR COMMUNITY MUSIC ACTIVITY

In 2004 the International Society of Music Education (ISME) published a documentation of its history (McCarthy, 2004). By personal request, its author, Marie McCarthy (2008), synthesized those aspects pertinent to the CMA and later fashioned a discrete article for the *International Journal of Community Music* (*IJCM*) outlining the CMA's growth and development. This study is important because it locates the commission both historically and conceptually. ISME, within which the CMA functions, was founded in Brussels in 1953 during a conference organized by the United Nations Educational, Scientific and Cultural Organization (UNESCO) in collaboration with the International Music Council. Over the years, those on the ISME board have committed the organization to music in all its forms and practices. This can be exampled through its seven special interest groups: (1) early childhood in music education; (2) education of the professional musician; (3) music policy (cultural, education, and mass media); (4) music in schools and teacher education; (5) special education, music therapy, and music medicine; (6) research; and (7) community music activity. At the heart of the society's mission, there has always been an attempt to recognize music in community life, lifelong learning in music, and education of the amateur. It is from this "promise" to its members, emulating from early talks in the late 1960s through the late 1970s, that one can locate the philosophical and structural framework of the CMA. McCarthy (2008) pinpoints four significant meetings that predate and influenced the CMA: Music Education in the Community (late 1960s); Education of the Amateur, Adult Education (1974); Out of School Activity Activities (1976); and Education of the Amateur Musician (1977). All of these meetings resonate with the development of community arts and community music in the United Kingdom and can be seen within a general cultural shift toward an emphasis on people and places rather than musical technique.

It was not until 1982 that the name "Community Music Activity" had been finally established. The first chairperson of the group was Norwegian music educator Einar Solbu, whose actions were paramount in establishing the group as a distinctive entity. Solbu was well placed for this role, not only because of his positioning in the international music education scene, but also because of his experience as a Norwegian music educator. As Veblen (2008a) points out, the Scandinavian countries have long histories of supporting community music initiatives. For example, the first Scandinavian community music schools were established in the 1930s in Sweden, Norway, and Denmark. After World War II, these schools flourished and continue to be an important part of the musical life, made possible in some part due to a funding mechanism that has been an accepted part of government mandates since the 1960s.[1] In personal correspondence, Sidsel Karlsen, a Norwegian music educator and an advocate of community music, supports this view, noting that almost all Scandinavian institutions for higher music education educate students to work as instructors within the community music field. With this context in mind, Solbu's initial concern, and thus his impetus for pursuing the development of the CMA, was unraveling the dichotomy between "the 'local' music enjoyed by every man, woman and child in a community, and the art of music, usually interpreted by the professional musicians" (McCarthy, 2008, p. 40). What had been troubling Solbu was the partitioning between the community music schools and the world of the professional musician and professional musician training. Solbu saw the CMA as an opportunity to explore these dichotomies through constructive dialogue with like-minded individuals.

During the 1984 ISME biennial conference in Eugene, Oregon, members of the newly formed CMA presented a policy statement to the board articulating its mission. Reflective of John Blacking's (1973) conclusions in his seminal text *How Music Is Man?* the statement read, "Music is a basic means of human expression and communication, [it] is one of the factors that creates social and cultural identity, and [that] music activity is in itself educational in the sense that it leads to personal and social development and self realization" (McCarthy, 2008, p. 40). It is the humanistic, psychological, and sociological dimensions articulated here that would influence and characterize the commission's work in the years that followed. As previously acknowledged, 1984 had been a pivotal year in the development of community music. While the community music movement was gathering momentum in the United Kingdom, links were being established internationally between those invested in education, community development, and music. Those in discussions used information and research to support their mission. These were gleaned from institutions, individuals, conferences, and the publication of a resource book on music education for adult beginners, compiled by Ingrid Olseng and John Burley (Burley, 1987; Olseng and Burley, 1987; Solbu, 1987; Taylor, 1987; Valøen, 1987). A year later, and in response to an emerging relationship between ISME and the European Music School Union, Solbu and the CMA were asked to investigate the current state of community music schools throughout the continent. This was the start of international community music conversation under the auspices of the CMA. ISME, with its global perspective, international membership, and interdisciplinary structures around all facets of musical culture, provided an intellectual stimulus through which the CMA's early pioneers could craft and shape a forward-thinking and responsive environment. Although the CMA was developing within a music education institution, a somewhat antithetical relationship if one reflects upon the growth of community music in the United Kingdom, I would say the support mechanisms and nurturing aspects of ISME enabled the CMA to flourish into an open and responsive international group.

Toward a Global Expression of Community Music

Since 1988, and based around a three- to four-day structure, CMA meetings have taken place every two years at a variety of venues across five continents. For those who had been part of the development of community music in the United Kingdom, including myself, the meetings could be a frustrating experience. Many of us felt that there was little progression on the formulation of a group voice that could express what community music is or does. The social activist trajectory inherent with the U.K. and Irish expression of community music was often at odds with an expression of community music that appeared to be describing "amateur" music making or ethnomusicological practices. McCarthy (2008) notes that "the issue of self-definition, which was an integral part of discussions in the early seminars, continued to be part of the discourse at seminar meetings" (p. 43). From the late 1990s and leading up the millennium, the U.K. and Irish "voice" dominated strategic proceedings. Those representing the United Kingdom and Ireland had confidence in their practice because many of the themes and issues had already been experienced through both practical project work and the formulation of their respective national participatory arts organizations. I recall that there were times when this did have a negative impact on other participants: saturating the discussions with a particular conceptual outlook, unsettling others' confidence, and freezing progression.

Adding to these challenges, the majority of those participating in the CMA discussions were employees of academic institutions. This was, of course, rather incongruous considering its grassroots heritage, and it became a major concern for many of the participants. During the 1990s, those aggravated by the ubiquitous representations of "professors" during the CMA meetings often made their point known, and it did, on occasion, cause personal concern to others. This unpleasant situation caused feelings of deficiency in areas of community music expertise, experience, and scholarly expression, all of which led to a disquieting and uncertainty regarding the commission's focus and mission. The suspicion toward the "formal," or institutionalized, world of music manifested into a polarization between the "real-world," the world of practice, doing, projects, funding, and people, and the "academic world," that of theoretical problem solving and conceptualizations. As a result, conceptualizations of community music as theory were marginalized and seen as "introspection," "navel-gazing," and a distraction to practice more generally. This outlook was initially blinding, because those that took up this position failed to recognize what participants from so-called formal institutions might bring to the discussion. Thankfully, this began to change with the collaborative writing of "key characteristics" that represented the heart of excellent community music activities. Produced in and around the final plenary session in Toronto in 2000, there were fourteen characteristics in all, outlining the nature of community music and prefaced with the phrase, "At the heart of excellent community music activities are the following characteristics":

1. Emphasis on a variety and diversity of musics that reflect and enrich the cultural life of the community and of the participants
2. Active participation in music making of all kinds (performing, improvising, and creating)
3. The development of active musical knowing (including verbal musical knowledge where appropriate)
4. Multiple learner/teacher relationships and processes
5. A commitment to lifelong musical learning and access for all members of the community
6. An awareness of the need to include disenfranchised and disadvantaged individuals or groups
7. A recognition that participants' social and personal growth are as important as their musical growth
8. A belief in the value and use of music to foster intercultural acceptance and understanding
9. Respect for the cultural property of a given community and acknowledgment of both individual and group ownership of musics
10. An ongoing commitment to accountability through regular and diverse assessment and evaluation procedures

11. Encouragement of a personal delight and confidence in individual creativity
12. Flexible teaching, learning, and facilitation modes (oral, notational, holistic, experiential, analytic)
13. Excellence/quality in both the processes and products of music making relative to individual goals of participants
14. The honoring of origins and intents of specific musical practices

Although rather cumbersome, these articulations began the process of relinquishing the dominance of the U.K. "voice" and providing an avenue toward a global understanding. Constructed away from the socialist spine that had initially defined the U.K. model, these statements resonated with David Elliott's (1998) paper presentation "Community Music and Postmodernity." Here Elliott tentatively makes the case for community music to be considered a postmodern enterprise.[2] Arguing from within this paradigm implicitly suggests that definitions, by their very nature, would unnecessarily fix, freeze, and limit the growth and development of the practice. This is reflected in a language that sets out characteristics and describes what community music does rather than what it is.

Networks

As a collection of people, the CMA has helped facilitate a number of regional network programs as part of its commitment to the development of community music worldwide. The first European regional network meeting to which the CMA contributed was held in 2003 at the Irish Academy of World Music and Dance (previously called the Irish World Music Center), in Limerick, Ireland. Phil Mullen, an Irish community musician living in London, was paramount in its organization and arranged a second meeting four years later at Goldsmiths, University of London. Mullen connected like-minded musicians from across the continent in order to share practice and thinking. The second meeting built upon the first with over forty community musicians from twelve countries including Norway, Denmark, Sweden, Austria, Hungary, Spain, Wales, Iran, Ghana, Canada, Ireland, Italy, and the United Kingdom. Participants considered issues on training, technology, collaboration, and project initiation and evaluation (Veblen, 2008b).

In 2008 the North American Coalition for Community Music (NACCM) was formed. The first meeting, held at Hewitt School in Manhattan, consisted of seventeen music educators from across the community music spectrum. In combination with the "Lifelong Learning and Community Music Special Research Interest Group" of the National (U.S.) Association for Music Education's (formally MENC), participants met to discuss the development of a continental organization focused entirely on community music practices. During their three days together, topics addressed included the following: What is community music in its broadest sense? Who are the people and groups most likely to effect a transformation to relevancy and accessibility, and how could this organization support those individuals and groups? Who would the organization benefit and represent? What organizations supporting community music practices and research already exist, and how would this one differ? What are the ways in which the organization could develop?

The Hewitt Commission, as it was called, determined that an American continental organization dedicated to the development and support of community music projects that advance accessibility and relevancy across age, ethnic, social, geographical, and political boundaries would be a worthy endeavor. The commission also concluded that such an organization would provide a voice and a network for the many diverse community music practices that currently did not have a forum for interaction and representation and would provide opportunity for all community music practices—including school music—to inform, learn from, and support one another (Bowles, 2008). Subsequent meetings in Minneapolis, Florida, and Texas, led by Don Coffman, have attempted to galvanize the group and give it direction. Other networks influenced by CMA participants can be found in Brazil, Australia, the Asia-Pacific region[3] and the Middle East.

Flowing from the confidence of a higher profile through regional networking, research, and practice, the CMA's vision and mission statements capture a global impression of community music practice. Here is CMA's vision statement:

> We believe that everyone has the right and ability to make, create, and enjoy their own music. We believe that active music-making should be encouraged and supported at all ages and at all levels of society. Community music activities do more than involve participants in music-making; they provide opportunities to construct personal and communal expressions of artistic, social, political, and cultural concerns. Community music activities do more than pursue musical excellence and innovation; they can contribute to the development of economic regeneration and can enhance the quality of life for communities. Community music activities encourage and empower participants to become agents for extending and developing music in their communities. In all these ways community music activities can complement, interface with, and extend formal music education structures.[4]

Here is CMA's mission statement:
The commission aims to:

- Facilitate the exchange of information on areas relevant to the field of community music.
- Encourage debate and dialogue on different international perspectives on community music and on current issues within the field.
- Encourage international cooperation.

- Where possible enter into dialogue with musicians and music educators in related fields.
- Disseminate research and other information

To reiterate the points made in the CMA's vision statement, the spirit of community music, as it has developed within the CMA, can be summarized with three succinct points:

- Community music activities do more than involve participants in music making; they provide opportunities to construct personal and communal expressions of artistic, social, political, and cultural concerns.
- Community music activities do more than pursue musical excellence and innovation; they can contribute to the development of economic regeneration and can enhance the quality of life for communities.
- Community music activities do more than focus on individual expressions of music making; they encourage and empower participants to become agents for extending and developing music in their communities.

What has emerged from the CMA's activities is a new, self-assured, mature expression of community music that seeks to respect community music histories alongside a wide variety of practices. This "attitude" toward a global expression found consolidation in 2008 in Rome, Italy. Here participants made presentations within an atmosphere that celebrated difference while maintaining an understanding of those dispositions that act as connective points (Coffman, 2008b).

EDUCATION, TRAINING, AND PROFESSIONAL PREPARATION

In previous chapters, I have suggested that the early growth and development of community music as intervention can be considered through the practices of musicians in the United Kingdom. From this standpoint, I will initially sketch a historical overview of training, education, and professional preparation from the perspective of the United Kingdom before widening the discussion to include developments from around the globe.

1990s to the Present

Those attending the Making Connections conference in 1989 at the Abraham Moss Center in North Manchester, England, drew boundaries around distinguishable areas of community music employment. They were categorized in four broad areas: (1) outreach work by professional music ensembles—for example,

orchestras and opera companies; (2) people working within a particular community—these musicians were often being called *community music worker* or *music
animateur*; (3) those working in music cooperatives or collectives; (4) freelance
workshop and project leaders (Joss, 1993). Once those working in the United
Kingdom had begun categorizing employment opportunities, issues of training,
education, and professionalization began to emerge. Influenced by these events,
the CMA met in Norway to talk about the training of a "new" music professional
and included a number of presenters who had attended the Manchester conference (Drummond, 1991).

Discussions surrounding professional development began to proliferate in the
United Kingdom through *Sounding Board*. An early example is Mary Keith's
(1992) explanation on the National Vocational Qualifications. Those working as
community musicians during this time began to form a clearer understanding of
what constitutes a community music professional and thus began to uncover the
value of their work. Specific competencies, such as musician, workshop leader,
project manager and instigator, and entrepreneur, helped form an understanding
of what a community musician did. This enabled community musicians to find
a language to articulate their practice more precisely and make them better
advocates of the work. The first courses that responded to this groundswell were
Music Performance and Communications Skills, run by the Guildhall School
of Music and Drama, and the courses for workshop leaders, run by Community
Music Ltd. in London, Cardiff, and Norwich. Those involved in community
music were keen for expansion, but not at the cost of its core values. Organizations
such as the Arts and Entertainment Training Council were in a position to enable
growth, but practitioners were hesitant. Their concerns oscillated around the
possibility that the curriculum might fail to fully reflect community music's core
principles, a discussion that had resonance with earlier debates surrounding
visual artists working in a community arts capacity (Braden, 1978).

Community music training in the United Kingdom found momentum around
1994. In spring of that year, there were eight training programs: Singing from
Scratch, Contemporary Music-Making for Amateurs, Music for Youth, Share
Music (working with young people with physical disabilities), Visions of Reality
(management skills for community artists), Local Distinctiveness in Action (the
celebration of local identity), plus programs providing professional orchestral
players with guidance and support in education work (Sound Sense, 1994). It was
also during this year that Pete Moser organized his first "Approaches to
Composition" weekend as part of the More Music in Morecambe project (Moser,
1994). This event has expanded over the years and has become a regular—and
much anticipated—training feature on the U.K. community music landscape.
Because of these program's beginnings, those working on them understood their
work as distinctive from formal music education. Largely rejecting a language
that used the term *education*, community musicians described their professional
development as *training*. This move was deliberate and created a polarity between

vocational and *academic* education. Echoing a national trend toward closer partnerships between potential employees and those within the employment sectors, training was seen as something different from education. For example, the initial advertisement for the Liverpool Institutes for Performance Arts degree in Community Arts described itself as being "unique in providing training in community arts within an integrated degree" (Owen, 1995).

Foregrounding this trend, Sound Sense, the United Kingdom's national community music organization, published a special feature about training in each 1995 issue of *Sounding Board* (Burgess, 1995; Higham, 1995). The growing interest in community music training accumulated in *Which Training?*—a directory of U.K. courses in community music (Deane, 1998). Describing itself as a "'hitchhiker's guide' to Community Music courses," the directory revealed nine specific community music courses, twenty community music modules within larger programs, seventeen modules or units that offered some aspects of community music practice, and four providers offering short training courses. During this time, a total of forty-seven different establishments offered community music training: twenty-four were higher education institutes (HEI), and five were music conservatoires. Only three HEIs—the Liverpool Institute for Performing Arts; Goldsmiths, University of London; and the University of York—were committed to delivering specific community music academic programs, while fourteen HEIs offered specific community music content and seven offered aspects of the work. At the time, only one conservatory, the Trinity College of Music, offered specific community music modules, and the remaining three conservatories—the Royal Academy, the Royal College, and the Royal Northern—covered some aspects of practice.

By 1998, community music in the United Kingdom was establishing a growing range of training opportunities. This continued with the development of programs and courses from local providers, such as Community Music East,[5] Community Music Wales,[6] More Music,[7] Sound It Out,[8] the Sage Gateshead,[9] and Music Leader, a support service that aims to increase the impact, value, and quality of music leadership throughout the country.[10] As music conservatories began to consider music in terms of a portfolio career (jobs that have multiple sources of income), traditional training establishments began to broaden their scope: for example, the Royal College of Music's Postgraduate Diploma in Creative Leadership,[11] Birmingham Conservatory and Leeds College of Music's master's in community music,[12] and Goldsmiths, University of London Certificate in Workshop Skills.[13] Universities also expanded their music programs such as the University of York's master's in community music,[14] the University College of Chichester's Contemporary and Community Musical Studies,[15] and the University of Edinburgh's master of science in music in the community.[16]

With those participating in the CMA acting as advocates for community music practice internationally, training opportunities in other parts of the globe were enriched or grew. For example, the Irish World Academy of Music and Dance has an established master's in community music going back to 1998.[17] The Steinhardt

School of Culture, Education, and Human Development at New York University began its first course in community music in 2003,[18] the University of Washington introduced specific community music content in 2008, and Boston University established its first course in 2011. In Japan, an organization called Creating Music Culture Foundation trains music facilitators for lifelong learning in community settings, running courses such as Principles of Lifelong Learning, Group Learning, and Facilitation; Art Management; Music and Society; Popular Music; Group Dynamics; Ensemble Work; and Japanese Music.[19] In Brazil, nongovernment organizations are utilizing music more frequently in their projects and are now providing localized training aimed to run concurrently.[20] In South Africa, the University of the Witwatersrand, Johannesburg, has created a lecturing position in community music with the aim of offering a degree program.

Although it has been recognized that those employing community musicians need help in selecting appropriate and qualified project leaders, there remains a healthy resistance toward professionalizing the field. One reason may be that the very idea of professionalization betrays community music's founding principles, particularly that of access. However, ask any seasoned community musician whether you can tell good work from not so good work, and they will surely answer "Yes." Unsurprisingly, practitioners will also be able to tell you what constitutes practice of excellence. In order to work with a commitment to good practice, embrace a range of training and education opportunities, and avoid saddling the "profession" with a set of standards or a concrete charter, MusicLeader and Sound Sense developed a Code of Practice to help ensure music practitioners provide high-quality music making and learning experiences for the people they work with. The code provides a set of quality statements concerning all aspects of music learning:

> Be well prepared and organized.
> Be safe and responsible.
> Have appropriate musical skills.
> Work well with people.
> Evaluate and reflect on the work.
> Commit to professional development.[21]

By adopting the code, practitioners demonstrate their commitment to quality work. By using the code as a benchmark, practitioners' employers demonstrate their commitment to requiring high-quality practice from their employees.

Community Music in Higher Education

The development of community music programs within higher education has meant that the notion of *training* and/or *education* has come under scrutiny.

Although not always conceptually well thought through, these terms are often used interchangeably, particularly from a European perspective. Bruce Cole (1999) described the relationship between community music and higher education as a marriage of convenience driven by a mutual need.[22] From a background immersed in the ideology of community arts in the United Kingdom, Cole had been responsible for the Lewisham Academy of Music, in South London, which had been a walk-in music resource for young people and ran from 1981 to 2000. It was at the invitation of John Paynter, at the University of York, that Cole became a teaching fellow in community music in 1986, developing what is now the master's program in community music. Keen to emphasize the potential partnerships between the university and its locality, Cole (1999) maintains that "there are powerful arguments for creating access to training for those already in the community," thus providing a benefit to student, professional musician, and those who are currently active within the community such as health-care workers and teachers.

However, there has been considerable suspicion among some community musicians toward higher education courses. This is underlined by Cole, who said, "The mere description of community arts as a profession could well be seen as a threat by those who see something insidious in the growth of accredited training courses; the establishment of a premier league of qualified practitioners who attract all the available funding and credibility" (1999, p. 150). As Cole points out, "There is no direct evidence that this is a likely outcome; funds, commissions and work opportunities are handed out—as everywhere else in the arts—on the basis of merit rather than qualification" (p. 150). Often in the instances of resistance, practical apprenticeships are seen as more vital because they concentrate on the fieldwork and place little or no emphasis on theory or written work. Among those who have suspicion toward tertiary-level courses, there is a fear that academia will somehow assume control of community music, colonizing a vibrant grassroots activity that thrives on relative informality. For me, this raises the following questions: What does higher education offer to community music? How can higher education courses be developed without creating two "classes" of community music practitioners, those with a degree and those without one? These concerns are not unique to community music. Simon Procter (2001) has similar worries for community music therapy, arguing that as the profession matures and makes a transition from radical, outsider group to accepted, establishment group through processes such as state registration, those that practice must be aware of the dangers of "professionalization." He continues,

> Preoccupation with rising professional status or eagerness to adopt the assumptions of more established disciplines can compromise our ability to offer clients our distinctive skills. . . . Music therapy has come from the outside, from radical musicianship. We must not merge entirely into a medicalised professional hierarchy: to empower and enable, wherever we work, we need hearing minds and radical hearts.

And if that means being regarded as mavericks or naïve, then so be it. (Procter, 2001, n.p.)

In 2009, an electronic discussion board was set up around the topic[23] of community music and higher education. According to the discussion thread, some university faculty and administrators are suspicious of the legitimacy of community music as a program of study. They believe that community music dilutes excellence by being broad-based rather than specialist and that, through its liberal ethos, it challenges the traditionally competitive and selective practices of formal music education. Added to this is community music's tendency to focus on popular art forms and challenge institutions whose curriculum is based on the Western classical tradition. One contributor to this thread claimed that it had taken him some twenty years to overcome the resistance of establishment thinking about musical values in order to implement a community music program. However, according to student evaluations, community music courses had been much more popular than the more traditional courses offered alongside them. Why? Because students felt that the courses were more relevant and grounded the practical reality of employment.

Kathryn Deane, in her contributions on the discussion board, is strong in her convictions that community music needs its academic wing—partly because it brings rigor to questions concerning its values, benefits, and ethics, and partly to validate both the practitioners as professionals and the practice as a profession. Cole (1999) concurs: "The strength of higher education is the staying power of its research programs, its teaching and evaluative skills and resource materials." But he adds, "Its weakness is that work is often building-based and lacking in public relations; it is difficult for university staff and students to tour, and work can be limited to a relatively small geographical area" (p. 149). From my perspective, it seems clear that community music is beginning to make significant inroads into music schools and university departments (Coffman, 2011; Mellor, 2011; Moran and Loening, 2011; Paton, 2011; Rohwer, 2011). It may not be ubiquitous now, but I believe that we will see more and more institutes of higher education respond to the changing ways people make and respond to music.

THE EMERGENCE OF A FIELD

As Marie McCarthy (2008) rightly suggests, community music as an academic discipline and area of research owes much of what it is today to the CMA. This forum has enabled both practitioners and scholars to come together in discussion and debate. Friendships developed through the CMA have turned into academic partnerships, such as my collaboration with David Elliott and Kari Veblen, which established the commercial publication of the *International Journal of Community Music* (*IJCM*) in 2008. The *IJCM* initially began as a peer-reviewed online journal in 2004. In this form, the journal was available for free and was run entirely as a nonprofit. In 2008, the journal moved to a professional publisher and became available both online and in print. The *IJCM* publishes research articles, project reports, reviews, and interviews. From the beginning, the journal's aims have been in tune with those of the CMA, holding both an open concept of community music and providing a responsive scope that is able to reflect the breadth of current international practice.

The format of the journal "book" and its scripted contents might seem somewhat at odds with the practical disposition of the community musician, so why is the journal important? The journal's growth is a manifestation of the field's emergent international maturity and confidence. As the education, training, and professional development of community musicians increase, so the requirement of scholarly research in the subject area becomes more necessary. This is important if community music intends to fulfill its political potential, a challenge toward those who preside over funding for music, music organizations, and institutions that engage people in music making, teaching, and learning. A more pertinent question might be, why go from a free, online journal to one that is subscription-based and published commercially? Doesn't this betray one of community music's prominent guiding principles, accessibility? In one way, this is true: the barrier of subscription might have had the effect of reducing access to the journal and thus readership. In fact, working with a commercial publisher has increased and widened the audience. In part, this is due to the cultural structures of academic tenure, the increased production values, and the current suspicion regarding the validity of online journal publishing. In resonance with its history, the *IJCM* is a political gesture, a desire to raise the profile of community music within a scholarly domain and recognize that this domain places considerable emphasis on the format of the journal. As the editor, I am charged with striking a balance between being a gatekeeper of such things as content relevance, originality, and soundness of scholarship, being a broker between an editorial board of twenty or so experts in their field, and having a desire to keep the journal connected to the current practice while pushing its boundaries. In order to reconcile these inner conflicts and remain authentic to the discipline, I try to think of myself as a "weak editor," someone who acts cautiously against the temptation to erect a claim about the one true context we should be living or thinking in (Vattimo, 1999). The notion of community music as *just* a practical endeavor has expired. The *IJCM*, this book you are reading, and those that will undoubtedly follow are a testament to that.

SUMMARY

This chapter has presented the CMA as a fulcrum in the history of community music. Through consideration of its beginnings in 1984, I have tried to show how its connection with the U.K. movement initially influenced its growth and output.

The positioning of the CMA within an organization solely focused on music education has, as you would expect, affected the way community music has developed as an international field. Interchanges and collaborations among seminar participants have meant a healthy broadening of both community music and music education but were initially restricted to an area of know-how bounded by the parameters of each. Over time, the CMA has been able to better represent an international set of practices that might now be classed as a *field*. Due largely to the emergence of the *IJCM*, a collaboration between a few friends who met through the CMA, the journal has established itself as an important vehicle for research and scholarly production. This has inadvertently supported the rise in training, education, and professional preparation, especially within higher educational institutes.

Through concise descriptions of fourteen projects from nine countries, the next chapter offers both a portrait and celebration of community music worldwide and reflects a growing visibility of community music as an international field of practice.

CHAPTER 6

Illustrations of Practice

Through concise descriptions of fourteen projects from nine countries, this chapter offers both a portrait and celebration of community music projects worldwide. The projects featured here have all been selected because of my personal exposure to them through witnessing the practice firsthand, getting to know the instigators and their work during the CMA seminars, or working with the community musicians in my capacity as editor for the *IJCM*. Each musician was contacted with an initial written outline and asked to validate the information. Additional questions were asked in order to elicit further information if necessary. As a collection, these illustrations are presented with little in the way of discussion because I explore many of the themes and issues in part II. They are then snapshots, bold statements representing the background, intent, practice, and future challenges of each project. Although each illustration resonates with my perspective of community music, there is great diversity among them. This is how it should be because, as I have discussed, community music is reflective of different people and places, and as such no two contexts are the same.

HOPE AND COMMUNITY THROUGH MUSIC

In 2006, Peace Corps volunteer Aaron Brantly, along with local teacher Nickolae Vladimiravich, founded the Kivsharivka Youth and Community Activity Organization (KYCAO), in Kivsharivka, Ukraine. Recent events, such as the end of the Cold War and the fall of the Soviet Union, have left many families in Kivsharivka in dire straits. As parents left home to find employment abroad, older children took on their parents' responsibilities. This situation frequently exposed the teenagers to an adult world of drugs, alcohol, and unprotected sex. As the drug problem worsened, it was not uncommon for used needles to turn up in the wooded areas surrounding the school and settlement. Because of this, the HIV infection rate among the youth population was reaching epidemic proportions.

The KYCAO functions as an after-school program, providing several hours of music learning and development per day. Brantly, who completed his Peace Corps service in 2007, and Vladimiravich organized music-making sessions, music lessons, and other cultural programs focused upon inspiring creativity, self-growth, and group synergy. This safe, alcohol- and drug-free environment provided teenagers relief from their heavy home burdens and became an outlet for their creativity. Students now had an opportunity to connect with their community and receive organized support to resist negative peer pressures.

Since 2006, KYCAO has served more than 6,000 youth, sponsoring music lessons, dances, and dramatic productions. Every night, the KYCAO provides several hours of open band practice and lessons for various music and dramatic groups. They also provide a game room filled with board games and art supplies. Each week, the KYCAO hosts a movie night so that students of all ages can watch a movie in a safe and warm environment. The movies are often thought-provoking films that inspire topical discussions among the students. The band practices, booked up weeks in advance, are attended by students with a passion for the latest sounds. Vladimiravich patiently works with the bands and helps them improve their musical skills and stage presence.

Of particular interest are the rock and pop bands that regularly practice there. In December 2006, KYCAO produced a community-wide concert, featuring five rock bands and a modern break-dance group. The bands performed all original music, written by the students, sung in both Russian and Ukrainian. The songs included lyrics about love, the future, disappointment, and hope. This first concert cost 2 Hyrvnia (50 cents) to attend and included a laser light show organized and run by the young people. Approximately 500 students attended the concert. At the beginning of the project, local residents had donated equipment, instruments, and space. Although the locals were generous, the project would have benefited from some robust financial assistance. A small-projects assistance grant was provided by the United States Agency for International Development (USAID) that enabled KYCAO to purchase extra resources such as drums, guitars, and amplification. Today, the project is funded by the continuing support of the parents and community as well as door receipts from concerts. Parents and guardians typically provide 20–50 Hyrvnia ($2–$5) per semester to support the ongoing programs. Contributions are required for only those who can afford to pay. Most support continues to come from local teachers and businesses in the form of in-kind donations of time and materials. Since 2007, there have been about nine concerts a year, ranging from traditional musical performances to rock concerts.

Unity through music has become the overriding theme in the KYCAO. Roman Tomah, a recent graduate of the project and an avid drummer, commented that the new drums, various guitars, and other equipment were a great addition to the school and that he and his friends, when they are in town, still go back to the school to play music and work with upcoming youth musicians. Parents, too, can see that the program provides a much-needed outlet for the children of the community, in particular providing a distraction from alcohol and drug use. They comment on how "fantastic" it is to watch their children perform at the different events.

As of 2008, the KYCAO became a department within the Kupyansk Youth Network (KYN), a larger nongovernmental organization. Because the region is served by eleven schools and two colleges and provides services for more than 10,000 children, the KYCAO has become a model from which other institutions have generated youth development approaches. For example, other schools have used the organizational model to promote such activities as HIV/AIDS awareness on World AIDS Day; collaborative projects on music, dance, and the arts; and journalism programs.

As always, funding is a constant problem, and securing funds for increasing capacity is difficult in Kivsharivka because so much of the population lives below the poverty line. Other challenges are cultural and are held over from the Soviet era, including attitudes toward personal property and more systemic problems such as alcohol consumption. Things have been especially trying recently due to the global economic decline, which severely affected Ukraine and Eastern Ukraine in particular. However, dedicated individuals, such as Nickolae Vladimiravich, Olga Vitaliyivna, and Lubov Petrovna, continue to volunteer for the betterment of the community.[1]

AT-RISK TEENAGERS REJOIN SOCIETY THROUGH COMMUNITY MUSIC GROUPS

In Israel, music teacher Vardit Sfadia provides community music opportunities and experiences for local at-risk teenagers. Sfadia works with these youth within two different projects, which link policy makers, community musicians, and teenagers. The overall objective for both projects is to "promote rehabilitation and reintegration to the normative peer group though creative music-making," thus offering an effective alternative to current rehabilitative programs for at-risk youth. During a music-making session, Sfadia aims for the children to encounter consistency, freedom (with few boundaries), individual attention, expression, success, and, occasionally, performing in public. In both projects, securing funding and qualified staff members are the most difficult obstacles, because funding is scarce and the musicians must have a combination of specific musical skills and experience alongside approaches to facilitate the process.

The first project, supported by the Ministry of Education, was established at Haifa High School, where Sfadia directed the regular school music ensemble. The student body consisted of middle-class teenagers living in the Central Carmel area in Haifa. In collaboration with the staff, Sfadia offered specialized music classes for teenagers with behavior problems. With a shared goal, the participants focused less on interpersonal conflicts and more upon the music making. Class became practice for life: students learned to cooperate, listen, and abide by rules within the group while drumming (darbuka, congas, and bongos). Through this group participation, two teenagers became proficient enough to become Sfadia's assistants and teach other at-risk children in the school. By the end of the year, the group of drummers, having learned to manage the pressure of performing and attained the self-control required to participate, performed with another selected school ensemble.

The second project, "Jasut ha Noar," is a part of an ongoing effort funded by the Youth Protection department of the Ministry of Welfare. The program operates all over the country, providing food and shelter (in hostels) to homeless children and teenagers gathered from off the streets. Once their immediate needs are fulfilled, the young people attend day centers, where specialized personnel run activities and classes; Sfadia manages one of the music-making groups. The first step in Sfadia's approach is to empathize with the musical tastes of the young people, hopefully creating a path for communication and trust. Sfadia knows how to set limits, enhance individual creativity, and enable each participant to create his or her own patterns to then seamlessly integrate into the group composition; in the process, Sfadia assists each participant to find their "voice."

After studying several case study participants in the Jasut ha Noar project, Graciela Sandbank (2006) noticed the

> process of musicalization of E, a youngster who discovered his musicality for the first time in his troubled existence, and found in music a means of creative expression and a catharsis for the suffering of growing in a maladjusted family. From being a street boy, surviving by petty theft and always in conflict with his peers and with the law, E become an oriental singer, learned to persevere and to get organized, got a job, participated and won a competition for oriental singers and finally was accepted for the army service, thus becoming a member of the normative society. The metamorphosis he went through can be seen in the change in his body language while he relates, dressed in his army uniform, how he learned to cope with the stress of being a soldier. The process . . . in E's case is highly influenced by the gradual formation of a musical identity. E is no longer a street boy, he is a singer.[2] (p. 124)

THE BUDDY BEAT: DRUMMING TO PROMOTE MENTAL HEALTH RECOVERY

In 2007, Jeanette Allan (lead occupational therapist for mental health for the National Health Service [NHS], district of Renfrewshire, Scotland) was introduced to the "traffic-light" model of social inclusion, aimed at assisting people with mental health difficulties to reintegrate with wider society as part of their recovery. Briefly, this model proposes three stages of activity:

> Red: closed—activities in mental health settings, attended by service users only
> Amber: supported—activities in everyday settings, for service users only
> Green: open—activities in everyday settings, accessible to all

With this in mind, Allan decided to establish a socially inclusive drumming project. She chose drumming because of her previous experiences working with community musician Jane Bentley, with whom she had run several successful short-term, hospital-based projects in the past.

Following this model, the project started at "red" with a series of workshops in the acute psychiatric admissions unit of two local hospitals. Bentley teamed up with an occupational therapist for each workshop, thus offering both musical and mental health support. Here, rather than focus on technique or performance, the emphasis was simply to engage people and build confidence by creating a safe musical space. In this mistake-free environment, participants were encouraged to form their own judgments about what it felt like playing in a musical group.

The drum sessions were neither a cacophonic free-for-all nor a stereotypical venting of emotions. Instead, group members were progressively encouraged to turn their attention outward from themselves toward the rest of the group, developing skills of listening and relational awareness as they learned to align their rhythms together. Because of the interactive nature of the music, this meant that participants related to one another in ways that mimic other forms of interaction (e.g., turn-taking, making eye contact, and sharing a mutual focus) without the specific pressures of self-disclosure that might occur in conversation. In this way, the music making constitutes a form of "social exercise," thus paving the way for more complex forms of social interaction. In an interview with Bentley, one group member, Laura, remarked,

> In the group, I have found things that I thought I would never find again after I became ill; total acceptance, true friendship and amazing trust. When I lost my job I lost all of these but have gained so much more than I ever had before. It is lovely to sit in the circle and know that no one is going to judge me and quite often I sit with my eyes shut—this I can only do when I feel totally at ease.

The amber stage of the model continues, with "The Buddy Beat" (a "buddy" is the local name for a person from Paisley, Scotland, where the group takes place)—a drumming group that meets weekly at the local arts center. Group members who are interested in continuing with drumming are encouraged to attend, on a day-release basis from the hospital, accompanied by occupational therapy staff. Additionally, they are free to continue after discharge, thus obviating the possibility of dangling a "carrot" of an engaging new activity during their hospital stay, only to find the opportunities withdrawn or inaccessible when they become well enough to leave.

The group's journey to the "green" stage happened a lot sooner than expected. During the fifth session, a passerby heard the music and, assuming that it was a regular performing drumming group, promptly asked Bentley if the group would perform for the opening of a local event. This posed a bit of a dilemma, because group members, in order to help build their confidence, had been repeatedly promised that no one would have to play drums in front of other people. However, it would also be disabling to stand in the way of potential opportunities, so the invitation was extended to the group, along with reassurances that such an event would be well within their capabilities. The music would be kept improvisational, thus masking any "mistakes" or lapses of attention. Everyone said yes—and loved it, for the chance to give something back and to be seen as a contributor rather than receiver. There was no mention of mental health—they were simply a drumming group.

Three years later, this has led to a twofold emphasis for the group: (1) anyone with a mental health diagnosis is welcome to attend the weekly workshops (which maintain an emphasis on social and communicative skills) commitment free; and (2) for those who want to, there are also a growing number of opportunities to perform. This has been enabled in part through Bentley's outside work as a community musician, as she is regularly invited to run large-scale rhythm "energizers" (imagine 300 people grooving together on a variety of drums and percussion) for conferences. This kind of event offers an ideal low-threat performance opportunity for the drumming group. They get to perform onstage to a large crowd, but they are not the sole focus, as everybody else is making music too. A further series of opportunities has arisen through invitations to work with groups of adults and children with special needs; group members have found this especially rewarding.

Group members have now taken ownership of the group—it was initially funded through the National Health Service but was later constituted as a voluntary arts group, and they now attract their own sources of funding. There is an "advanced" group for longer term members who want more of a musical challenge, and a monthly evening workshop that is hosted by the group for the general public. They have also run a workshop assistants' course to enable members to further support music workshops for vulnerable groups, and there are plans to develop a drumming project involving older people with dementia.

The challenges that remain are, as ever, to maintain funding sources for the group, but also to keep enabling the progression from "red" to "green" by returning to the hospital to encourage new members. One of the most distinctive features of the group is that no one is asked to leave after six weeks. The result of this is that members have formed extremely strong, cohesive social networks that have carried beyond the drumming and into everyday life: Bob, a group member, exclaimed, "I have pushed all my friends away over the years until I had none to speak of and not only has Buddy Beat taught me that it is okay to have friends but also that it is also okay to keep them. That is priceless!"[3]

"JUNK" INSTRUMENTS, ENSEMBLES, AND MUSIC MAKING

The PickleHerring Theatre Company was started in Liverpool, United Kingdom, in 1994. Working alongside funding agencies such as Arts Council England, local government, and environmental organizations, PickleHerring produces performing events that promote environmental issues such as recycling and waste management. Described as "spectacle and surprise," performances grow from local concerns and take place in spaces that reflect the issues the group is dealing with— for example, a shopping district, an abandoned warehouse, or a recycling plant.

Using an interdisciplinary approach to community music (including theater and movement), PickleHerring seeks to foster the creative and innate musician in each participant. Matt Smith, the artistic director, underscores these ideas by encouraging inclusion, creativity, and ownership.

PickleHerring runs a variety of projects and workshops for children, teens, and adults. In these sessions, participants invent instruments out of "junk" and engage in junk music-making ensembles. The ensembles play music from many genres, including blues, folk, rock, world music styles, and original compositions. Musicians who work for PickleHerring act as facilitators, loosely organizing the group and then gently guiding the process along the way. This enables the participants to take charge of their own experiences.

Because musical instruments are made of "waste" materials—such as cups, plates, pieces of plastic, and scrap metal—participants feel free to experiment, playing with sound unhindered by notions of technique. Smith notes that participants do not seem to be worried about breaking a junk drum, and this enables their relationship with the instrument to be more playful and carefree. One of the implications of this work is that participants can invent their own technique and eventually become a virtuoso on their own creation. The junk instruments allow participants to find a freedom that has, in many cases, been previously missing within other music-making encounters. Participants instantly invent sounds and often easily connect with fellow participants. The sound seems raw and noisy but has an energy that can bring public spaces to life. Smith suggests that everyone can develop his or her own technique for a junk instrument: "Everyone can be a junk musician."

With a focus toward democracy, creativity, and collaboration, Smith describes the pedagogical approach as "radical"; the pedagogy is based on the idea of the active participant and draws upon the work of Paulo Freire and Augusto Boal. PickleHerring creates projects and workshops for environmental agencies and continues to draw artists and participants together in order to make sound and protest throughout English cities.[4]

THE HONK! FESTIVAL IN DAVIS SQUARE

Since 2006, hundreds of street bands have gathered in Davis Square, Somerville, Massachusetts, for a weekend in October to perform free brass and drum music in Davis Square, on the border of Cambridge, Massachusetts, United States. The idea for the festival emerged from shared goals and dreams between the Second Line Social Aid and the Pleasure Society Brass Band. The HONK! Festival's mission is to "reclaim public spaces with loud, joyful music and spectacle, and to inspire and embolden our audiences in support of progressive causes in our communities" (Leppmann, 2010).[5] The weekend objective has been to bring street bands together for free, outdoor, family-friendly music. At the heart of HONK! is the notion that culture should be part of everyday life and that everyone can and should participate (Garafalo, 2011).

A local committee manages and administers the HONK! Festival, debating and making collective decisions about meeting participant needs and how to allocate their limited resources. The HONK! Festival committee chose Davis Square because the location offered good accessible performance spaces within a context of a strong, supportive arts community. The festival relies heavily on community and participant volunteers due to a small budget. In the first year, the festival was open to any nonprofessional band willing to participate. Unfortunately, the committee must now turn bands away because of limited space or insufficient resources.

Over the years, the HONK! Festival has offered new and innovative programs. In 2007, for example, there was a parade of community groups, and in 2007 and 2008, the addition of school workshops and a formal symposium enriched the events. Most recently, the committee added several Friday shows in nearby underserved communities and a Sunday night, all-band program at Davis Square's renowned Somerville Theater. The HONK! Festival has also spread to other cities, including a post-HONK! East Coast tour through Providence (PRONK!), western Massachusetts (Brass Mayhem), Brooklyn, and New York City (BONK!), as well as brass-band convergences in Seattle (Honk West), Texas (HONKTX), and Montreal (Congrès de l'insurrection Culturelle). The largest challenge remains in attracting and maintaining donors.

COMMUNITY BANDS IN THE SUBÚRBIO FERROVIÁRIO SECTOR

Community bands (wind and percussion concert bands) in Brazilian villages are often the only source of instrumental music education for young people. They provide music instruction and significantly contribute to the cultural life of the community. The majority are civic organizations, but some are associated with the military, some are maintained by governmental agencies, and a few are connected to schools and nonprofit NGOs (nongovernmental organizations).

Barbosa (2008) describes the efforts of three projects in the Subúrbio Ferroviário sector of Salvador City, Bahia, Brazil, an area of high social vulnerability and oppression, low income, and high unemployment. These include the Sociedade Primeiro de Maio (NGO) partnership with the School of Music of the Universidade Federal da Bahia (UFBA) to develop the Filarmônica Ufberê wind band; the Orquestra da Juventude de Salvador (OSJS) orchestra, financed and coordinated by the Municipal Secretary of Social Development (SEDES), and the Fundação Gregório de Matos (the Municipal Secretary of Culture); and the School of Music Maestro Wanderley, financed by the Casa das Filarmônicas (NGO). Professors and students from UFBA provide instruction to young people, who subsequently earn some money by performing for dancing shows, anniversaries, and weddings, or by teaching privately. Some students gain enough skill to participate (and receive pay) in the state youth orchestra. Barbosa observed that these groups provide a lot more than music instruction, because they contribute toward emancipating youth from the social oppression they experience:

> Through the direct contact with the university professors and students and public authorities, in addition to the participation in significant events and important places, the community [music] student understands the world deeper, beyond his community. He [sic] goes into prestigious places and events where his parents have never had the chance to enter. He gets to know people who ascended socially and financially and the way they did it. He sees the possibility of ascending as well, or he sees himself already ascending through the participation in the music group by using and improving his talents. His vision of community and society and his perspectives and paradigms of living expand. He comprehends that he, with and within the music ensemble, has cultural and artistic values that may serve as capital to negotiate with the richer communities from which he used to feel excluded. Now he knows that he can be an important part of the society, playing a worthy role in it. When he understands this, he also sees the necessity of making his capital to be worthier, looking for ways to improve his musical abilities (going to the university, for instance). (Barbosa, 2008, p. 100)

These bands exemplify the intentions of many of community musicians who seek to bring social uplift and economic regeneration to marginalized or disadvantaged populations. In such instances, the social and personal well-being of participants becomes at least as important as the music making, if not more.

The bands described here have faced three significant challenges that have at times seemed insurmountable:

1. *Funding.* Although the project received a little money to buy some instruments, payment of music facilitators continues to be a problem. This has been compounded by several university strikes that have eliminated student music

teachers for months at a time, a funding system that works on a yearly application cycle, and a new mayor who revoked his promise to support the projects and thus left the participants frustrated and disillusioned.

2. *Rehearsal space and off-site practice.* During the first four years, rehearsal space was an issue. The only available room was accessible for only a few hours a week. In addition, because of the area's high crime rate, the youth were not allowed to bring the instruments home in order to practice.

3. *Mental health.* Barbosa admits that at the beginning, the team did not think participants would need any psychological support. However, the relationships among some of the students became difficult because some of them had seen and suffered such abuse and violence that they had developed mental health problems. Those working on the project did not initially know how to deal with this. Now the projects are linked with the public Center of Psychosocial Service and the young people are getting the help they need.

Recognizing some of the mistakes that have been made during the development of these projects, Barbosa notes that projects must start with a

clear decision of what its objectives are. We never knew, or discussed even, if we were a social project with music or just a music project. When some students decided to be a professional, we realized we plant dreams. But they were not prepared to pass the public university's entrance examination, in subjects such as Portuguese and Mathematics.[6]

Although there have been difficulties and frustrations, the project continues and Barbosa's team continues to look for solutions in a context that often mitigates against them.

INTERETHNIC CONNECTIONS AT A YOUTH MUSIC FESTIVAL

In Kumanovo, a city in the former Yugoslav Republic of Macedonia, the local youth held a summer music festival in 2008. The youth, under the auspices of the nongovernmental organization Centre for Intercultural Dialogue (CID), instituted the Youth Open Festival (YOF) to confront, and hopefully ameliorate, the local conflicts between young people of various ethnic origins, due to perceived differences.

Today, the postconflict[7] city population is divided between the Macedonian majority and the Albanian, Roma, Serbian, and Turkish minorities. Although they all live within city boundaries, there are few interethnic connections or interactions: for example, each subgroup attends its own schools, gathers in separate spaces, and lives in distinct neighborhoods. Perceptions of ethnic difference, as well as linguistic, religious, and cultural distances, contribute to constant interethnic tension, hostility, and violence.

During the 2008 festival, more than 100 volunteers, from all ethnic groups in Kumanovo, participated in joint artistic activities, culminating in a concert. Well-prepared, young staff members (average age 22), from all ethnicities in the region, managed the festival and ensured safety and equality. The festival, funded by the "Youth in Action" program of the European Union, took place at the public square of the cultural municipal building in the city center.

During the YOF, ethnomusicologist Alexandra Balandina worked as a facilitator and researcher, coaching a music ensemble of twelve volunteers. The participants ranged from 14 to 22 years old and were from different races, religions, socioeconomic backgrounds, and ethnicities, including Macedonian, Albanian, Roma and Serbian. Balandina envisioned *intercultural musicking*,[8] which refers to the musical activities of sharing and learning across cultures and celebrates things commonalities over differences. Employing peer learning and rote imitation, the teenagers taught one another traditional and contemporary music and dance that represented their own cultural heritage. The participants also learned and performed popular music and hip-hop from the English-speaking world. In the end, all twelve participants together composed a multilingual rap song, "Ajde Site" ("C'mon All Together"), as a finale, which highlighted and emphasized the purpose of the festival.

Intercultural music making and collaboration provided the opportunity for dialogue, understanding, and peace building. A unified musical purpose built relationships among participants, eased interracial tensions, promoted respect, and empowered the youth. Commenting on the total experience, one participant said,

> This is the first time we befriended one another. I could never imagine that we could enjoy so much the music workshops and the concert. It is sad that the festival ceases. I am not sure whether we will hang out together, but I can tell and I hope that at least we who participated in the music project will never fight or assault each other on the streets. (Balandina, 2010, p. 241)

Lack of funding has been the largest obstacle, preventing this project from growing into a yearly event and hindering research on the positive effects of the project beyond the duration of the actual music event. In addition, due to the deep-seated historical and political ethnic tensions and violence, improving interethnic relations and promoting reconciliation necessitates multidimensional peace operations and both bottom-up and top-down contributions.[9]

VIRTUAL COMMUNITY MUSIC IMPROVISATION

For nine years, Steve Dillon, Andrew Brown, and their colleagues have conducted an ongoing research project aimed at increasing access to meaningful music-making experiences via media channels. The research project grew from a theoretical examination of the educative power of meaningful music making and the creative leverage of algorithmic processes for musical engagement. Observations about the transformative opportunities of information technologies for collaborative music making led to them deliberately extending the use of music technologies from production to performance using real-time algorithmic systems. The work has been supported financially by the Australasian Cooperative Research Centre for Interaction Design (ACID), Apple Computers Australia, the Apple University Consortium, and the Queensland University of Technology's Institute of Creative Industries and Innovation, along with many community centers, schools, and universities that have provided in-kind support.

Dillon and Brown designed and developed the computer program *jam2jam* to implement their vision, and since then *jam2jam* has grown into a "family" of collaborative media performance software programs. Since the beginning, Dillon, Brown, and an interdisciplinary project team have brought *jam2jam* to several thousands of youth and people with disabilities in Europe, the United Kingdom, the United States, and the Asia-Pacific region.

The *jam2jam* program allows inexperienced music makers to electronically gather and collaborate on music projects. The program is distinct from other music technologies because it focuses on communal creativity with computers and primarily considers the computer as an instrument, the network as an ensemble, and the Internet as venue for performance. With *jam2jam*, there are multiple forms of possible relationships among members of a virtual ensemble. Performers can be colocated, using a local area network or USB controllers around a single computer, or geographically distributed, communicating and performing together in real time over the Internet. Participants form ensembles, organize performances, explore instrument capabilities, improvise collaboratively, and "jam." *Jam2jam* turns a computer into an "instrument," allowing users to quickly "play" musical parts and learn about musical concepts. The software enables those with little music background to easily operate instruments, mix sounds, and become "performers." Even those uncomfortable with technology can quickly navigate the program.

Jam2jam operates somewhat like a video game, in which players, using a mouse, keyboard, or external controllers, change the music's timbre, volume, texture, density, and pitch range. Instrument options vary depending upon which "scene" is selected, but typically include drums, percussion, bass, guitar, and keyboard. The *jam2jam* AV version includes the live manipulation of video and digital images as another performance instrument so the user can perform like a VJ (video jockey) as well as a DJ. Performances with *jam2jam* can be saved as audiovisual movies for review or sharing.

The music in *jam2jam* is not limited to one culture; however, most music created through the program reflects its digital origin in rock, pop, or techno. Jam scenes or styles are often designed specifically from information gathered from users' cultures: for example, a Canto pop (Cantonese popular music) scene was created for a Hong Kong event, and reggae and country music scenes valued by Indigenous Australian communities were created for the One Laptop per Child (OLPC) XO computer program in Indigenous Australian communities. Commissioning expert practitioners from a culture to create the content can enhance the cultural fluidity of the scenes for *jam2jam*. This is particularly important to maintain an ethical approach to cultural appropriation of musical and visual content while providing content that is immediately engaging and valued by users. Engagement with *jam2jam* performance is designed to be personal, social, and cultural and promote a relationship with the music and the process of communal creativity through performance.

Throughout the research project, there have been numerous trials of several different versions of the software in the United States, United Kingdom, Europe, Asia, and Australasia. Each version of the software tailors the music making to a different population or culture. To facilitate this diverse usage, the program utilizes icons instead of words. This allows the system to be used across cultures and with semiliterate participants. Versions for people with disabilities have incorporated controllers and sensors that initiate expressive change in instruments and their parameters. Of particular interest in this area is the documenting and assessment of the value of enabling these kinds of nonverbal and nonpresent relationships and determining the relational pedagogies required to facilitate these experiences.

In the future, the *jam2jam* team will need to conquer technology and funding challenges to ensure expansion and provide software support. Current funding cycles for *jam2jam*'s development have recently been completed, and the research outcomes will be summarized and published over the coming years. *Jam2jam* software, as it stands, is robust but operates on particular hardware platforms. Its uptake as a research prototype is increasing at a steady rate, in many countries and for many different reasons. The idea of using generative technology to enable a virtual ensemble that allows easy access to performance is still relatively new, and each innovation inherent in *jam2jam* has its own disruptive effect on its use and research. Dillon and Brown suggest that generative media tools like *jam2jam* present three ideas that are challenging and disruptive: the computer as instrument, the network as ensemble, and the Internet as venue. Each challenges the perceptions of what music making and performance are, especially what is accepted as "music" in institutional settings.

As digital media becomes more accessible and ubiquitous, researchers expect to be able to focus more on theoretical and pedagogical findings, rather than on software development, to evaluate the social and musical benefit of generative media performance. In terms of software development, data visualization software has been recently developed that provides a display of activity data collected during a jam and aligns it with playback of a video recording of the jam. This kind of use of software, which provides visual summaries of performance choices and relationships among players, is enabling Dillon and Brown to further gather evidence abouthowpeopleengagewithmusicmakingindigitalcommunities.Consequently, research efforts in the future will focus on relational pedagogies, analytical feedback, broader access through controllers, and the Internet as venue.[10]

A VIRTUAL CLASSROOM

Special education music teacher Donald DeVito launched the Virtual Classroom for Students with Disabilities Project (VCSDP) in 2006. The VCSDP's goals are as follows: to virtually connect institutions, public schools, and community musicians; enhance music education majors' skills and proficiency in teaching special education; supplement public school special needs music instruction; promote cultural interaction; and expand formal education structures. DeVito initially worked alongside university students to create adaptive music lessons for students who attend the Sidney Lanier School, a public school for children with moderate to profound disabilities that include autism, cerebral palsy, Down syndrome, among others. Working directly with students with disabilities and their families affords university students the opportunity to engage with a different population of their community.

The first full-scale project was developed with community musicians DeVito had met during his time in Singapore with the CMA. These included Emma Rodriguez Suarez at Syracuse University, David Akombo (Kenya) from Weber State University in Utah, and Magali Kleber from the Universidade Estadual de Londrina in Brazil. During this project, university students were paired with Sidney Lanier students, meeting regularly during the semester through Skype (a free Internet video communication program).[11] The music sessions varied depending on the context, but usually included the university students individually preparing and facilitating music-making workshops that were appropriate for the students of Sidney Lanier. Workshops ranged from learning original Brazilian songs, learning to perform the beat to Kenyan music, and performing and singing folk, spiritual, and patriotic songs directly from the cultural source. As the project organizer, DeVito provided feedback to all of the participants guiding the process and responding to individual needs.

In May 2010, the project, DIScovering ABILITIES, culminated in a performance held in Weill Recital Hall at New York's Carnegie Hall. Local teachers, students, and the general public were invited to the performance. During this mixed evening of music, the Sidney Lanier students played with the Santa Fe College Jazz Band directed by Steven Bingham; David Akombo led the Syracuse and Sidney Lanier ensemble in the Kenyan folk song Jambo Bwana; and Magali Kleber performed the songs "Marche de Pifano" and "Meu Balaeo," which had been taught through the Virtual Classroom. Lansana Camara, founder of Group Laiengee, a music ensemble that assists in providing food and housing for children with special needs in Conakry, Guinea, West Africa, was brought to the concert along with several other guest musicians thanks to a grant from the National Endowment for the Arts. In the future, the Virtual Classroom project aims to combine *jam2jam* interactive performance technology with DIScovering ABILITIES in online concerts with the CMA members and participants.[12]

BREAKING DOWN BARRIERS

In February 2010, three religiously, socially, and culturally differing, yet geographically close, choirs performed in a concert, *Blessing*, in a relatively small performance venue within the Franciscan Custody of the Holy Land monastery, in East Jerusalem, Israel. Shortly thereafter, the Franciscan monastery and administration offered a five-day conducting course for Arab and Israeli conductors.

Both the concert and conducting course arose as projects within the Conductors Without Borders (CWB) program, founded in 2007 by the International Federation for Choral Music (IFCM). Among many goals, the CWB seeks to "answer the needs of choral conductors and leaders who require access to professional guidance and mentorship," "share a common philosophy of choral singing, repertoire and experiences," and "build a community of local partners furthering co-operation and an exchange of information."[13] The Eric Ericson International Choral Centre (through the Carpe Vitam Foundation) and the Franciscan order supported this activity together with the participating choirs.

The three choirs—the Efroni Choir from Israel, the Sawa Choir from Shefar'am (the Palestinian part of Israel), and the Yasmeen Choir from East Jerusalem—performed individually and collectively within the concert. Andre de Quadros worked with each choir individually for a day, then all together for a daylong rehearsal, dress rehearsal, and final concert. The singers were unused to collaborating against the backdrop of political tensions, so a number of communal and social activities were organized to enable a friendly and harmonious atmosphere to develop.

During the concert, each choir sang a set of pieces that were later combined for the final three numbers. Separately, the choirs sang a wide variety of culturally and musically meaningful pieces, representing their own traditions and ancestry. The combined repertoire consisted of three significant pieces: a contemporary Australian piece, "Goolay Yali" by Stephen Leek; "Kom" by Monica Aslund; and "Oye" by Jim Papoulis.

The concert as a whole, and the combined choir itself, became a manifestation of peace and social inclusion in a city wrought with violence and separation; the backdrop of the city was a foil for the concert, which highlighted the potential of music to cross social, cultural, and religious barriers. One participant from the Sawa Choir noted that this was "a dream of a moment of joy and peace, that will help us remember that we have more in common than we think."

During the conducting course, young and experienced Arab and Israeli conductors worked with de Quadros in developing conducting skills and techniques, vocal ability, and sight-singing skills. Emphasis was placed on the development of a community of aspiring conductors while excavating the philosophical dimensions of conducting. The conducting course had an effect on participants that was similar to that of the concert course: one participant from East Jerusalem commented, "I would not trade this week for any other. There was no tension whatsoever, I always realize that in doing music or through music itself we forget differences and just want to enjoy the heavenly sounds that we can make through peace alone."[14]

COMMUNITY MUSIC PROJECTS REVITALIZE A SEASIDE RESORT

Since 1993, More Music has been organizing and producing hundreds of community-wide music activities, projects, and classes.[15] More Music resides in the northern U.K. seaside resort town of Morecambe, but it also provides opportunities for communities in the subregion of northwest England. Over the past eighteen years, led by its founder Peter Moser, More Music has grown from one employee to twenty-two full-time employees, gaining a national and international reputation along the way. In the process of supplying hundreds of music programs and enabling young and old people to participate in active musical doing, More Music has significantly contributed to the revitalization of Morecambe.

The community music sector in the United Kingdom has grown since the mid-1980s, due to the Arts Council's development priorities, social regeneration programs, lottery funding, and creative education initiatives. More Music's funding initially came from local stipends and grants. Since then, its funding base is a combination of earned income, donated funds, and governmental financing.

More Music began when a local arts manager, Tom Flanagan, invited Moser to Morecambe to create and run a community music development organization. In the first three years, More Music created a new community carnival band, several songwriting programs, and band festivals. In the next five years, the hiring of community music trainees and several key administrative positions led to larger projects, including contemporary music projects with teenagers, a song cycle performed at a self-produced choral festival, a nationally commissioned choral work that toured (creating new local community choirs), several special needs projects, and a set of professional training weekends.

In 2001, More Music became a charity and company limited by guarantee,[16] which initiated expansion and growth in music programming and planning and the refurbishment of a rented local office and workshop base. In the next several years, More Music capitalized upon this stability and added early childhood classes, adult education courses, evenings for teenagers, carnival band sessions, an afternoon elderly club, and elderly music outreach sessions. More Music also ran several themed summer festivals and published *Community Music: A Handbook*, a compilation of professional training weekend ideas from seven main contributors. In 2006, the More Music employees created a new vision for the organization and divided into four departments: Creative Production, Education, Regeneration, and Young People's Projects.

Participants have found acceptance, vitality, and delight at More Music. One participant said, "I now realize that my ideas are important and that people want to hear them." Another remarked, "The Hothouse [More Music's venue] has transformed my life. The Thursday sessions are literally keeping me alive." And a parent exclaimed, "My daughter never stops singing!"

Moving forward, More Music faces both opportunities and challenges. Having just purchased its current building, the organization is looking to first create a venue and new multifunction spaces, and then expand the educational programs, outreach opportunities, and innovative creative production projects. Simultaneously, it faces substantial funding challenges: the current government is cutting available funding and trusts, and foundations are investing less and less in arts organizations (due to the trend of declining returns on investment). Moser also faces the challenges of running a growing organization. The balance between finance, budgeting, and music making are difficult in times when "if the money doesn't work, then everything falls apart." There are also challenges in managing a workforce. Entering a business because you love making music with people through the process of facilitation and then finding that you need to direct and manage staff has presented, at times, a conflict of interest. However, More Music is determined to survive and to remain a beacon of imaginative music making for the nation.[17]

MUSIC MAKING IN AN ENGLISH-LANGUAGE SCHOOL

In preparation for mainstream schooling in the Australian state of Victoria, incoming refugee and immigrant children from countries such as Somalia, Afghanistan, Vietnam, China, Iraq, Burma/Myanmar, and Sudan can attend intensive English-language school for between two and four terms. Funded by the Australian government through the Victorian Department of Education and Early Childhood Development, the English as a Second Language (ESL) program in Victorian schools aims to provide educational support to culturally and linguistically diverse students who are learning English as a second or additional language, and in particular those with a refugee background who have little or no prior schooling.

The support needed by new arrivals can vary. Some children will enroll at English-language school with age-equivalent education from their country of origin (albeit often within a very different school and classroom culture than that which they encounter in Australia). Others, in particular refugees who have been exposed to extreme violence and traumatic events, will have had very little or no prior access to schooling, or their opportunities to attend school have been frequently and persistently disrupted. All new arrivals of school-age children will undergo an intense and often overwhelming and confusing cross-cultural adaptation, in addition to grappling with a new language. Thus English-language schools provide an important range of supports, building students' confidence and competence in English (both oral expressive and receptive language, and English literacy) in a curriculum context, and familiarizing students with the expectations, systems, and social culture of school in Australia. In Victoria, the number of newly arrived students requiring intensive English-language classes has increased each year from 2002. During the same period, there were significant increases in the number of refugee and humanitarian entrants enrolling in primary and secondary schools in Victoria who had little or no prior schooling, the cohort that is most strongly in need of intensive, focused educational support.

Gillian Howell (2010) has worked as a community musician within the context of one of these schools, the Collingwood English Language School, since 2005. The school is funded by the Song Room, an Australian not-for-profit organization committed to supporting creative and arts education in disadvantaged Australian schools. Howell's objective is to support English-language learning, encourage musical growth and expression, and assist emotional journeys through group composing. From the commencement of the program, music quickly becomes one of the students' weekly highlights, providing them with opportunities to learn new skills and work collaboratively and socially toward group outcomes. For many, the weekly music class is a chance to shine and experience success in school—this is most strikingly the case for some of the young students from the Horn of Africa whose limited prior schooling experience leaves them ill-equipped to handle their academic work when they first arrive in Australia, but whose experience in music making in their communities sees them take on leading roles in Howell's music classes. The classes work each week toward whole-class compositions, often taking themes of transition, journeys, change, and identity as starting points for musical work. Although the children may not know it, they are composing, and the process leads toward a greater sense of joy and self-esteem, accompanied by laughter and opportunities to work collaboratively in a social and relatively informal context.

Working with children between the ages of five and sixteen, Howell facilitates composing and creating original music material, placing emphasis on student choice and input, creativity, and social interaction. Students may create original songs, brainstorming words together using vocabulary that is often pretaught by their classroom teacher or words and phrases from the different languages represented in the group. Tuned and untuned percussion, guitar, and drums usually accompany these songs, and thus students also develop sophisticated ensemble and performance skills, singing and playing contrasting parts in a piece. Instrumental pieces also play an important role: inspiration for these may be taken from stories or themes the students are exploring in their classroom work. For example, a project inspired by the children's book *Aranea* (by Jenny Wagner), which tells the story of a spider's web being destroyed in a storm, offered a powerful parallel with the children's experience of seeking shelter and safety in their own lives, and their original music formed a powerfully expressive arc through the drama and intensity of the storm, the strangeness of the new place of shelter, and the optimism of starting to rebuild.

The music that the students compose typically does not fall into a genre, however; music that children introduce from their own culture is encouraged and prioritized in the classroom composing. These ideas may be revealed in response to direct questioning or suggestions from Howell or the teacher, but they may also be revealed unconsciously: for example in the way a student experiments with an instrument for the first time or as students sing or tap a pattern to themselves during downtime in the lesson. Students may bring in a piece of music that they like from their country of origin, such as a Somali pop song. The class will learn a riff or melody from this recording aurally, and then develop their own composition using the borrowed material as the starting point. Sometimes students develop songs from individually improvising sung melodies on a single line of text. The ideas offered by different students frequently reflect their musical cultures, and Howell then combines these phrases to create melodies that are fusions of musics of the different cultural groups represented in the class.

At the end of each school term (ten weeks), the class performs the compositions to an audience of students, teachers, and parents. This performance coincides with the end-of-term celebrations and certificate presentations for students now ready to move on to mainstream school. Thus the students feel a strong sense of occasion and achievement attached to these performance events. The students are also frequently invited to perform in community events, such as Refugee Week celebrations and local government events.

Every cohort of refugee students brings their own unique set of circumstances, experiences, and responses. Australian teachers from the late 1970s to early 1980s will still vividly recall the wide-eyed, silent, frozen responses of the children arriving at schools directly from their traumatic experiences of escaping Vietnam by boat. One of Howell's challenges is to keep the music making relevant and appropriate to the needs of each group of students. Participation and engagement can take many forms when students come from a diversity of traumatic experiences, and it is vital that the community musician remain sensitive to the cautious or tentative, boisterous or diffident ways students may demonstrate their engagement.[18]

A music participant in the United Kingdom uses a microphone to amplify his voice and the lyrics to his new song. A community music project in the United Kingdom provides opportunities to would-be DJs.

Courtesy of Sound It Out Community Music, www.sounditout.co.uk.

Yakama musicians from the United States perform and record their new song in a cluttered room of a local community center.
Patricia Shehan Campbell.

Young musicians are engaged in a music workshop in Ireland. The community music facilitator explains the next stage in the process of writing new songs.
Maurice Gunning.

Using technology to bridge a geographical divide, a community music facilitator and participant are engaged in a face-to-face encounter with a musician from another culture.
Don Devito/Sidney Lanier Center.

A rock band performs in front of an audience as part of a youth music festival in Ukraine.
Aaron Brantly.

As part of an arts festival in the United Kingdom, a community music facilitator improvises on the Djembe drum alongside a young participant. Through acts of hospitality, the facilitator welcomes musical interaction from the young drummer.
Courtesy of More Music.

Parading down the street at a HONK! Festival in the United States, the community band What Cheer blast out their arrangements with celebratory attitude.
Photo by cmurtaugh. Creative Commons.

Four musicians representing different musical traditions and genres work collaboratively to find points of musical union. Using a mixture of instruments from across the world, this U.K.-based community music project encourages cultural democracy by valuing the heritage of those who live in the area.

Courtesy of Sound It Out Community Music, www.sounditout.co.uk.

Young people from an Irish traveling community present some of their work on an open-air stage at the end of a community music project.

Maurice Gunning.

A music participant listens intensely as the community music facilitator addresses the group during a gamelan residence in an Irish university.
Maurice Gunning.

As part of a drumming circle, a community music facilitator and participant are engaged in a welcoming encounter that opens up musical and social possibilities.
Tom Chalmers.

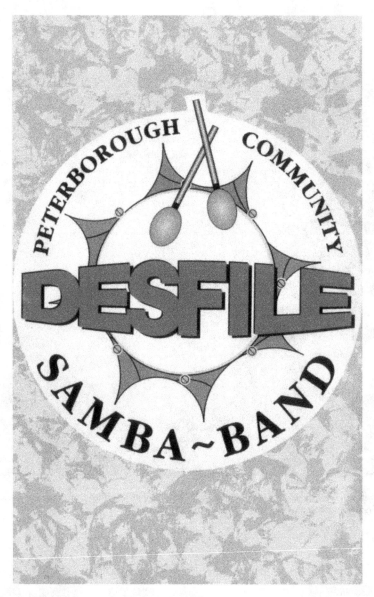

Peterborough Community Samba Band's logo, which was designed for them by a local magazine company. The word *desfile* means "parade" in Portuguese.
Lee Higgins.

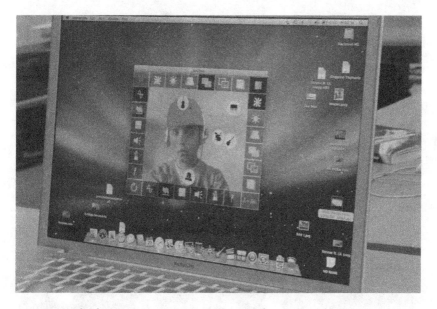

Using music technology, young musicians engage in musical invention and interactive jamming in Australia.
Steve Dillon.

A community music facilitator leads a group workshop in China. The intergenerational group beats out rhythms on sticks while sitting in a circle, a preliminary event before collaborating on a joint music adventure.

A community music project in the United Kingdom has its closing performance on a professional stage. Representing a cross-section of the local population, this group has a momentary reprieve from their drumming as they prepare for the final chorus of the evening.
Courtesy of More Music.

Consisting of music facilitators, health workers, and participants, this music group, which meets weekly to take to the streets in Scotland, is prepared to entertain anyone who walks by.
Tom Chalmers.

An Australian community musician engages a young participant in moments of music invention and discovery in East Timor.
Gillian Howell.

Laying their hands around a circular drumhead, participants find a physical, social, and emotional connection before playing a new piece especially created for their socially and musically inclusive ensemble.

Photograph © Musiko Musika 2012 www.musikomusika.org

In a local Brazilian community center, a youth group is having their weekly wind band rehearsal as admirers look on.
Filarmônica Ufberê.

The author leads a 140-piece bucket-drumming ensemble on the streets of Princeton, New Jersey.
Brock DeHaven.

LEARNING MUSIC IN A LARGE COMMUNITY CHOIR

In order to create a place where people could freely sing for the enjoyment of singing, Shivon Robinsong launched the Gettin' Higher Choir (GHC), an intergenerational, nonauditioned choir in Victoria, Canada. Robinsong created the choir at the request of some Victorian residents who had been to Cortez Island and heard her impromptu choir there. About five or six people came to a planning meeting in Robinson's Victoria home, and when the first official rehearsal was held, forty people arrived. It was later discovered that many of them had learned of the meeting through word of mouth. Since its founding in 1996, the choir has grown to more than 300 member singers. The singers range in age from late teens to over eighty years old, with the majority in their forties and fifties. The choir attracts members from all socioeconomic backgrounds and professions. Singers pay a session membership fee, which covers director and administrator salaries, and the choir offers scholarships to those who cannot afford the biannual fee.

During rehearsals, the director and codirector create an enjoyable and light atmosphere, in which singers learn in an informal context. Singers attend one of three evening rehearsals per week and then combine for the dress rehearsal and concert. The directors teach with a mixture of note and rote learning methods, and participants possess both scores and lyric sheets in their binders. The repertoire ranges across all genres, from secular to sacred, and across all styles, from polyphonic to homophonic. A portion of the repertoire is designated as "core," and it is rehearsed each session. Singers reportedly love and prize singing in harmony. The GHC requires that members memorize all music and singers refer to themselves as the "off-book" choir. The choir and directors rely on veteran members as role models for newer members; this ensures that the traditions and sound of the choir transition to the next generation and allows newer members to acclimate more easily to choir expectations and repertoire.

Along with regular concerts, the GHC participates in several community outreach projects responding to invitations from community organizations to provide music for their events. These community "sings" are called SWATs (Sing When Asked To), and a portion of the choir will attend on each occasion. In another vein, the GHC supports local and global outreach projects, which the singers call "performing with a purpose." The GHC donates concert profits to organizations such as the locally run program Power of Hope (art programs for youth) and the global initiative Kapasseni Project (to build a school and other necessary buildings in a Mozambique village). Singers describe feeling empowered when they sell concert tickets, and they perform with passion and heart onstage, knowing their efforts make a difference in the world. The success of the choir has led to the creation of two sister choirs and leadership-training courses. The sister choirs are High Noon, which provides a daytime choir option, and Soundings, which offers an auditioned choir option with more challenging repertoire. The Community Choir Leadership Training Course (CCLT) trains participants in establishing and running community choirs in their towns.

Through surveys and interviews conducted during a study of the choir in 2006, Mary Copland Kennedy (2009) discovered singers who professed that they found their voices and themselves by participating in the choir. Other members claimed that participation in the choir brought healing, inspired spiritual connections, and triggered transformative experiences. In the future, the GHC faces two primary challenges: managing membership (in any one session, one third stay, one third take a break, and one third are new) and keeping membership dues as low as possible. In addition, the size of the choir is an issue: at 300 members, the choir has reached its maximum size and, as one informant noted, is "self-regulating." At present, the choir is going strong and all signs point to a healthy future.[19]

RECIPROCITY IN A TRAVELING ELDERLY CHOIR

In 1991, Elsie Briscoe established the Yarra Valley Singers, a traveling group of elderly vocalists. The mission was to perform for senior residents in care facilities and patients with dementia throughout Victoria, Australia. Today, the senior citizen choir operates under a new name, the Happy Wanderers, but with the same initial mission.

Funding for this group comes from the community-based organization Dandenong Ranges Music Council (DRMC).[20] The DRMC seeks to "provide opportunities for people of all ages and abilities to learn, participate in, listen to and perform music in the Yarra Ranges." The government endows the DRMC on three levels: the federal Australia Council for the Arts, the state Arts Victoria, and the local Shire of Yarra Ranges.

Self-described as "dedicated" and a "happy group of people," the Happy Wanderers have ten singers and one accompanist, all in their sixties and seventies. The accompanist, Sam Derrick, is visually impaired and plays by ear. As a group, they perform in nursing homes, aged and dependent care facilities, day centers, and Vision Australia facilities,[21] and for hostels and senior citizens' groups. They have a busy schedule, performing in around 110 concerts annually. The group has a repertoire of more than 600 solo, duet, and ensemble songs, consisting of classics, oldies, folk songs, and famous international tunes.

When performing for an audience, the choir aims to entertain, stimulate memories, and provide brief relief from current ailments. The group also seeks to involve and engage the audience; as Win Kent, the current director, noted, "We sing the songs that people like and we try and get them to join in"

(Southcott, 2009, p. 147). One member remembered a memorable, or perhaps miraculous, moment when performing:

> We have … such wonderful experiences, like one time there was this lady [who had] had a stroke and she was lying back in her chair, I always remember her two daughters were with her and she had not spoken since the stroke. And I went up and I knelt down and I held her hand and sang "If you were the only girl in the world" and she started to sing. And the two daughters are crying and I was crying just about, and can still cry over it, it's so beautiful. (Southcott, 2009, p. 151)

The Happy Wanderers enhance the lives of both audience members and themselves. The choir has been a haven for the performers. After observing and interviewing members of the choir, Southcott noticed that through performing the singers gained a sense of purpose and fulfillment, acquired and maintained meaningful relationships, and realized opportunities for personal growth. The Happy Wanderers face many challenges as they move forward, including aging members, continuously learning new music, staying relevant to their audiences, and maintaining funding.[22]

CHAPTER 7

Crossfields

The purpose of this chapter is to acknowledge three areas of musical discourse that have synergy with community music and, in doing so, point toward possible connections, meeting points, and differences in order to invigorate future conversations. But first, I reflect on two areas of school-music education that have been of particular interest and influence for those involved or interested in community music practice.

DEMOCRACY, LIFELONG LEARNING, AND SCHOOL-MUSIC EDUCATION

Since the end of the Cold War, education theorists have expressed renewed interest in the relationship between education and democratization (Perry, 2005). It is probably accurate to say that this has become one of the "hot" topics in the field of music education, especially in the United States. This relationship is complex and means many different things to different people. In order to progress the discussion, I think it is useful to consider education and democracy in the following two ways: first, educational structures and practices that promote democratization in the broader society, and second, schools that function democratically. The latter addresses a macro-level perspective that takes into count widespread literacy and mass schooling that is not "democratic" in and of itself but is correlated with the democratization of society, whereas the former has a micro-level view that considers education important for citizenship, human rights, and tolerance.

I have previously noted that the first wave of musicians working under the auspices of community music in the United Kingdom felt that school-music education had been dominated by the Western canon and was largely irrelevant to the musical worlds of their participants. Most music teachers of the day were considered "out of touch" with the changing trends of music making, creation, and performance. School music did, however, begin to change in the late 1970s, and certainly by the 1980s both schools and music colleges were much more catholic in their musical content and methods of inquiry (Pitts, 2000). This meant that those working in community music had less of a reason to be resistant toward the school music ethos. Coupled with the changing funding structures, a situation that began to encourage community music collaborations, community musicians decided to go "back to school" (Peggie, 1997, 1993). This was not without its problems. A major concern that school music advisers had with community musicians was that they lacked experience and understanding of the education process, particularly on the issue of evaluation. However, many community musicians did work in schools, particularly with composition and performance projects. Community musicians were also hired to deliver in-service teacher training. Over the last three decades or so, there has been a steady increase in the interaction between community musicians and schools. This has fostered mutual respect: community musicians have benefited from employment, gained exposure to the pedagogical process, and learned a range of approaches to evaluation, while school music teachers have been exposed to a greater diversity of musics and different processes of music making.

> Community music-making practices have had a profound impact on the way class teaching is organized and taught—and of course have had an impact on musical content itself. Musicians working in this field were often less conventionally skilled or had embraced other musical genres as part of their own musical development and found that folk traditions, popular forms and more sociable musical practices offered an almost instant way in to collective music making, where instrumentation and technique were infinitely adaptable to ability, notation was unnecessary, and speech and movement were natural companions. (Hennessy, 2005, p. 218)

This is not the same in the United States, where much of the current music education system has been dominated by three traditions: band, orchestra, and choir. As David Myers (2008) states, "The sacred model of elementary general music leading to large performing ensembles supplemented by occasional chamber music and jazz bands formed the non-negotiable structure within which research and curricular change were undertaken" (p. 52). This "fixed" structure has a strong emphasis on "end" results, an idea of schooling that has been supported by the No Child Left Behind Act of 2001 and the movement for national standards. Here, as Randall Allsup (2007) says, "students are aggregated as statistics rather than understood as individuals" (p. 52).

In an effort to revitalize the public, or one might say the community, in public schooling, music educators such as Allsup (2003a, 2003b, 2003c, 2007), Heidi Westerlund (2008; Karlsen and Westerlund, 2010), and Paul Woodford (2005) have been working under the philosophic framing of John Dewey (1916), Maxine Greene (2000), Paulo Freire (2002), and bell hooks (1994). To some extent their work has been building on notions of American community music. I suggested in chapter 2 that community music as a strategy for human development, democracy, and change was alluded to in the United States from around the mid-1920s to the mid-1950s but lost its impetus, visibility, and consequently its momentum during the 1960s. With a history that can be dated to the Settlement House Movement, New Deal, Popular Fronts, and Progressive Education, contemporary expressions of community music have consonance with the ideas and actions of these movements. To some extent they share a philosophical heritage. Those music educators, who are seeking to reignite and reimagine a Deweyan sense of democracy within the music classroom, provide an important and powerful strand through which to engage the music education community in conversations about how things might be different. In this situation, community music can and has provided another stick with which to prod the current state of American music education. Although there has been some careful consideration given to the notion of "community" in American music education (Jorgensen, 1995; Froehlich, 2008; Bowman, 2009), it is Allsup's (2003a, 2003b, 2003c, 2007) thinking that is most closely connected with community music as described in this book. From his perspective, schools are seen as ideal "societies" for fostering democracy and "the full and unfettered development of one's talents, abilities, and gifts is its primary aim, 'an ideal' to live by but also an ongoing way of life" (2007, p. 52). These sentiments have a strong resonance for those actively advocating lifelong learning.

As a principle, or organizing concept, lifelong learning resists preaching a set of values, policies, and rigid processes (Maehl, 2000). The European Lifelong Learning Initiative defined *lifelong learning* as "a continuously supportive process which stimulates and empowers individuals to acquire all the knowledge, values, skills and understanding they will require throughout their lifetimes and to apply them with confidence, creativity, and enjoyment in all roles, circumstances, and environments" (Watson, 2003, p. 3). Jannette Collins (2009) usefully paraphrases these sentiments: "It never stops; it isn't done alone; it's self-directed and active, not passive; it's more than what we know; it happens from our first breath to our last; it's not just for knowledge's sake; it's a positive, fulfilling experience; and; it applies not only to our chosen profession, but to our entire life" (p. 615).

In his exploration of American school music education, Myers (2008) notes that many schools have lost sight of the ways in which people engage in music throughout their lives. He is critical of how the "profession" has often managed to "bifurcate the topics of adult and community music from school music," therefore leading to philosophical and practical divisions that hinder the preparation and professional development of music teachers (p. 54). The consequence of this, according to Myers, is that we see a reduction of the skills that underlie personal music making and thus a decrease in the opportunity to form a basis for more relevant school programs. Myers argues for a life-span perspective on music teaching and learning, and is quite right when he says that meeting the needs of an aging population through intergenerational learning and community collaboration may, and more importantly should, challenge the status quo of how music education is implemented in schools. Thickening the conceptual apparatus through which to discuss this issue, Patrick Jones (2009) reminds us that this is a longitudinal conception and by adding the notion of "lifewide" to lifelong, there is an enrichment that more accurately portrays the complex and multidimensional situations that exist between school and community, child, youth, and adult learners.

As a general consensus, those who advocate lifelong learning in music education assert that the frameworks in operation throughout schools, plus the current approaches to teaching and learning, must change (Mantie and Tucker, 2008; Smilde, 2008; Pitts, 2009; Rowher and Rowher, 2009). This agenda is strongly supported by those who think that formal music education is no longer sufficient to cope with our rapidly changing society that they therefore favor an informal approach to music education (Mark, 1996; Jaffurs, 2004a, 2004b; Batt-Rawden and DeNora, 2005; Green, 2008; Smilde, 2009; Wright and Kanellopoulos, 2010). Congruent with many of the characteristics of community music, the current debates in lifelong learning have introduced pedagogical models that have provided leverage for greater insight into community music practice (Lave and Wenger, 1991). The New Horizons International Music Association for older adult bands, orchestras, and choirs presents an excellent example of how a musical and social organization can flourish within a lifelong learning framework (Coffman, 2008a, 2002; Dabback, 2008; Kruse, 2009). My next point may be controversial, but one might say that the success of the New Horizons bands may be the result of failings in the American music education system. Although anecdotal, many New Horizon players were once enthusiastic school band players. However, with a relentless rehearsal schedule, an emphasis on competition, and reduced opportunities upon graduation, many simply forgot why playing once had been so important. The New Horizon bands have provided a fresh environment for older adults to reconnect with their past musical lives.

COMMUNITY MUSIC THERAPY

Although music therapy may mean different things to different people for a myriad of reasons, it has, for many years, "seemed less preoccupied with larger social forces or cultural contexts" (Ruud, 2010, p. 121). According to Simon Procter (2004), music therapy has not always been this way. During the 1950s and 1960s, music therapists considered their work to be both practical and communally focused, but during the 1970s and 1980s there was a tightening of the boundaries coinciding with the professionalization of music therapy. The turning point came in 2002, at the Tenth World Congress of Music Therapy held in Oxford. It was here that participants explicitly emphasized community and spirituality as two marginalized aspects within "traditional" music therapies.

Community music therapy, or CoMT as it is often abbreviated, particularly resonates with the Paul Nordoff and Clive Robbins (1971, 1977) approach. Their work with disabled children moved comfortably between intense private work and public performances of musical "working games" and musical plays. Coming from a background in the anthroposophical movement,[1] Nordoff and Robbins saw their role as providing individual therapy for the children they worked with in preparation for a full and meaningful community life.

As an evolving practice within music therapy, CoMT is a way of doing and thinking about music therapy in which the larger cultural, institutional, and social context is taken into consideration (Ruud, 2004). As a collaborative and proactive approach to health, development, and social change, CoMT involves an awareness of the broader systems that music therapists work within and is characterized by collaborative and context-sensitive music making focused on giving "voice" to the relatively disadvantaged. This form of collaborative musicking has a distinctively musical-therapeutic agenda, although it is understood by those whose lead its activities that the participants would have interest in, or a love for, music (Stige et al., 2010).

The development of CoMT as an articulated practice can be linked to an openness toward music, culture, and society (DeNora, 2000; Kramer, 1995; McClary, 2007). Like community music, Christopher Small's (1998) notion of musicking is of particular significance, providing many of its practitioners with a conceptual fulcrum through which to discuss music as a performance activity. As such, CoMT provides challenges for major reassessment of performance's place within music therapy. As Gary Ansdell suggests, CoMT is developing "a more nuanced understanding of the affordances and varying suitability of the private and public aspects of musicking within broadly-defined therapeutic contexts" (Stige et al., 2010, p. 186).

Simon Proctor's work at Way Ahead presents a good illustration of CoMT. Located in London, in an environment that has high levels of unemployment, crime, and incidences of mental illness, Way Ahead is a nonmedical community resource center for people with experience of mental health problems. Not part of any statutory services, it is funded by a yearly grant from the local health authority, social services, and an assortment of charities. A management committee, which includes service users and local people, runs the center, endeavoring to create an environment in which members can value their individuality and their culture through a sense of community. The center is designed to help people experience their capacity for well-being, rather than focus on their medical illness. In an effort to alleviate isolation, there are no doctors, nurses, or patients—just members. There are no experts—just workers. There are no case history files and no classification of members on the basis of diagnosis. Members are welcomed to the center based on *who* they are rather than a personification of a history or diagnosis. Way Ahead is, as Procter describes, "a haven from psychiatric orthodoxy" (Procter, 2004, p. 224).

Extending Christopher Small's (1998) notion of "musicking," Procter engages with each member in such a way to draw him or her into "co-musicking," with all the interpersonal and creative demands that this presents: "Our co-operative relationship, at the center of all we do, is that of musicking together, or co-musicking" (Procter, 2001). Through co-musicking, Procter seeks to create a shared musical history that is not documented for others to pick over, but experienced by each musician in his or her own unique way. For the most part, and certainly in the United Kingdom, music therapy has not engaged with attempts to build publicly accessible nonmedical mental health services. Procter suggests that perhaps this is due to suspicion among users that music therapists place too much emphasis on psychiatry. The suspicion cuts the other way also. For example, some music therapists see the type of work described here as not maintaining rigorous boundaries between client and staff. Procter illustrates this with two examples: an impromptu performance with a former member that draws a crowd in a public space and an improvised piece in a public art gallery. Although music therapy in this setting is not part of a medical treatment model, neither is it really just playing music. Procter's musical engagements cause him to reflect on the members' well-being in order to offer intervention, "changing the ways I played and the suggestions I made in response to my musical observations of our co-musicking" (Procter, 2001). Without interventions, Procter believes that he could not offer his co-musickers significant opportunities for empowerment and enablement.

CoMT attempts to promote health within and between various layers of the sociocultural community and/or physical environment. Its practice includes a focus on family, workplace, community, society, culture, or physical environment; these interlinking aspects of life are described metaphorically as an ecological perspective. An ecological theory of music never sees musicking as alone or abstract. Instead, performance takes a key place through emphases of people and context. This is illustrated nicely through the work of Norwegian music therapist Venja Ruud Nilsen. Working for several years with female prison inmates, Nilsen's work generated a culture of rock music making within the prison. This has meant that many of the women have become proficient rock musicians. Nilsen, not restricting herself to the confines of the prison, has organized and supported participatory music opportunities for women after their release. As Ruud (2010) notes, "Working both within the institution and out in the community, the music therapist creates a bridge between prison and society" (p. 132). This "bridge" helps support the person in maintaining a prison-free life. Through her work both on the "inside" and on the "outside," Ruud creates a safe space, providing a friendly atmosphere, a continuing social network, and a drug-free environment.

So what makes CoMT different from community music? This question is considered directly by Ansdell (2002) during CoMT's infancy. Ansdell recognizes that both fields of practice flow from a broad belief in musicking but points toward working territory, theoretical explanations, institutional legitimacy, and resourcing as areas of divergence. One of the key differences is that those working in CoMT have built up a body of experience and expertise through working toward the promotion of health. However, through a practice that directly considers the individual-communal continuum, CoMT has challenged tightly bounded definitions of music therapy (Wood, Verney, and Atkinson, 2004). This is illustrated through the work of Harriet Powell (2004), who once worked as a community musician and later trained as a music therapist. She assumed a new identity, understanding music therapy as a more narrowly defined field. She now sees CoMT as a way of "coming out," a chance to work with a broader identity that enables greater breadth in her professional life.

CULTURAL DIVERSITY IN MUSIC EDUCATION

The purpose of this section is to hone in upon an aspect of music education that has, in more recent times, played a significant role in the development and promotion of community music practice. Four people have been major contributors: Patricia Shehan Campbell, Huib Schippers, David Elliott, and John Drummond. These four, very different people have all shared a keen sense of advocacy for cultural diversity in music education and community music.

According to Schippers (2003), the term *cultural diversity* is understood as a dynamic concept, a neutral indication for the presence of more than one culture in any given situation. The term is being used here to refer to (1) content—that is, music from various cultural backgrounds, and (2) people, especially a mix of ethnicities. For my purposes, cultural diversity references different approaches to music making or systems of musical transmission and learning. Although it is beyond the scope of this chapter to offer an extended history of cultural diversity in music education, it seems important to at least offer a working framework through which I can characterize significant traits that connect to community music.

As an orientation within the broader area of music education, cultural diversity emerges through the growth and developments of multicultural education (Banks, 1996; Gibson, 1976; Grant, 1977; Pratte, 1979; Sleeter, 2005). Multicultural education is most often understood as emerging from the ferment of the civil rights movement of the 1960s and early 1970s (Sleeter, 1996; Banks and Banks, 2001). It was during that period that sociologists began to highlight the blind spot of this prevailing approach by suggesting that educating children in the dominant culture privileged those who came from that culture (Bourdieu and Passeron, 2000; Bowles and Gintis, 1976). Following Bourdieu, Drummond (2005) reinforces this point by suggesting that schools are locales through which the dominant culture engages in "symbolic violence" against socially disadvantaged groups. Multicultural education arose from the diverse courses, programs, and practices that educational institutions devised to respond to the demands, needs, and aspirations of the various pressure groups, such as the women's rights movement, those advocating equality for the disabled, senior citizens, and the gay communities. Grounded in a vision of equality, multicultural education served as a mobilizing site to support and advocate social justice and democracy.

During the 1980s, however, complacency and backlash began to replace a general sense of optimism. It was argued that the *multicultural curriculum* was insufficient on its own to redress disadvantage among students from minority backgrounds. Programs that supported the values and practices of *cultural pluralism* (a term used when smaller groups within a larger society maintain their unique cultural identities) were added to the mix but had little impact on the continuing transmission of the dominant culture within schooling (Drummond, 2005). Valuing democracy with diversity in ethnicity, language, lifestyle, and tradition, cultural pluralism rejects the notion of the cultural "melting pot" and characterizes the multicultural condition (Duarte and Smith, 2000). The increased attention toward the idea of cultural pluralism, ignited by both ethnic and women studies, for example, broadened the conceptual field through interdisciplinary debates that resisted assimilation because it emphasizes cultural sameness rather than cultural diversity.[2] The demand for structural changes within institutions created pressure that eventually led to the creation of new kinds of educational settings for learning about a range of musical cultures (Drummond, 2005).[3] Institutions such as the Conservatory of Amsterdam,[4] Copenhagen Rhythmic Music Academy,[5] Malmö Music Academy (Sweden),[6] Queensland Conservatorium (Australia),[7] and the World Music and Dance Center, Rotterdam,[8] serve to illustrate this.

Although the term *world music* was initially linked to globalization, commoditization, and consumerism, its roots are housed in "the sheer love of discovering new and exciting music" (Schippers, 2009, p. 17). It is here, through the site of playing and performing, that issues arising from cultural diversity in music education find a synergy with community music practice. In short, there is an intrinsic value given to the transmission process, what Marie McCarthy (1999) might describe as "passing it on." Characteristic of the teaching and learning experience found in those institutions committed to world music is that practice often goes before theory (Kors and Schippers, 2003). The inclusion of world music into a more general music education curriculum has much in common with the way other forms of popular music, such as rock and jazz, have found their way into the classrooms (Folkestad, 2005). The attention given to playing by ear, collective processes, and informal environments of engagement highlight Trevor Wiggins's (2005) point that for many years, emphasis has been given to exploring the nature of the learning activities that contribute to the development of skills, knowledge, and self-validation as a musician. Through an initial investigation into the learning styles of popular musicians, Lucy Green (2002) has been influential in championing the informal music learning processes. Green (2008) notes that "until very recently, music educators have not recognized or rewarded the approaches involved in informal music learning, nor have they been particularly aware of, or interested in, the high levels of enthusiasm and commitment to music displayed by young popular or other vernacular musicians" (p. 3). This is not, however, true of community musicians, who have long since found effective ways of celebrating participants' enthusiasm and commitment to popular, vernacular, and newly composed music.

From a music education philosophical perspective, it is the work of David Elliott (1995) that most strongly resonates with notions of cultural diversity in music education and community music. Elliott's (1989) "dynamic multicultural-ism" offers a "pan-human" perspective to a broad range of world music and world peoples and is important because he has taken an active role in community music through his attendance and contribution at the CMA and his role in establishing the *IJCM* (Veblen, 2005). Cultural diversity in music education helps students to find a place for music in their lives and to understand that members of diverse cultural groups have commonly shared need for art making generally and music specifically. As an empowerment strategy, and through transformative educational goals, cultural diversity in music education can serve as an effective vehicle for social change and emancipation. As a way of seeing the world and one's place in it, cultural diversity in music education helps enable students to develop skills and insights needed "to question some of the latent assumptions and values within the mainstream society, to think critically about the gap between the nation's ideals and realities, and to develop a commitment to act to help create a just human society" (Banks, 1992). One might conclude that cultural diversity in music education promotes a general shift from teaching to learning and consequently from teacher to learner. This represents a change of focus to how one engages students in content and consequently informs ways of learning. As Goran Folkestad (2005) stresses, the most important issue is how the music is approached: there is an emphasis toward an artistic/musical framing rather than a pedagogical one. This perspective pushes against the didactic approaches educational institutions generally favor (Wiggins, 2005). With an emphasis on practice and musical doing, cultural diversity in music education has, as Schippers notes, "deep implications for thinking, designing, and realizing music education across the board" (2009, p. 167). Community music also provides these opportunities and challenges.

APPLIED ETHNOMUSICOLOGY

As a field of study that joins the concerns and methods of anthropology with the study of music (Shelemay, 2001), ethnomusicology has followed the anthropological lead in its utilization of the prefix "applied" (Ervin, 2004). Described as "elusive to define,"[9] applied ethnomusicology, like community music, is best understood through the work that it *does* rather than any attempt to describe what it *is*. However, like any emerging scholarly discipline, it needs a working statement that outlines its agenda and the key characteristics of practice. A good starting place is the International Council of Traditional Music (ICTM) study group on applied ethnomusicology. As a collective, the group suggests that applied ethnomusicology is an approach guided by principles of social responsibility that extends the usual academic goal of broadening and deepening knowledge and understanding (Pettan, Harrison, and Usner, 2007).[10] The ICTM advocates the use of ethnomusicological knowledge in the influencing of social interaction and courses of cultural change.

As a discipline, ethnomusicology grew through the academy (Nettl, 2002), and was, as Jennifer Post (2006) notes, "once used to identify academically trained professionals who predominantly engaged in ethnographic research and taught college and university classes" (p. 2). This reflects the onetime view of ethnomusicology as an objective science whose practitioners aimed not to interfere with the musical culture under study (Stock, 2008). Because it is a rigorous academic enterprise, those working in ethnomusicology cultivated significant expertise in appropriate methods of research. Like anthropology, ethnomusicology relies on the ethnographic account as its principal mode of research. Jeff Todd Titon (2003) explains that although modern ethnomusicologists have largely abandoned claims of scientific objectivity, "most have not abandoned ethnographic fieldwork" (p. 173). Ethnomusicologists, although not abandoning ethnography, have attempted to reform and reshape the cultural study of music based upon postmodern and poststructuralist thought, such as continuums of subject/object, self/other, inside/outside, and author/authority (Barz and Cooley, 2008, 1997).

Because of changes in the political, social, and economic landscapes, there are now many more ethnomusicologists engaged in applied work with a primary intended output of musical or social benefits, rather than in the increase of original scholarly knowledge. Kathleen van Buren (2010), in organizing a World AIDS Day event in Sheffield, United Kingdom, illustrates this. Emerging from van Buren's fieldwork in Nairobi, Kenya, and building upon her experiences of partnerships between African musicians and a host of Kenyan and foreign institutions focused on local, national, and international development, van Buren cemented a partnership of her own back in the United Kingdom. Teaming up with the National Health Service (NHS) Center for HIV and Sexual Health, van Buren organized a daylong event that combined performances by a variety of local performers with a keynote speech from a health professional. In a similar vain, Samantha Fletcher (2007) documents her benefit concert in support of the refugee and social justice committees at the Unitarian Church, Vancouver, Canada, while Angela Impey (2006) explores the operational interface between ethnomusicology, environmental conservation, and sustainable development in South Africa.

Writing the introduction to a collection of essays under the banner "Music, the Public Interest, and the Practice of Ethnomusicology," Titon (1992) suggests that applied ethnomusicology has its awareness in practical action rather than the flow of knowledge inside intellectual communities. Along with a special issue of *Folklore Forum*, edited by John Fenn (2003), these seminal groups of papers explore issues on applied ethnomusicology and music law, careers, collaboration, and strategies for action. The latter source usefully articulates four strategic areas through which applied ethnomusicologists attempt to solve problems: (1) developing new "frames" for musical performance, (2) "feeding back" musical models to the communities that created them, (3) providing community members access to strategic models and conversation techniques, and (4) developing broad, structural solutions to structural problems (Sheehy, 1992, pp. 330–331). As a collection, they represent a decade of development and growth. During this period, Dan Sheehy (1992), then director for Folk and Traditional Arts at the National Endowment for the Arts, describes applied ethnomusicology as "perhaps most observable as an implacable tendency, first to see opportunities for a better life for others through the use of music knowledge, and then immediately to begin devising cultural strategies to achieve those ends" (p. 324). Applied ethnomusicology is therefore not so concerned with the research and the dissemination of knowledge inside intellectual communities, but rather, the development of projects in the public sphere that involve and enable musicians and various musical cultures to present, represent, and affect the dispersion of music (Titon, 1992). Practice-informed theory, a desire to communicate ideas and findings without generating disengaged and remote scholarship, takes precedence.

Illustrations of this can be seen in the work of Samuel Araujo (2008) in Brazil. Over a four-year period, Araujo and his collaborators, the Ethnomusicology Lab of the Federal University of Rio de Janeiro in partnership with the Center for the Study and Solidarity Actions of Maré, a nongovernmental organization (NGO), engaged in participant action research. The research team built a public database and developed outreach programs within Maré, an area of Rio with high rates of unemployment, drug trafficking, and violence. Using collaborative research, they mapped out the musical culture of its residents, some 135,000 people. This led to increased awareness of the community's preferred musical styles and interests and finally resulted in a new kind of interaction both socially and musically.

Other examples of collaborations leading toward research presentations and cultural organizing are the West African Community Cultural Initiative that Tom van Buren (2003) began in 1995. In this project, artists and scholars from the Arab, Albanian, and Dominican communities of New York developed field research, documentation, and performance programs in collaboration with the center. Tina Ramnarine (2008) highlights collaboration between university departments and local schools. She reports on New York University's partnership with the NGO Harmony, a group that aimed to bring music teaching to an underserved young population in the city, and Royal Holloway University in London, which partnered with the Cultural Co-operation[11] to provide inclusive approaches to both Andean and Indonesian musics. Van Buren (2003) underscores these types of relationships: "The lesson of true collaboration in applied ethnomusicology is that we must maintain integrity in our dealing with others" (p. 75).

In the United States, the field can be divided into three general areas: (1) the public sector of national-, state-, and county-level arts agencies, museums, and archives, (2) commercial applications, such as publishing, or music productions and promotion, and (3) the research and public organizations, often known as folklife centers (van Buren, 2003). Relevance beyond the academy can take many forms, including advocacy, enterprise, therapy, policy making, journalism, archiving, museum work, concert organization, producing teaching materials, and public performance (Ramnarine, 2008). Post (2006) notes that although "advocacy and music have been linked for years, especially through the music education field, ethnomusicologists have only recently actively embraced the subject to relate it directly to their own research" (p. 10).

Svanibor Pettan's work is an exemplary illustration of what Post (2006) describes as "advocacy ethnomusicology," community-based action using knowledge and experience drawn from fieldwork and utilizing the ethnomusicologist's specialized understanding and interest in a region or culture. The root of Pettan's musical advocacy grows from a commitment to establish tolerance and justice after the dissolution of the former Yugoslavia. He states, "My interest in applied ethnomusicology stemmed from my wish to understand that reality of 'war at home,' especially the potential of the field to explain the war-peace continuum" (Pettan, 2010, p. 91).[12]

One example is a project that brought together Bosnian refugee musicians and Norwegian music students. Based in Oslo, it operated on three levels: research, education, and music making. Concerts of the ensemble Azra, formed from both Bosnian and Norwegian musicians, raised a wider awareness about the war in Bosnia and Herzegovina and in doing so generated some much-needed funds for the humanitarian effort in Pettan's own country. In a second project, Pettan created a photo exhibition, video documentary, CD-ROM, and book to highlight the integrationist role of Romani (Gypsy) musicians living in Kosovo before they became victims of the Albanian-Serbian conflict. The project had two principal purposes: first, to raise awareness and funds to support the physical and cultural survival of the Roma in Kosovo, and second, to recognize the legacy of the Romani musicians through a wide dissemination of information.

As an early advocate of applied ethnomusicology, Charles Keil (1982) believes that beyond the scholarly pursuit and performance orientations of ethnomusicology, there should be a third area. This, Keil says, should be termed *applied* because "it suggests that our work can make a difference, that it can intersect both the world outside and the university in more challenging and constructive ways" (p. 407). Maureen Loughran (2008) documents "community powered resistance radio," work that resonates with Keil's thoughts and with the work of the community arts movements discussed in chapter 2. Broadcasting within tight neighborhood boundaries, the radio station serves many functions within the community: as a forum for discussion of neighborhood issues, an outlet for local musical expression, and a catalyst for community activism. In addition, the founders of the station, as well as the station DJs, all have connections to the local music scene, either as musicians or activists. More specifically, it is through the urban music traditions of punk and hip-hop that residents situate their activism. Alongside projects such as Keil's 12/8 path bands,[13] the activist street bands of the HONK! Festival (see chapter 6), and Music for Change,[14] Loughran's project presses for grassroots, nonprofit events made possible by local residents and businesses. It is here that the work of the applied ethnomusicologist intersects with the early "spirit" of community music.

SUMMARY

CoMT, cultural diversity in music education, and applied ethnomusicology represent approaches to music making that enable a deeper understanding of community music. Like community music, CoMT seeks to reduce hierarchy and authority, through an inherently participatory, performative, resource-oriented, and actively reflective practice. Community music and CoMT originate from a common belief in "musicking" as a means of working with people, each approach seeking to reclaim music for everyday life as a central force in human culture. By working more frequently with those within the community or at well-being stages, rather than with those who fall into the acute illness/crisis and rehabilitation stages of the health-care continuum, there are considerable signs of similarity between the respected approaches.[15] Ansdell (2002) calls for dialogue between the two areas of practice but points toward a lack of "serious" community music literature, or lack of equal territory on which to dialogue, as currently preventing deep mutual accommodation and progression.

This has not been the case with those working under the banner of cultural diversity in music education. From the political implication of multiculturalism, cultural diversity in music education became a crossroads for knowing music, education, and culture (McCarthy, 1996; Campbell, 2003). Resonating with the pedagogic approach of the community musician, those working in this area are interested in a holistic musical education, which includes the thought that Western art music is *world music,* another tradition like the many others. Occasions for community musicians to work in school settings have flowed from these developments, capitalizing on the many world music "affinity groups" found in cities around the globe and led by community music facilitators.

Emanating from a political perspective, both community music and applied ethnomusicology emerged from the cultural upheavals of the late 1960s. With a turn toward public projects that emulate from the desires and voices of the community members themselves,[16] applied ethnomusicologists involve themselves in community projects because of their concern for the political and pedagogic opportunities as well as the social and cultural riches that arise from exploring a range of repertoires (Seeger, 2008; Ramnarine, 2008). The term *applied* evokes *intervention* and subsequently *change*, a push for music projects that have a desire and heart for transformation (Hemetek, 2006). Applied ethnomusicologists and community musicians understand that music can play a vital role in community development through education, income generation, and self-esteem.

As I have shown, subfields of music therapy, music education, and ethnomusicology, CoMT, cultural diversity in music education, and applied ethnomusicology draw upon a history that includes philosophical and conceptual frameworks, research methodology, established outlets for discussion such as conferences, journals, and book publications, and pedagogic methodology. As siblings to larger fields, CoMT, cultural diversity in music education, and applied ethnomusicology have been asking awkward questions about the contemporary role of each respected practice. I believe that in order for the field of community music to contribute more effectively within those domains that it intersects with— music therapy, music education, and ethnomusicology—there needs to be a conceptual framework with which one can argue for both its relevance and its vital and dynamic force. Part II of this book, "Interventions and Counterpaths," takes on this challenge. It is in the next four chapters that I attempt to outline a theoretical framework that might enable a conceptual understanding of community music. I see this as an imperative, a chance to articulate a conceptual springboard for others to build on, or knock down, an opportunity to spark dialogue and conversation among those in the field and those who work in other areas.

PART TWO

Interventions and Counterpaths

CHAPTER 8
Acts of Hospitality

One might say that *to be* is to inherit: "the *being* of what we are *is* first of all inheritance, whether we like it or know it or not" (Derrida, 1994, p. 54). Through an exploration of the development of community music from the late 1960s through to the present, in part I, "Inheritances and Pathways," I responded to this idea. Underlining this was a proposition that any musician, advocate, or researcher who evokes *community music* becomes heir to this legacy. Inheritance, therefore, is never a given: it comes to us as a task; it is an injunction to which we must respond. As an heir to this history, I offer *my* response in part II, an opportunity to present inventive thoughts and gestures that might enable those who already work in community music, as well as those who are coming to the field for the first time, a way to describe and understand the phenomena. Many of the ideas and concepts presented are inextricably interwoven. I therefore intend to gradually thicken the philosophical lexicon by introducing new ideas and recapitulations as I go. This will, I hope, provide the reader with an increasing array of ideas and concepts that can be understood as emerging from both community music history and the illustrations of practice.

The purpose of this chapter is to explore the concept of *community* as it relates to the larger concept of *community music*. My overall goal is to suggest that those invested in community music might like to reimagine how the term *community* operates within its name. I begin with an etymological analysis of the concept, suggesting that the *community* within *community music* is best understood as *hospitality*, as initially articulated by Jacques Derrida (1999, 2000, 2001). My proposition is that *hospitality* encompasses the central characteristics of community music practice, broadly understood as people, participation, places, equality of opportunity, and diversity. I do not argue that hospitality should replace the term *community*, but that hospitality evokes the practical meaning of community in the work of community musicians. From this perspective, I propose that *community*, conceived actively as "an act of hospitality," runs deeply through the practice of community music, and that an acute awareness of its production will expose the distinctiveness of community music within the musical discourse more generally.

I will use two questions to guide my explorations: How can the concept of community be understood in practices named community music? How is community made manifest through community music? I will address these questions in three sections: (1) an etymological consideration of the word *community*, (2) community in the twenty-first century, and (3) rethinking the status of community music as a hospitable act of welcoming. The chapter concludes by suggesting that it is the act of hospitality, a welcome to would-be music participants that gives community music its distinction.

COMMUNITY

The term *community* became particularly important to nineteenth-century social theorists, including Ferdinand Tönnies (2001), Max Weber (1947), and Emile Durkheim (1984). At that time, society was caught up in rapid changes of industrialization and urban development, and sociologists were concerned with the potential disintegration of traditional ways of living. Cultural upheavals, including the French and American Revolutions, nineteenth-century industrialization, and most recently the onslaught of globalization, have produced changes in the ways people live together and communicate today. This may account for why the word *community*, and its associated concepts and meanings, became popular during the 1950s, spurring developments in community services and later community arts and community cultural developments, which were discussed in chapter 2.

As a contested concept, *community* is both problematic and powerful. The use of *community* as a prefix to music gives *community music* not only its distinctive name but also an opening toward its characteristics of practice. An explanation of the word's etymology provides a springboard for later discussions. In an analysis of the German word *gemeinschaft*, often translated as "community," Kant (1998) makes a distinction in Latin between *communio*, an exclusive sharing space protected from the outside, and *commercium*, the processes of exchange and communication. Following Kant, Tönnies, who was perhaps the first to clearly describe the term, explores *gemeinschaft* (community) in relation to *gesellschaft* (society), suggesting that both terms are different forms of associated living brought about by human will. His influential conclusions suggested that modern societies have replaced *gemeinschaft*, the site of traditional cultural values, with *gesellschaft*, an expression of modernity, as the primary focus for social relations. William Corlett (1995) considers the word *community* from a slightly different stand point: first, *Communis*, com + munis, meaning "common" and "defense," as in "with oneness or unity," favored by the communitarian theorists, and *communes*, com + munnus, meaning having common duties or functions, emphasizing the doing of one's duty, "with gifts or services."

In the field of anthropology, the term has been usefully isolated with three broad variants: (1) common interests between people, (2) a common ecology and locality, and (3) a common social system or structure (Rapport and Overing, 2000). More specifically, in *The Ritual Process*, Victor Turner (1969) begins his analysis of the word *community* with *communitas*, the Latin expression for belonging, which is irreducible to any social or political arrangement. Philosopher Philip Alperson's (2002) description of community articulates the most general etymological understanding: community as a state of being held in common. Alperson advocates that, both ontologically and structurally, community refers to a relation between things. Charting the term's changing patterns of application and understanding, the fields of anthropology and sociology provide a variety of perspectives. These include community as loss and recovery (Rousseau, 1993; Gutek and Gutek, 1998), belonging (Block, 2008), communitarianism (Christodoulidis, 1998; Lehman, 2000; Stone, 2000; Etzioni, Volmert, and Rothschild, 2004), citizenship (Demaine and Entwistle, 1996; Beiner, 2002), multiculturalism (Giroux, 1993; Kernerman, 2005; Nagle, 2008), symbolic structure (Cohen, 1985), globalization (Adams and Goldbard, 2002; Rupp, 2006), diaspora (Brah, 1996; Angelo, 1997; Matsuoka and Sorenson, 2001; Najam, 2006), nationalism (Williams and Kofman, 1989; Bhabha, 1990; Vincent, 2002), and the imagined (Anderson, 1991). A review of this literature reveals that the concept of community is constantly changing, functioning differently depending on the context of its use.[1] Given the above, it is clear that different uses and applications of community are in some ways unavoidable. This is so because the root of the word designates a social phenomena and a sense of belonging and identity, both of which are context bound and are always in a state of fluidity. This makes it difficult at best to "define" its meaning and locate its use within the name *community music*.

COMMUNITY IN THE TWENTY-FIRST CENTURY

Recent anthropological discussions tend to emphasize *difference* as a guiding idea in exploring tensions between fixed social and political relations within communal frames and the considerable pressures toward individuation, fragmentation, and border identities (Barber, 1996; Brah, 1996; Hannerz, 1996; Wilson and Donnan, 1998; Olthuis, 2000; Donnan and Wilson, 2001; Amit and Rapport, 2002; Childs, 2003; Vila, 2005). One might think of these ideas as contesting *community*, because they challenge our most comfortable notions of what is meant by the term. Understood through postmodernism's critique of modernity, these perspectives maintain that communities are not static or bounded, but rather organic and plural. Music philosopher Wayne Bowman (2009) argues this point: "Who 'we' are, and with whom we identify most strongly are open questions whose answers are plural, fluid and grounded in patterns of influence" (p. 111).

Illustrative of a contemporary sociological perspective, Gerald Delanty (2003) suggests four categories within which one might reconsider community in the twenty-first century:

1. *Collective identities:* bursts of time, such as dropping the children off or picking them up from school, or the hours spent with work colleagues in the office.

2. *Contextual fellowship:* times of emergency or grief—for instance, the terrorist attacks on the World Trade Center or the death of Princess Diana. Contextual fellowship can also be said to have taken place in times of travel delay or cancellation. It is during these times that people find a common bond that momentarily links them together.

3. *Liminal communities:* a sense of the transitional, those "in-between" times that have importance in people's lives. For example, the ritualistic morning coffee in Starbucks, the train journey to and from work, or the Saturday morning yoga class. These moments have a consciousness of communality.

4. *Virtual communities:* most often associated with technologically mediated communities such as chat rooms, Facebook, and Myspace, but could equally be extended to websites such as eBay.

When the term *community* is opened in these ways, the phrase *community without unity* seems an apt one. In this formulation, *without* designates an open sense of the word *community,* a community of possibilities rather than a limited horizon of visibility and gathering. From a line of thinking that has a trajectory from Georges Bataille (1988), Maurice Blanchot (1988), Jean-Luc Nancy (1991), and Jacques Derrida (1997b), this formulation has a resistance to one unified and authoritative identity because the communality at the heart of community provides internal contradictions. The very concept of the "common" (*commun*) and the "as-one" (*comme-un*) becomes a problem for the politics of pluralism. Community without unity is then a descriptive attempt to recognize the importance of diversity in the modern space of communal relationships (Brent, 1997).[2] There is, therefore, an acute contradiction between the word's etymology and its general usage in today's society.

In the international field of community music practice, the general use of the term *community* is a ratification of community music's participatory ethos—an emphasis on creative endeavors toward music making through workable agreements and conversation. In short, community musicians strive for understanding among individuals with common (albeit diverse) goals despite cultural, class, gender, economic, and political differences. The work of community musicians attempts to provoke discourse, stimulate active participation, and enable a sense of "voice," both for individuals and those complicit groups or communities of which they are part. In the pursuit of socially conscious music-making experiences, the traditional notion of community, as explored in the origins of the word, can often be at odds with the practice. From a perspective of Western European history, the word can be seen as dangerously advocating a group consensus that has historically fed into visions of fascism, fundamentalism, discord, and war (Derrida, 1995a).

As a prefix to *music*, the meaning *community* is open to many interpretations. One might argue that this has helped the growth and development of community music. For example, the CMA sponsors a wide gamut of projects under its umbrella and serves to support this point. However, open definitions are not always satisfactory. Huib Schippers (2009) reinforces this sentiment by noting that one of the contributing factors to the confusion surrounding the definition of community music is that there is a tendency to "mix descriptions of specific practices with organization, artistic and pedagogical approaches, and sets of beliefs underlying the activities" (p. 93). My exploration of community music's growth and development in part I reveals this also. However, unlike Andrew Peggie (2003), who suggests that we take the C-word out of community music, or Anthony Everitt (1997) who states, "It is time to ditch the term [community music] and replace it with 'participatory music'" (p. 160), I am not advocating a rejection of the word. Why? Because although I do find aspects of its historical use problematic and out of sync with contemporary practice, I believe that a "rejection" of the word will not help the development of the practice and those that work within it. As with the term *democracy*, which I will consider in chapter 11, I think it is important to acknowledge what the term does provide and respect its historical use.

The challenge becomes to understand the production of the idea or concept within the context it is being used today. From my research and practical experience, the term *hospitality* articulates a contemporary meaning behind the prefix *community*. Conceptually arriving at this point through the notion of "community without unity," an idea that recognizes that community is as much about struggle as it is about unity, *hospitality* acts as a verb that describes the actions and desires of community musicians who seek to provide *authentic* music-making opportunities for people. In order to shed light on the word as I intend to use it, I will begin, as I did above with the term *community*, with a brief explanation of its origins and meanings.

COMMUNITY AS HOSPITALITY

As an action, hospitality begins with the *welcome*, etymologically derived from *wilcuma*, an exclamation of kindly greeting, one whose coming is in accord with another's *will*, from *willa* meaning pleasure, desire, choice, and *Cuma*, "guest" related to *cumin*, "to come." As a gesture toward another, the welcome becomes a preparation for the incoming of the potential participant, generating a porous, permeable, open-ended affirmation of and for those who wish to experience creative music making. In this context, the welcome of the community musician refutes the closure inherent within notions of the gated community, enclaves that contain restrictive perimeters that are tightly controlled and which monitor participant's entrances and exits.

As an initial gesture given by community musicians to those who wish to participate in musical doing, the welcome invites and causes a reflecting on hospitable action. In Ancient Hebrew, hospitality derives meaning from the word *philoxenia*: *philos* meaning "love," and *xenia* meaning "stranger." It is an old word that can be found in many biblical commands and examples within the Old Testament (Exodus 22:21; Exodus 23:9; Leviticus 19:10; Leviticus 19:33; Leviticus 19:34; Leviticus 24:22; Deuteronomy 10:18 New International Version). Although today the word is not used in the same way, it still shares common antecedents and mutual influences. Taking its form from the French *hospitalité* and the Latin root *hospitalitas*, the general use of the word today designates a friendly and generous reception of guests or strangers or of new ideas. Its associate *hospitable*, from the medieval French *hospiter* and the Latin root *hospitare*, to entertain, means "giving, disposed to give, welcome and entertainment to strangers or guests" (Phipps and Barnett, 2007, p. 238). It should be noted that hospitality could paradoxically mean both "host" and "stranger," its root common to both "host" and "hostile." It is from within these tensions, a welcome from the host while hostile toward the stranger, that community music practices operate.

As a preparatory thought and consequential gesture, the welcome toward a potential music participant is an invitation: the making of time for another and the invitation to be included. It is an ethical action toward a relationship to another person, a philosophical position drawing from the thought of Levinas (2006), who would describe this as a humanism of the other according to which being-for-the-other takes precedence over being-for-itself. As an example of hospitable community music, consider Bambini al Centro (literally "Children in the Center"). Across Europe, there are many music projects that form a vital role in combating the modern challenge of social exclusion. Bambini al Centro represents an example of this aspect of community music.[3] Andrea Sangiorgio and Valentina Iadeluca are community musicians who have hospitality at the center of their practice. They had always imagined a place where children in poor or difficult situations could use music as a language to express themselves: to create, to get in contact with others, to learn to play respectfully, and to cooperate. This would be a place where children, parents, and grandparents could encounter music and dance together, an environment where the welcome sign was always switched on.

In 1999 in Rome, Italy, Bambini al Centro opened its doors with money from the national fund for infancy and adolescence. Its two directors, Andrea Sangiorgio and Valentina Iadeluca, had created a recreational musical space devoted to children (birth to 12 years) and their families. The principal goal of the center was to provide an opportunity for encounters, relationships, sharing, and global growth with, and through, music and dance. Housed in a public elementary school in one of Rome's northeastern suburbs known for its economic difficulties, Bambini al Centro hosts between 120 and 160 children and their families each year. At the heart of its service is the aim to promote the well-being of children and their parents through the experience of making music in groups. One of the center's key services was the playroom, which supported families by offering children a suitable after-school alternative to loneliness, television, computer games, or wandering about the streets. Activities included early childhood music (for children birth to thirty-six months and their parents); music and play, incorporating active music making with Orff instruments (ages four to six years); or utilizing voice and percussion instruments (ages seven to eight years); and music theater (ages nine to twelve years and their parents). The demand was high and pushed the limits of the resources.

After ten years of activity, the service was so well known in the local area that the requests largely exceeded the possibility of reception. This growth was a surprise for the directors: their project exceeded their expectations. Many people came to the center through personal contacts. Many others were referred through the center's social services network and with the nursery and primary schools of the area. Often social workers or schoolteachers contacted the center to point out specific cases of children with difficulties or problems. The center welcomed the children, treating them as the most important users of the center, rather than overlooking them and putting them on a waiting list. Although maintaining this openness is sometimes difficult given the practical of running a business with limited space, personnel, and resources, the center held fast to its policy of hospitality until the lack of government funds forced its temporary closure.

This type of hospitality suggests unconditionality, a welcome without reservation, without previous calculation, and, in the context of community music, an unlimited display of reception toward a potential music participant. As such, unconditionality approaches a transcendental idea, one toward which we might aspire, even though it remains inaccessible. I am suggesting that by reaching out beyond what may be thought possible, new and interesting things can happen. An example of this is the recent interest in prison choir programs (Silber, 2005; Cohen, 2007a, 2007b, 2008; Shieh, 2010). It is here that the "unconditional" hospitable welcome can contribute to reducing the tensions felt by the prison population, both among themselves in the prison and between themselves and those on the "outside." Drawn from data collected and presented by Mary Cohen (2010), the hospitality offered by musician Elvera Voth serves as an example of "excessive" hospitality in action.

In 1995, Elvera Voth volunteered to conduct a secular prison choir in Lansing, Kansas, United States. Voth, a native Kansan, worked as a choral music educator in Alaska for over thirty years and also prepared choruses for Robert Shaw. In addition, she founded numerous musical organizations, including the Department of Music Education at the University of Alaska, the Anchorage Boys' Choir, and the Alaska Chamber Singers. Upon retirement, she returned to Kansas to put her considerable music skills to good use in an area of need. During a reunion of a Mennonite men's chorus, she shared her vision of working within the criminal justice system with a former student, Janeal Krehbiel. Krehbiel's brother-in-law, a deputy warden of Lansing Correctional Facility, arranged a meeting between Voth and David McKune, warden of the prison. McKune granted Voth permission to begin a men's chorus at the minimum-security unit called the East Unit. The chorus took its name, East Hill Singers, from the unit's name.

Voth posted a sign inside the facility advertising the choir, stating simply, "Forming a Singing Group." There were no expectations for joining the group, merely an open invitation. This was her act of unconditional hospitality, a gesture toward a future that was unknown. The limits of her welcome were tested immediately when the participants asked whether they could form a rap group. Perhaps not surprisingly, this was something Voth felt she could not facilitate. However, the openness of the initial call enabled a level of communication that formed the beginnings of a fruitful and relevant music-making experience. It was Voth's ability to allow herself to be exposed to an unforeseeable future that enabled the subsequent prison singing programs to happen.

Ordinarily, *unconditional* refers to a situation not limited by conditions. Within this context, there is a break from the Kantian idea that describes the unconditional as an absolute, a sovereign instance, or an archetype, a supreme, preeminent, or indisputable something. Kant's (1998, p. A 567/ B 597) sovereign instance is removed from time and space and completely given to itself, a logic that suggests fixivity. In the context used here, unconditionality is accepted as residing at the very origin of the seminal concepts that give the West its history, politics and culture (Wortham, 2010). The unconditional is therefore always entwined with what is conditional and must be recalled in order to rethink and transform commonly accepted ideas and concepts. The unconditional is not therefore sovereign and becomes intrinsically linked to a future that is unforeseeable.

For example, a community musician may have prepared a series of workshops for a local arts center but, an hour before the first session is due to start, finds the expected group of music participants will now additionally include five young refugees from Haiti who have been relocated to the area and have shown interest in music. The unexpected change takes the community musician by surprise and requires the ability to augment current plans and make room for another possibility. The consequence of this type of change has implications for the relatively foreseeable future plans of the music director such as next week's band practice, the instrumental assessments, and the difficulty in resourcing next year's classes.

In short, unconditional hospitality embraces a future that will surprise and shatter predetermined horizons. Much like the improvisations of Ornette Coleman or Derek Bailey, the sonic assaults of Napalm Death or Meshuggah, or the inventive break from traditions that can be found in the music of Arnold Schoenberg, the Beatles, or Jimi Hendrix, the unconditional implies a sense of "violence" toward that which is stable, fixed, and comfortable. In other words, something that is violent is not to be taken as a fatal corruption of a pure origin, a fall from some fundamental integrity (Derrida, 1997a). Used here, violence operates as the "machinery of exclusion" and implies an essential impropriety that does not allow anything to be sheltered from risk, failure, and forgetting (Hägglund, 2008).

It therefore follows that the community in community music, as described here, does not subscribe to an idealistic community, understood in terms of a desire for that which has no imperfections. This would be a utopian dream of pure plenitude existing as a sovereign lament while betraying the practical realities that surround the work of community musicians. If *coresponsibility*, in the sense that group members are responsible for one another without their personal or individual responsibilities being reduced in any way, describes a relationship between community musicians and the participants they work with, then the desire for a utopian community would not be responsible, a theme that will be explored in chapter 11. This is essential thinking for practical reasons. For example, if I did not discriminate between whom I did and whom I did not welcome into the workshop space, it would denote that I would have renounced all claims to be a responsible music facilitator. It might also mean that I would have opened myself to whatever is violently opposed to me without reservation. Unconditional hospitality is not to be desired beyond what can be known or realized. It is not transcendental in the Kantian sense of an absolute or sovereign thing.

As described above, the use of the word *community* can often evoke a sense of closure, a bounding of a group that defines who is included and who is excluded. Sangiorgio and Iadeluca's unconditional hospitality exceeded this, but there is always a chance they will have to refuse someone at the Bambini al Centro because the practicalities demand it. However, their vision exemplifies unconditional hospitality as they attempt to push back at these customary definitions of community boundaries. Over the years, many people have told Sangiorgio and Iadeluca how important Bambini al Centro has become in their everyday life; it is a trustworthy place where they can take their children, knowing they will be respected as human beings and encouraged to develop their music skills. The future was always uncertain for Bambini al Centro, and it is sad to report that it was forced to close in the middle of 2010 due to financial and political problems.

The open invitation can become a genuine human expression and an ethical moment that community music facilitators generate. This can result in an experience of connectivity among participants, and between participants and the music they make and listen to. It is the hospitable welcome that encourages participants toward creative music making and can produce lasting impressions on both community musicians and participants. It is vital in every socially interactive musical experience, in every context. The implication behind thinking of the word *community* as a hospitable welcome becomes a refusal of any interpretation of community that privileges "gathering" over "dislocation." These sentiments do not advocate the destruction of unity, as there can be an "open" gathering. Instead, the challenge is for notions of "pure" unity and "absolute" totality because these ideas significantly reduce negotiation, conversation, and movement. As an act of unconditional hospitality, community music is a promise of the welcome, a commitment to a "community *without* unity," a chance to say "yes" without discrimination against any potential music participant.[4]

However, Voth's desire for unconditional hospitality is often challenged by the conditional realities of working within the criminal justice system. Inmates must be at a level three on a three-level behavioral incentive system in order to leave the facility for public concerts. If they do not maintain that level, they cannot go out into the community with the group to perform. During the public concerts, many inmates recount personal narratives to the audience. According to Voth and volunteer singers, these narratives are a key element of any concert. The narratives explain details about the choral selections and describe how singing in the chorus is meaningful to the inmate singers. They describe the hospitality and welcome that is needed to enable the choir to function. Concerts occur almost exclusively in Kansas churches, although concerts have taken place on the campus of Washburn University in Topeka and at the 2008 Kansas Music Educators Conference in Wichita. Through a *reimagining* of the word *community* in community music, there is a foregrounding of its key characteristics, a sharpening of the distinctive traits that make its operation different from other musical discourses. Community music describes a field that is hospitable and open, a set of practices that look ahead in order to generate environments that can be accessible and participatory.

SUMMARY

Communities can be based on many things, including ethnicity, religion, class, gender, or politics. They can be located in villages, towns, cities, or cyberspace. Communities can be large or small, local or global, traditional, modern, or postmodern. However, this "warmly persuasive word" has at its heart the search for human belonging (Williams, 1985, p. 76). It is through the embrace of unconditional hospitality that musicians Andrea Sangiorgio, Valentina Iadeluca, and Elvera Voth can exert a welcome that fertilizes a network of shared relationships, creating what is generally understood as a sense of community. As Maurice Blanchot (1988) says, "This sharing refers back to the community and is exposed in it" (p. 19). Such networks echo Levinas's (1981) notion that, "the community with him begins in my obligation to him" (p. 11), and Blanchot (1988) reinforces this sentiment by stating, "If I want my life to have meaning for myself, it must have meaning *for someone else*" (p. 11). With the help of community musicians, participants of the Bambini al Centro and the East Hill Singers prepare themselves for the arrival of new music participants; their community making is porous, permeable and open-ended. I have suggested that the concept of *community* in *community music* resides as an act of hospitality, a welcome (given by those that name themselves community musicians) to those who want to participate in active musical doing. This is an attempt to conceptualize its distinctive characteristics based on an understanding of what constitutes both conditional and unconditional hospitality rather than define it. This perspective suggests that the strength of the term *community* within *community music* lies in the welcome it extends to others, rather than in any codification of the word.

Community as a prefix to *community music* is a gesture toward an open-door policy, a greeting to strangers, extended in advance and without full knowledge of its consequences. New participants do not simply cross a threshold with the intention of joining a community music project. Any new *welcome* is always also a direct challenge to what has been currently constituted. This challenge surprises and calls into question prior group identity and predetermined community borders. One might say that the promise of the welcome constantly puts the "inside" in doubt—and this can be scary for both the group leader and the participants. From this formulation, the outside, or the excluded, affects and determines the inside, or included.

A good example of this can be drawn from the Peterborough Community Samba Band, which was highlighted throughout chapter 4. As a group, they always tried to anticipate new members. This had a direct effect on everybody because it was rare to have the same participants from week to week. The preparations of both the music facilitator and the participants were such that they could never become too comfortable. New people would come and go, "disrupting" the equilibrium of the group on a regular basis. This was not only tolerated; it was at the heart of their constitution. You could say it was why the band existed. This is also true of Bambini al Centro and Voth's prison work. The open welcome is a challenge to those who are already participants because you must be ready to be hospitable yourself to provide a space for more.

If community musicians can acknowledge desire for unconditional hospitality, this may prevent the closure characteristic of a determinate community and thus provide an enhanced ability to say, "Yes you are welcome to join this music workshop." Community musicians concerned with creating accessible and diverse music-making opportunities might look at their approach toward inclusion and ask, "Do I create an environment of unconditional hospitality?" "Am I open to new and different possibilities?" "How welcoming are my music workshops?" In short, community music as hospitality requires the embrace of those who wish to participate in music making within the limits of what is not known to be possible. Community musicians might think beyond comfortable understandings of what usually constitutes community and as a result may be more successful in providing increased and richer opportunities for participants' voices to be heard. In the next chapter, I expand this discussion by focusing on approaches of community music practice.

CHAPTER 9

Approaches to Practice

I n order to generate music-making environments that are accessible for those
who wish to participate, community musicians generally adhere to particular
strategic approaches that reflect an "act of hospitality." This chapter sets out to
explore these strategies excavating desires[1] and tensions inherent within facilitating or leading community music workshops.

THE MUSIC WORKSHOP

In order to activate music making, community musicians have relied on particular and determined approaches to practice. Although ideas surrounding community music have many orientations, community musicians have emphasized the
workshop and facilitation as key strategies for practice. The term *workshop* is
most often associated within educational settings as a site for experimentation,
creativity, and group work (Aston and Paynter, 1970; Paynter, 1982, 1992; Self,
1976; Schafer, 1975, 1976, 1992).[2] In resonance with these classroom practices,
community musicians pursued the workshop as their means of achieving a *democratic* space favorable to creative music making. Although *creative* is a complex
word, "being creative" in this instance means generating new ideas and concepts
from both individuals and groups (Webster, 1996).

As a spatial and temporal domain, the contingent structure of the workshop
enables an open space to foster active and collaborative music making. Music is
an open structure that permeates and is permutated by the world, and as such the
workshop can be an ideal site through which one can create a deterritorialized
space to foster and harness human desires for musicking. Following Gilles
Deleuze and Félix Guattari (1988a), deterritorialized workshop spaces also
produce change by freeing up fixed physical, mental, and spiritual relations, while
seeking the opportunity to expose new relationships. In conjunction with deter-
ritorialization, the notion of musicking is also useful because it has its focus on the
relationships among those who take part in musical events. One can say that the act

of musicking has its primacy in the social dimensions of face-to-face or face-to-group encounters (Small, 1987).

Through an openness and focus toward relationships, the workshop can become a touchstone through which diversity, freedom, and tolerance might flow. Consequently, pedagogical practices that work within *workshop* or *laboratory* structures are actively involved in the pursuit of equality and access beyond any preconceived limited horizons. For example, consider the community drumming workshops organized by Powers Percussion in the northwest United States. Run by community music facilitator Mark Powers, his "Sights and Sounds of Ghana" workshops focus on the music and culture of the Ewe people of West Africa. Drawing on Powers's studies in the village of Kopeyia in 2003, in these workshops he explores life, music, and school in Ghana with the participants. In his "Junk Jam" workshops, Powers then works alongside the participants to discover "found sounds" and explore the percussive possibilities within everyday items such as five-gallon pails, garbage cans, automotive brake drums, and soda can shakers. Using a similar process to those of the PickleHerring Theatre Company, illustrated in chapter 6, workshop participants learn how to creatively transform ordinary objects into musical instruments. From a pedagogical perspective, Powers's workshops aim to expose participants to different musics from around the world, and also their cultural contexts. His enthusiasm toward accessible music making demonstrates an act of hospitality, an open welcome activated through the workshop space that often results in a vibrant integrated arts experience (Higgins and Bartleet, 2012).

Another powerful and widespread form of community music activity that serves to illustrate this point is group songwriting. Like drumming workshops, songwriting workshops can also provide empowering and transformative learning experiences for participants. David Denborough describes the power of song:

> As holders of community knowledge and pride, songs can lift the spirits and hold them aloft. The physical act of singing together, of making music together, can also be transformative. This seems especially so if the process resonates with cultural traditions of community song-making and music making which exist in the vast majority of communities. In this way, not only can the song itself act as a musical documentation of the alternative stories of the community, but the community performance of this song can act as a demonstration of the continuation of a joyful and inclusive tradition. (Higgins and Bartleet, 2012)

The Dandenong Ranges Music Council in Victoria, Australia, has been funding community music in this region for thirty years and has made a major contribution to providing learning and performance opportunities for musicians of all ages and abilities. At the heart of the "Fire Cycle Project," which had its focus on issues that have significant local interest, such as fire prevention and water conservation, there were a series of informal songwriting workshops with local schools, fire brigades, and park rangers. Community music facilitator and song-writer John Shortis and a local community music therapist ran songwriting workshops. They were designed not only to educate participants about fire prevention but also assist them to express their grief over the devastation that was caused by the bushfires. In the local schools, Shortis brainstormed ideas and issues with the participants about what had happened, their feelings and reactions to the events, and incorporated their words and ideas into the resulting songs. He followed a similar process with a group of local firefighters, who then wrote a song about fire education and prevention. The songs that resulted from these workshops were then recorded with a local school choir and adult choir and launched at the Torchlight Parade. As an approach to community building through an act of hospitality, the songwriting workshops not only enabled participants to cope with the grief and bewilderment they felt about this tragedy on an individual level, but also taught them the importance of connecting with their local communities through music in order to rebuild their lives.

Both Powers's and Shortis's workshops can be understood as *events*. One usually describes an *event* as something that happens or is regarded as happening, something that usually occurs in a certain place during a particular interval of time. One might say that it is an occurrence of some importance that calls for new modes of experience and different forms of judgment (Malpas, 2003). According to Jean-François Lyotard (1991), the event disrupts preexisting frames or contexts, giving opportunity to the possible emergence of new form and voices. Bill Readings (1991) summarizes it as "the event is the fact or case that something happens, after which nothing will ever be the same again" (p. xxxi). In this way, the workshop can mark the point at which something happens, a potential location to shatter prior ways of making sense of the world. In Powers's drumming workshops, this manifested itself through new cultural insights and exhilarating musical involvement. In Shortis's songwriting workshops, there were moments of connection that revealed a new perspective through which to consider home. One might say that the instance of the workshop is not known until it is over because it occurs as a disruption. As *event*, the workshop becomes a singular disruptable happening that challenges with intention to transform. Although guidance is needed within workshop events, it is imperative that the structure remains porous and open in the same way that the term *hospitality* predisposes us to welcome those we have yet to meet. As a manifestation outlined here, the workshop space becomes a site for experimentation and exploration through a deterritorialized environment. Although the space is bounded, it is not a tightly controlled location that fixes parameters with rigidity and barriers. Spaces set up in this manner enable change and transformation. Within the workshop situation, one might consider this as freeing up fixed and set relations, physically, mentally, and spiritually, while seeking the opportunity to expose new relationships. As metaphoric "lines of flight," the workshop event releases criss-crossing pathways that connect the most disparate and most similar happenings.

There are no roots as such because community music processes operate as a haecceity within a rhizomatic structure, paths of networks with a multiple of entryways.[3]

FACILITATION

Within any possible workshop situation, the community music facilitator might strive toward unconditional hospitality. It is this implication that creates conducive opportunities through which to generate a creative music-making experience, or, as one might say, a venture into the unknown. Musical doing of this sort should not be predictable: the creative experience is to come, a future event as yet unknown. Following the notion of a "community without unity," the music facilitator here gives privilege to "dislocation" over "gathering." In this sense, the concurrence of harmonization through collective gatherings is understood as a limiting process. Dislocation, however, requires continuous negotiation, and in these situations new rules and idioms must be found on which to phrase disputes or conversation (Lyotard, 1988). As a positive action, dislocation celebrates all types of music and all types of "participatory discrepancies" (Keil and Feld, 1994). From this perspective, the music workshop leader has the potential to host participants, so that neither the individual or collective, nor the power of the facilitator, is diminished in any way.

Derivative from the French *facile*, "to make easy," and the Latin *facilis*, "easy to do," facilitation is concerned with encouraging open dialogue among different individuals with differing perspectives. Exploration of diverse assumptions and options are often some of the significant aims. Christine Hogan (2002) usefully describes a facilitator as a "self-reflective, process-person who has a variety of human, process, technical skills and knowledge, together with a variety of experiences to assist groups of people to journey together to reach their goals" (p. 57). As a complex practice of what Mirja Hiltunen (2008) calls "agency," facilitation grew throughout the second half of the twentieth century in areas such as business, education, and development. Its evolution extends from educators such as John Dewey,[4] Maria Montessori,[5] Alexander Sutherland Neill,[6] Kurt Hahn,[7] and Malcolm Knowles.[8] It also includes Edgar Schein's[9] "process consultancy," the radical developments within action research discourse from practitioners such as Jean McNiff and Jack Whitehead[10] plus person-centered counseling, the approach pioneered by Carl Rogers.[11] Robert Chambers[12] has also been influential in developing participatory methodologies for use in the developing worlds. One should also mention the work of Paulo Freire,[13] who attacked the "banking" concept of education while championing concepts of reflexive lifelong learning not governed by set curricula.[14] From this trajectory, there are now many good writings that offer methodological approaches and strategies. For example, texts such as those by Frances and Roland Bee (1998), Jarlath Benson (2010),

Allan Brown (1992), Tom Douglas (2000), Dorothy Whitaker (2000), and Christine Hogan (2003) all underline the current importance of facilitation as a structure for creative group work.

From the perspective of the community musician, facilitation is understood as a process that enables participants' creative energy to flow, develop, and grow through pathways specific to individuals and the groups in which they are working. Facilitation does not mean that the community musician surrenders responsibility for music leadership, only that the control is relinquished. Within any group setting, there is a fine line between leading and controlling, but the two processes are very different and therefore provide contrasting results to the group experience. For example, in controlling the group journey, there is a strong sense of the beginning, middle and end, and the expectations and needs that must be met. However, in facilitating the group experience, there may certainly be a starting point, but the rest remains uncertain. Community music facilitators offer routes toward suggested destinations and are ready to assist if the group journey becomes lost or confused, but they are always open to the possibility of the unexpected that comes from individuals in their interactivity with the group. These possibilities cannot be predicted, and that is the excitement of facilitated music that grows from the group, be they a class of young children, members of a youth garage band, inmates in a detention center, or adult members of a drum circle. Anything can happen when musical events are proposed and facilitated but not directed in the manner of the top-down conductors/directors tradition.

At times, the group will look to its facilitator for reassurance, clarity, direction, encouragement, guidance, or shaping. Facilitators are able to find a comfortable balance between (1) being prepared and able to lead and (2) being prepared and able to hold back, thus enabling the group or individuals to discover the journey of musical invention for themselves. Facilitators are never static in one approach or another but move in and out of roles as the group dictates. Facilitation necessitates trust in the ability of others as well as submission to the inventiveness of others. Community musicians develop this trust as they learn to listen to others while maintaining the skill to enable the participants to work together and steer a course for their group. Trust is, as Caputo (2000) points out, an "expectation of hospitality" (p. 57). By establishing a secure but flexible framework from the outset, community musicians often give over the control to the group and trust in the direction it takes. In giving up control, the possibilities emerge for musical outcomes that are unpredictable and evident only in their unfolding. Music becomes an invention personal to the participants, owned by and meaningful to the participants, with the potential to generate an experience that can shape, create, and have an impact on identity formation (Green, 2011). In short, music-making experiences such as these can be uncompromising, personal, and "alive," a process that evokes a telling of "their" story over those of the music facilitator. The self-worth that comes from being "enabled" to invent is powerfully affirming.

For those whose musical practice has been tied up with directing, conducting, and "calling all the shots," the parent-child relationship may be a useful mirror of the facilitator-group relationship. A young child needs clear instruction and boundaries to feel safe and secure; this is the premise for the child to begin to grow and develop. As he or she becomes older, the parent needs to step back a little. The child must face some milestones alone but is always able to return to the security of the caring parent who is ready, waiting, and expecting to offer comfort, support, guidance, and perhaps redirection. As the child moves into adolescence, so the parent needs to release the reigns further, enabling the young adult to overcome challenges, encounter new discoveries, and develop self-assurance. With the aim of enabling the development of autonomy, the diligent parent will carefully consider when to sensitively step in with offers of support, guidance, advice, or comfort (Higgins and Campbell, 2010).

As children, we may have experienced a parenting style that was intrusive and gave us little freedom to discover ourselves. Alternatively, we may have experienced a childhood in which the adults in our lives adapted their parenting style to suit our changing needs. It is this ideal that most closely reflects the community music group-facilitator relationship: the ability to sense what is needed and to be able to offer an accurate response in all situations. Those who have been recently exploring an "informal" approach to music education have also been interested in this type of approach (Jaffurs, 2004a, 2004b; Söderman and Folkestad, 2004; Folkestad, 2006; Green, 2008). The "informalization" toward musical teaching and learning has been championed within the Musical Futures project.[15] As an example of the type of work they support, the Guildhall School of Music's Connect project closely resembles what I am describing here (Renshaw, 2005). Using a delineated vocabulary that labels the learning context as (1) the *formal* sector, schools, college, or statutory music provision; (2) the *nonformal*, statutory provision led by adults; or (3) the *informal* activities organized and led by young people with no adult supervision, those involved in Musical Futures have sought to change the nature of the musical learning environment and the relationship between participant and facilitator (Price and D'Amore, 2007). Operating inside a formal context but utilizing nonformal procedures, the Connect project, as reported by Peter Renshaw (2005), offers "a rich opportunity for the 'voices' of its young musicians to be heard and acknowledged. Performances are characterized by a strong sense of ownership, motivation and shared responsibility" (p. 2). Renshaw outlines the underlying principles as follows:

- Knowing how to work musically in a group that incorporates any instrument brought to an ensemble by the young musicians;
- Knowing how to work effectively in mixed groups varying in size, age, technical ability and musical experience;
- Knowing how to make music in a genre-free ensemble, where its musical material reflects the shared interests of the leaders and participants;

- Knowing how to engage in music-making virtually without notation;
- Knowing how to create music collaboratively. (p. 2)

Renshaw's insights into the pedagogic approach strongly echo that of the community musician.

SAFETY WITHOUT SAFETY

The workshop as a space and facilitation as a strategic approach to music leadership provide community musicians with opportunities to imagine and invent *new* things alongside participants. As a notion closely aligned to that of the *event*, the word *invention* has traditionally meant the coming of something new: something to come that is different from what has come before (Derrida, 2007b). From the Latin root *venire*, "to come," this is a call that signals the arrival of the unexpected and therefore has close associations with the *welcome*, a theme I will expand on in chapter 10. Although inventive possibilities have yet to arrive, when they do, they can be disrupting, challenging, and anachronistic. Musical doing that advocates this type of thinking and action is not often predictable. Through the welcome, the facilitator can create a pathway toward a genuine invention, an authentic and meaningful adventure. As a strategy, facilitation is employed in order to evoke this imaginative and inventive atmosphere, encouraging and nurturing a rapport with fellow human beings. This action requires that the working space be a *safe space*, in which the music facilitator attempts to create an atmosphere that is mindful of the participants' range of abilities but challenging enough to stimulate all concerned. In this way, the community musician creates deterritorialized spaces in order to open opportunities for the workshop event to become a place of conversation, negotiating, and play. Drawing from these concepts, I suggest that workshop facilitators might think of their work as exhibiting "safety *without* safety." In this instance, boundaries are marked to provide enough structural energy for the workshop to begin, but care is then taken to ensure that not too many restraints are employed that might delimit the flow or the becoming of any music making.

For example, as part of my work, I run improvisation workshops (Higgins and Campbell, 2010). At the beginning of these workshops, improvisation is treated as *free*: the structures are loose, and the emphasis is on *play* rather than performance. Following Derrida's thinking, *play* is understood as a gesture that works against the ideas of self-sufficiency and absolute completion: its emphasis is on participation and/or process rather than performance and/or completed product.[16] Play is therefore closely connected to the spirit of every music workshop event, in that exploration, experimentation, and invention are encouraged. Play is seen as challenging and disrupting what might be regularly thought of as music performance, a finished and final project. Likewise, the participatory process is upheld and maintained as central to every event, such that the interaction and contributions of each individual participant to the whole is more important than a polished performance. Of course, it is possible that playful participation can result in a "peak" musical product too, but the critical factor is that music is not held at a distance and objectified but is a process into which all members of the group enter, experience, and enjoy. All events might be thought of as playful and evocative of a musical freedom within rules and limitations. There are rules, but they are bendable, and just like children's games, the rules can change during the course of play.

Through open-ended musical structure and a promise toward the welcome, participants from a range of musical traditions are often able to liberate their playing from past parameters that have restricted this sense of free play. Music making in this way is nonhierarchal, "a process of lateral connections between sounds, genres and musicians" (Gilbert, 2004). This puts *danger* into the heart of music-making workshops. The security of the familiar is replaced with the safety of the workshop environment. The workshop facilitator can advance success through the possibility of failure. This is not an unwelcome possibility or an exposure to harm. It is an attempt to generate excess that supersedes the mundane and the predictable while recognizing a duty to care. In order to encourage and maintain a frame of mind that enables both participant and facilitator to venture into new territories, judgments tied to old existing definitions of what is viewed as acceptable in each context must be suspended. If the facilitator can create a safe climate for risk taking, then this may release the group, or individual, to try the untried. In these instances, "failures" are celebrated and community music becomes, as community musician Martin Milner (2007) suggests, "a path of no mistakes": experiences that are not to be understood as devastating but as important moments of learning within the creative process.

Safety without safety gestures enable community musicians to operate within a code of appropriate facilitation practice but to also allow for excesses beyond the workshop's spatial-temporal realm. In this formulation, the *without* does not just separate the particular from the general.[17] There is no attempt to think of a universal safety parameter within which individual examples are exempt. As a freedom from danger or risks, safety is always in the process of arriving: like the welcome, it is to come. As such, it is synonymously linked to invention and is at the heart of the creative process.

If we combine the ideas presented so far—community music as an act of hospitality, the workshop as an event, and the desire to facilitate inventive music-making opportunities through the gesture of safety without safety—there is both a structural imperative and a process of engagement for the music facilitator. In the next section, I will attempt to bind these ideas together by suggesting that the music facilitator encounters the participant through the act of gift giving. That is, the giving of time and space but also the giving of quality experiences and skills.

THE GIFT

When community musicians welcome their participants, they generally do so with a sense of hospitality, a readiness or liberality in giving of some sort. The giving of oneself and encouragement for others to give has been previously illustrated through the work of Sangiorgio, Iadeluca, Voth, Powers, and Shortis, plus many of those featured in chapter 6. Gift theory acknowledges this type of *hospitality* as well as complementary attributes such as empathy and care. However, the gesture of the gift also reminds us of less positive characteristics that lurk within such human transactions: these include self-interest, systems of debts, and expectations of reciprocity. I like to think about these types of exchanges within the character of the circle. The circle is a significant feature in community music because music facilitators organize participants within the circle's "democratic" geometry. As such, the continual exchange between facilitator and participant, plus the spatial location of the group and their environment makes the circle a significant metaphor. It is interesting to note the word *cadeau*, gift, comes from *catena*, meaning "chain."

Marcel Mauss's *The Gift* (1990), first published in 1924, is often regarded as the starting point for contemporary discussion surrounding the gift. Mauss notes that a gift is never free, entailing as it does a triple obligation—to give, to receive, and to reciprocate. Within anthropology, Mauss's book has been critiqued and reinterpreted many times (Firth, 1963; Lévi-Strauss, 1969; Sahlins, 1974; Hyde, 1979; Gregory, 1982; Bataille, 1991), but as Alan Schrift (1997) suggests, it is only recently that the theme of the gift and gift giving has emerged as a central issue in a wider range of fields and practices. Helen Nicholson's (2005) book on community drama and theater offers a fine example of this. The emergent interest of gift and gift giving may be, in part, traced back to the publication of Derrida's *Given Time: I. Counterfeit Money* (1992). Challenging Mauss's circle of obligation, Derrida examines the economy implied in the idea of exchange and explores the circularity inherent within gift exchanges, noting that circular economies are understood to bind the receiver to a debt of gratitude, while the donor receives gratitude either from the gift receiver or from her or himself (consciously or unconsciously). The resultant tensions are that the donor, instead of giving something, has received and the receiver becomes indebted. One might say that gifts are given to enhance the social role of the giver and to impose an obligation on the receiver. Gifts therefore bind others to gratitude and consequently lead to reciprocation. In this way, expressions of thanks never find rest: a gift is something you can never be truly thankful for. As a circular economy, both theoretically and practically, the music workshop operates through reciprocity and may create binds and debts. Any belief the music facilitator has regarding altruistic desires is also brought under question through this analysis.

Like the tensions implicit within the word *hospitality*, the gift too carries conflict within itself. For a gift to be an unconditional, there must be no reciprocity: no return, no exchange, no counter-gift, and no debt. Gifts are exchanged and are therefore a self-limiting concept forming circular economies caught within trading networks. In one sense, it is this logic of exchange that annuls any gifts we care to give. If one applies this line of thought to the music workshop event, one concludes that it too carries its own opposition: the workshop as both a poison and a present.[18] As a *poison*, the workshop becomes a disappointment and a negative experience, making false claims and raising hopes. This type of experience might reinforce the participants' belief in their lack of musicality. On the other hand, as a *present*, it becomes a springboard for positive creativity, exploration, and future happenings, generating a safety without safety space in which to nurture participants' potential, an atmosphere where possibilities appear limitless.

Although we can acknowledge the impossibility of the workshop as unconditional gift, it should not mean the end of thinking about its gesture. In fact, it alerts us to its structure, and our antennae become sensitive to its laws of operation enabling a greater sensitivity within its many movements. A conscious awareness of the circles of gift giving may make the music facilitator more effective through a process of self-reflective practice. In short, the gift reinscribes in terms to greater openness, a call, and a welcome that ignites trust, respect, and responsibility, three themes I will explore in the next chapter. Through this gesture, the workshop leader's responsibility is to create situations that are beyond debt, or at least to be thought of in this way. As a music facilitator, one might aim for group togetherness, respectful collaboration, and open negotiation. These may be partly met but can never be truly fulfilled unconditionally: the economic cycle will always close down these desires. As I have discussed, and all too often experienced, any workshop event will always carry imposed conditions and structures that limit any creative music-making activity. However, within the circle of exchange between facilitator and participant and between participant and participant, the desire to give something without getting anything back ignites the economy of exchange and pushes the music workshop into motion.

SUMMARY

Building upon the suggestion that the *community* in community music can be understood as an act of hospitality, this chapter had as its focus the approaches of community music practice that make this idea concrete. As the community musician's modus operandi, the workshop was conceptualized through the notion of *event*, a caesura or interruption that disrupts and shatters prior ways of making sense of the world, while facilitation was seen as a strategy of musical leadership. As a practical occurrence, the workshop presents itself as a *democratic* event: namely, that the ownership is not vested in a single individual (the workshop facilitator) but lies with everybody. This can be seen at the beginning of most music workshops, as the most common starting point for any facilitatory process is that of the circle itself, a condition of space that reduces hierarchical structures. The reduction of a dominant force provides fertile ground for "future-producing" moments that can be transformative, evoking possibilities of change immanent to any given territory: physical, mental, and/or spiritual. Self-aware exchanges within a gift system have the potential to transcend their given limits and in turn may sharpen a facilitator's emphasis on a "bottom-up" rather than "top-down" approach to creative music making. The music workshop event becomes a practical framework for participation, equality of opportunity, access, and development. It has the potential to be a formidable tool of engagement, but its potential as a poisonous present is often overlooked. If those who facilitate musical doing could understand that their workshops are not *gifts* to be returned, perhaps this would limit those structures that generate predictable musical and procedure outcomes.

Finally, the idea of safety without safety reminds community musicians of their responsibilities while alerting them to the desires for full, breathing, and creative interactions. Safety without safety reinforces a drive toward dynamic music-making experiences that embrace risk and undecidability. There is a traditional South African community song that calls "VeLa, VeLa," meaning "Come, come, we want to see you." It is this type of embrace that encourages community music participants to take creative risks. Through an unconditional welcome, the community musician calls "VeLa," liberating opportunities for authentic creative experiences.

With a shift of focus toward those individuals who make up groups, the next chapter explores the one-to-one encounters that happen between music facilitator and participants and vice versa. Using data gathered from visits to ten locations committed to acts of community music, I examine the interactions between individuals and explore the themes of trust, respect, responsibility, and friendship.

CHAPTER 10

Face-to-Face Encounters

I have established that community musicians facilitate active and creative musicking through a welcoming workshop environment. Through acts of hospitality, the music workshop as event, evokes collective and inventive conversations that aim to encourage music making that is open, creative, and accessible. In short, participants who commit to community music projects do so because they want to be "worked with" rather than "worked on." In this chapter, I focus on one-to-one relationships between the community music facilitator and the participant, making the claim that the face-to-face encounter emerges as a *friendship* that challenges those mutual and reciprocal structures commonly associated with ordinary conceptions of the word. The primary data underpinning this chapter, gathered in the spring of 2008, represents visits to ten locations committed to acts of community music. During that time, I interviewed music facilitators, and music participants, both individually and in small groups. I asked the music facilitators, how do you, as a facilitator, understand the relationship between yourself and the individual group participant? I asked the participants, how do you, the music participant, understand the relationship between yourself and those leading the music workshop? Four key themes flow from the data analysis and serve as an organizational frame: (1) the individual participant, (2) working together, (3) trust, respect, and responsibility, and (4) friendship.

THE INDIVIDUAL PARTICIPANT

Although collaborative music making represents the most common form of community music practice, it is the interaction between the facilitator and the individuals that enables functional group work. Sean, the director of a choral group open to those aged fifty years and older, emphasizes this: "Unless you have the individual relationship then you don't have a group." He further adds, "[Groups] are made up of individuals and you have to deal with them as individuals." Patty, director of a community music center makes this point also: "I [as the facilitator] should listen to the participants' emotions and should feel the group [so that]

I can ask them how they are, what they are doing." A freelance community musician reflects on her practice, noting that "in order to be a good facilitator you need to know where everybody is at." She qualifies further by suggesting that solid relationships enhance the possibility of being creative within the music workshop. On this very point, Michael, the manager of a youth music organization, states that "inevitably after one or two sessions you begin to know the individuals and then you get a better idea what works for that person and what particular journey they are going on." Chloe, a freelance community musician, stresses the importance she puts on "getting to know everyone ... getting to know their characteristics and strengths" and therefore understanding that "they are all different." With particular reference to work within the special education sector, one music facilitator stated, "I feel that I have a very strong relationship with them all," going on to note that her individual relationships increase the chances of creating an authentic space for music-making experiences.

Everyone I interviewed and observed had a commitment toward the music making and social well-being of individual participants as well as the group as a whole. Their work was consistent with the key dispositions that characterize community music practice explored in part I, such as person-centered facilitation processes, access for all members of the community, a recognition that participants' social and personal growth are as important as their musical growth, and an acknowledgment of both individual and group ownership of musics. Through my experiences, it has become clear that in order to respond to these ideals, community musicians need to take a certain ethical stance. Community music practice begins with the welcome, and it is here that the participant is first exposed to an ethical moment. For example, I asked a variety of community musicians to describe some of their significant community music recollections. The responses espoused strong connections to a sense of humanity and the "just": what I have already described in connection with hospitality as a humanism of, and for, the other (Levinas, 2006). A music facilitator from London, recounting a moment from his work in a young male offenders' institute, said, "These guys have never touched an instrument before," adding that "they felt so good about it." Another music facilitator told me that participants with challenging behavior had been "really opening up and looking into themselves." The music-making activities had boosted confidence and, in one case, led an individual, who was having a disruptive effect on other participants, to cement the group through outstanding leadership, both musical and emotional. There were many such celebratory narratives, including several young people who were recommended to attend a National Youth Agency mentoring program,[1] individuals who received a stipend to attend weekend music school, and those who had grown more confident through the opportunities for musical self-expression. One particularly touching story involved a senior member of the choir group. One evening, after the weekly music workshop, this senior choir member left a bottle of wine and a card for the facilitator saying, "Thank you for giving me my life back after my husband died."

Through his critique of Heidegger's ontological notion of "the 'they,'" Levinas proposes that there is a danger that people may become just colleagues, associates, or coworkers, rather than sources of compassion, admiration, or desire.[2] From this scenario, relationships might become nondescript and dull, lacking a fire that ignites a passion for life. The loss of vital human interactions would mean that human beings may just fail to acknowledge the humanity in each other. In the context I am discussing here, the individuals who constitute community music groups become just a crowd. Music participants become nothing special: they are to be "worked on" rather than "worked with." They are viewed as a "bunch" of people who evoke no acknowledgment, a group that arrived at the workshop space and were not greeted with a welcome. Jackie, from a community music project in the north of England, captures these sentiments when she recalls, "As you feed off of the stories and humanity [from those you work with], the ideas and the person that they are [travel through you] and in a way it goes back to them." A music facilitator working on a project in the United States stresses this point when she notes that "if you view the relationship with your participants as just participants, I think the relationship can be pretty cold. So I think it is very important to get to know them as friends get to know each other." Coldness is seen as a negative attribute because it suggests detachment rather than friendship, which is understood as warm and caring.

Beginning with the welcome, the ethical aspect of community music practice calls into question the music facilitator's ego or consciousness and challenges his or her motivations for action. Music workshop facilitators who desire the "outside" to impact on the "inside," a manifestation discussed previously as a promise of the welcome, regularly, if only momentarily, put their ego aside. Ethics, as the term is being used here, does not seek to tell us how we ought to act, nor does it claim to offer a normative system or procedure for formulating and testing the acceptability of certain maxims, judgments, or values. In the context of community music, ethics is simply the hospitable gesture and recognition that the one-to-one relations between facilitator and participant cannot be reduced to full comprehension; difference is always celebrated (Critchley and Bernasconi, 2002). Reflective of the points made by Bowman (2001, 2002), the ethical encounter, as described here, questions the liberty, spontaneity, and cognitive undertaking of the community musician who seeks to reduce otherness. In short, the ethical encounter in community music practice should mark the location of a point of musical interaction, creativity, and expression.

My observations of choral director Sean illustrate this point. During his session, he was demonstrating a rhythmic phrase. One of the participants, an ex-music teacher, challenged Sean's rhythmic accuracy and was quite right in her correction. What followed was an ethical response. Sean, in front of fifty or so participants, relinquished his ego by admitting that he did find this section particularly problematic. It was because of this encounter that the relationship with the participant deepened. Why? Reciprocal trust and respect was heightened because Sean welcomed constructive critique and in the process showed vulnerability. Sean explained that although the action was conscious, it demanded a certain level of confidence and maturity brought about through years of facilitating. Continuing, he remarked that this type of situation had not always been easy for him: "At first I thought, why aren't I better at this? Now I think, if they can help, and we make a joke of it, we can do it together." He went on to stress that it was important to know whom to trust from the group, affirming that this "comes right the way back to the individuals knowing each other however big your group is—you have to take time to do that." This is reminiscent of Ansdell's (Stige et al., 2010) descriptions of a community music therapy project in which he suggests that musicking is exemplary of collaborative "respect-in-action" (p. 281). Through further conversations with Sean, it became apparent that exchanges of this nature had been difficult for other community musicians he had occasionally employed: "We had a guest facilitator who came in once and one of the ex-music teachers got out of her seat and started playing the piano part because he [the guest facilitator] had been getting it wrong. Now she [the ex-music teacher] would have thought she was helping!" This was a crushing blow for the new music facilitator, who, with perhaps more experience or a greater confidence in showing vulnerability and relinquishing their ego, might have resisted difficult confrontation.

WORKING TOGETHER

Those who choose to participate in community music workshops do so because they wish, or "call," to be "worked with" rather than "worked on." The following three bullet points summarize the encounter as I see it. This is not meant to be restricted to the first meeting but rather describe an ongoing cyclical structure.[3]

- The participant makes the decision to attend a music workshop. He or she meets the community musician (face-to-face encounter).
- The participant is ready to make and create music and expects to do so (call).
- The community musician is open and ready to work with the participant to enable a meaningful music making experience (welcome).

This structure sets up and ignites the ethical experience and is *active* rather than passive.[4] I describe this relationship as being organized through a structure of the call and the welcome. For example, one participant I interviewed was a regular attendee at a local community music service and decided to sign up for a half-term project led by an external community music agency, although he was not sure whether he would like the offered music experience because he was into heavy metal and the project did not specify its musical genre. This was the "call." The community music facilitator greeted the potential participant and

Apr 19th
Do the quiz
Class Drawing
go over the reading

...olved in the creation of a new piece of music. This ...le example, the community musician had met the ...p to the project with approval, not in the sense of ..., but as a hospitable beckoning. The "welcome," as ...tion of kindly greeting, one whose coming is in ...discussed in the previous chapter, the welcome ...the potential participant and seeks to restrict ...hat reduce participants' musical capacities. In this ...d that the facilitators were "always pleasant to be around—they are never grumpy and never shout at you . . . like friends might." It is through the call and the welcome that individual participants reveal themselves as themselves while resisting a diminishment of individuality that may lead to their vanishing within the overall group milieu.

Placing both the facilitator and participant in an active structure of the call and welcome suggests that the relationship is heteronymous and forces a confrontation with the notion of autonomy. Directly challenging Kantian ethics, Levinas advocates *heteronomy*, generally understood as the condition of being under the obligation of an outside authority, rather than *autonomy*, an independence or freedom to give law to oneself.[5] *Heteronomy* as used here is not to be understood as a brutal gesture that allows domination of external laws, as defined by Kant (1964), but rather as a silent heteronomy that is unknown. The community musician, knowingly or not, often embodies this heteronomy by relinquishing his or her ego, activating an ethical encounter that does not originate in self-interest. This is not easy to put into practice because it reverses the natural impulses and primacy of concern for oneself, as Levinas (1969) suggests: "To welcome the Other is to put in question my freedom" (p. 85). In this formulation, those involved in these relationships have an investment in each other. This type of "investment" creates environments conducive to meaningful music making. The illustrations of practice in chapter 6 are a testament to this claim.

TRUST, RESPECT, AND RESPONSIBILITY

As an expectation of hospitality, trust and respect are significant ideas. In synergy with an ethics of care, as articulated by Nel Noddings (1992, 2002), I observed community music facilitators consciously cultivating environments of trust and respect through an overarching desire to "hear" the others' "voices."[6] One facilitator explained that "if you establish the relationship based on respect, listening, and all the things that make groups work, then they [the participants] will also trust you implicitly." Trust and respect are understood here as intertwined and inseparable ideas that work when participants, or facilitators, are able to rely on the actions and decisions of each other. As anticipated situations directed toward the future, gaining the respect, or a positive feeling of esteem, for one another enables individuals and groups to experience the creative process.

Establishing trustworthy and respectful relationships is the result of skillful facilitation but can challenge the boundaries of the music facilitator's role. The ethical exchange requires a demarcation between the participant and facilitator. In some instances, this can be very faint, a specter even, but without such a boundary, the ethical musical experience is in jeopardy. Contrary to the semantics employed by my interviewees, the relationship between facilitator and participant is *not* an equal one. It is built upon inequality and structured through (1) the facilitator's responsibility as leader of the process, and (2) the participant's call that reaches beyond the capacity of those who lead. I will now explore this theme through the notion of responsibility.

According to many of the people I interviewed, music was adept at "leveling the playing field" and "blurring the boundaries" between participants and facilitator. A freelance musician-composer said, "The relationship [between the facilitator and participant] is stronger because they know they are being treated as an equal," while community musicians working in a school suggested that "it's an equality thing. It's not, 'I'm the teacher,' I think of myself as equal with the children." One musician explained, "the most important thing [is] the minute you say teacher and student you are not having the full musical interaction: It starts to put up barriers." Adamant on this point also, another community musician notes that "when you are [playing] in a [school] band [for a musical or show] we are all working as musicians together. You work with people on a musical level rather than a teacher/student level," qualifying his point by adding, "When we play together [in school bands] we are all musicians." A community musician working at a high school in the Midlands concurred with this sentiment, stating that "with the older kids I don't see myself as a teacher, we are all musicians in a classroom," further adding, "They are teaching me. After all they are better than me at their chosen instruments—rapping, emceeing—I can't do that—so they feel empowered."

The relationship between facilitator and participant cannot be equal. It is the facilitator's responsibility to ensure some boundaries and as such they hold some power. However, community musicians and participants often described their relation as equal. How can this be, and how might one understand it through an exchange that is activated by the ethical experience of the call and welcome? In the terms of Levinasian phenomenology, relationships have a responsibility to the "infinite," meaning any given relationship can never be totalized (Levinas, 1985).[7] Ethics is understood not as a spectator sport but rather an active experience; in the case of community music, this involves a call and a welcome. These demands cannot be completely met or avoided. The implication, then, is that relationships happen as asymmetrical bonds: relationships are built on inequality in order to ignite the ethical experience inherent within the structure

(Critchley, 2009). Take, for instance, the remark above that "the minute you say teacher and student you are not having the full musical interaction." The implication is that it is an "equality" that enables the musical conversation to begin. This is not so because the community musician has said "yes" to the participant's call. The "yes" involves a responsible decision, a promise to work alongside the participant with care and respect. The interaction constitutes an act of "faith" between the community musician and the participants. Why? Because in order to say "yes" to an act of hospitality, to agree to be involved in a music project or work with particular individuals and groups, one must understand that the decision takes place across a structure that has a multitude of possible outcomes (Derrida, 1988). Although the decision requires a "leap" into the unknown, it is not an act of indeterminacy: it is a responsible welcome that oscillates between conditional and unconditional hospitality.

Following this, it might be said that relationships are never equal: there are no straightforward correlations, and there is no equilibrium. However, my research supports the idea that the notion of being equal is an important one for both music facilitator and participant. How can this be explained? Grounded in what American psychologist Carl Rogers (1994) would describe as "empathic understanding,"[8] the facilitator enters the relationship without presenting a front or a façade and encourages the participant to do likewise. This opens the possibility for both to journey together, a chance to venture "safely" into the unknown. Indeed, both parties' experiences, expertise, and knowledge may be different, their goals may also be different, but through a facilitative process that puts faith in the realness of the relationship, trust, respect, and responsibility flow. Responsibility is therefore made concrete through professional boundaries, demarcations that vary in thickness but nevertheless challenge any notion that there is equality between facilitator and participant. This means that the hierarchal structure is not a simple binary construction but one of inequality marked by the participant's call and the facilitator's welcome or vice versa. Empathic understanding nurtured through the workshop as event reflects the "give" and "take" between the self as community musician and the other as participant. It is here, from this vantage point, that the perceptions of being equal are imagined.

FRIENDSHIP

Responsibility, trust, respect, and individuality are all aspects of what is commonly understood as friendship.[9] During my interviews with community musicians, I posed the question, how do you understand your relationship with the participants? The majority of those I asked talked explicitly about the idea of friends and friendship. For example, those facilitating a project in the Midlands agreed that "you really want them [the participants] to be your friends."

One facilitator commented, "I think I would like to see them all [participants] as my friends." A community musician working on a project in London understood her relationships as, "kind of like an older friend, someone you can look up to." Further comments included "Totally with that [idea of friendship]" and "If I run a primary school choir I want them to feel that they are my mate [friend], without any question that is the person I am in those situations." For a significant portion of those I interviewed, notions of friendships were seen as intrinsic to facilitator-participant exchanges. One person remarked, "You are more confident in sharing amongst friends," while another noted, "You try things among friends because they trust you—they are honest relationships." In resonance with these remarks, other community musicians explained that "creating the friendship is important because we are all on the same side," meaning that we are all musicians working toward the same musical or performance goal.[10]

In order to create a vibrant and active music environment, most community musicians agree that this requires that you go the extra mile. The "extra mile" was a phrase I heard a number of times and is often associated with interacting with participants outside the framework of any given workshop or creating extracurricular music opportunities within school settings. This can be understood through the economy of the gift, discussed earlier, an extra special effort that may reap a number of benefits for those who give the time. Within nonformal music making environments, friendship circles were both expanded and consolidated. Participants attending Sean's choir program suggested that their director was "a friend more than a teacher." Young musicians taking part in a project described how they viewed the music facilitators. Aziz said, "Yeah, I see them as friends." Some of the young people I interviewed compared their image of the facilitator-friend to their regular school music teachers. In these instances, music teachers were seen as "obstructive" and "unapproachable," whereas the music facilitator appeared to care for them and their music. For example, one such participant says, "[The facilitators are] like friends really. Never grumpy," whereas another participant explains that, "they are always pleasant to be around [they are] like your friends." Participants on one project explained, "There're like friends. . . . By the way they talk . . . they tell you that they are always there for you." Other participants suggested that facilitators are "like a friend that will always try to give you the right advice . . . they will explain things to you that you don't know [and] give more confidence in yourself by saying you are good."[11] In one interview session, I allowed the music facilitators to listen to the responses of those participants I had just interviewed. In hearing the friendship affirmations, one music project leader replied, "I think that we have done our job properly—I think that is the best thing they could have said because that means they see us as equals and that is exactly what should be going on."[12]

Not everybody I interviewed conceptualized or agreed with the notion of facilitator-participant friendships. For example, one facilitator was adamantly opposed to the idea: "You must remember you are not their friends. . . . [Y]ou are not their mates." Olivia was unsure: "I was going to say that what I do not want to do is be their friend. Maybe it is not a good idea at the end of the day.... [B]eing a friend is different. I suppose there are different kinds of friendships?" These were fairly isolated cases because the majority of those I interviewed spoke to the "idea" of friendship. How, then, might we conceptualize and understand the idea of friendship within the ethical structure of the call and welcome described above? I begin answering this by making some general comments on friendship then proceeding toward my own conception of the friend within community music practice.

For those who have written on friendship, including Cicero (1967), St. Augustine (1977), Thomas Aquinas (1989), Michel de Montaigne (1948), Ralph Waldo Emerson (1841), C. S. Lewis (1960), Kant (1964), Nietzsche (1969), Maurice Blanchot (1997), and Derrida (1997b),[13] Aristotle (1938) provides the touchstone, dividing friendship into three types: utility-based, pleasure-based, and excellence or goodness. Although Aristotle (p. 371, VII.2.13) says that "there are many kinds of friendships," it is the friendships of excellence that are most significant for him. In this instance, friends "love" each other because of who they are, not because of their utility (e.g., as employee, boss, or doctor) or their pleasure-based role (e.g., as a member of a sporting team or as a lover). Friendships of excellence embrace each other's innate goodness; one might say that they long to know each other. Once established, friendships built on such bases will tend to last: as Aristotle notes, "It is clear that from this that the primary friendship, that of the good, is mutual reciprocity of affection and purpose" (p. 373, VII.2.16). Today, we typically use the notion of friendship to characterize personal relationships of a certain kind. Neera Kapur Badhwar (1993) provides a clear articulation of this when she states that "friendship is a practical and emotional relationship of mutual and reciprocal goodwill, trust, respect, and love, or affection between people who enjoy spending time together" (pp. 2–3). As I have illustrated, community musicians and participants actively seek to go beyond the utility of a functioning working relationship. Trust, respect, and responsibility ignite a desire to be more than just friendly toward each other. However, the ethical encounter constituted within the structure of the call and welcome is inherently unequal. How can community musicians and their participants have friendships beyond utility and pleasure within a structure of fluctuating inequality?

Speaking on the podcast *Philosophy Bites*, Alexander Nehamas (2008) suggests that what is essential about friendships is that one does not simply treat everybody the same: friendships are inherently based on inequality since you give your friends preferential treatment over others. Since the Enlightenment, it has been popular to identify all values with moral values, and those values enjoin us to treat everybody equally. If the values of morality are values that depend on our commonalities and similarities, then values of friendship are those that distinguish us from one another. They are what make us distinct and interesting individuals, differentiating one person from another. This is so because our friends guide us to become one kind of person or another and help us to understand who we are. Although both sets of values are crucial for living, the values of commonality have dominated over divergence and difference.

However, as I argued in chapter 8, contemporary notions of community may be understood through a postmodern perspective that maintains that communities are as much about struggle as they are about unity. Radically different from Aristotle's *Polis*, modern societies are fragmented, and as such those who live in them are caught in their intersections. Both Derrida (1997b) and Blanchot (1997) emphasize this by suggesting the separateness in friendship gives friendship its authenticity. Following this, friendship becomes inherently an ambiguous relationship in which a union or fusion between people is merely an illusory ideal, and here *illusory* means a commitment to the idea that friendship consists in a complete synthesis. Sandra Lynch (2005) suggests that the sense of connection between friends might be best understood as a "useful fiction" rather than illusion (p. 87). As disparate construction predicated on freedom of choice, friendship might therefore be understood as less stable than more formal relationships in which we engage. Perceptions, motives, and goals appear to us only as fragments and thus imply that friendships are a potential fragile and unstable enterprise "preserved by silence" (Derrida, 1997b, p. 53).

Borrowing Badhwar's (1987) classifications, friendships within the community music setting could be seen as "instrumental" friendships rather than "end" friendships. What this means is that most friendships formed within a community music project are based on features that are tangential, or accidental, to the facilitator or participant, and are motivated primarily by each person's independently defined goals.[14] Describing friendship within the framework of an ethics of care, Tove Pettersen (2008) suggests that friendship implies a special sort of attitude, "a mutual and recognized attitude between two or more persons" (p. 130). It is through such an attitude that both symmetrical and asymmetrical relations take place. One might say that symmetrical friendships reflect Aristotle's friendship of character because of its reciprocal balance, whereas asymmetrical friendships take place in relationships in which one part is superior in power, resources, and competences, and in which this superiority influences the exercise of caring. In other words, the friendships found in community music are both asymmetrical and instrumental and support the claim that they are unequal—although there is a desire and a perception for things to be otherwise.

Structured by the call and the welcome, friendships between community musicians and participants try not to relinquish or diminish the other's individual responsibility. As Levinas (1981) stated, "Responsibility is a bond," and it is through an understanding and an awareness of this bond that facilitators and participants experience friendships (p. xix). The value of a model of friendship predicated on difference rather than similarity is, as Lynch (2005) describes, a recognition of difference that "encourages a view of the other as separate from ourselves; it alerts us to the possibility that the friend's desire, motives and concerns might conflict with our own and that we might need to tolerate some friction, or accept difference and perhaps some disappointment" (p. 191). From a position of value and self-worth, participants announce a stronger belief in who they are, both as musicians and as social beings. For example, Stephanie says, "They [the facilitators] make you believe in yourselves . . ., [the music workshop] boosts your confidence, really [bringing] you out of yourself." On another occasion, Mark said, "I'm more confident in talking to people than I was."[15] Because the ethical encounter is heteronomous (albeit silent) rather than autonomous, responsibility precedes individual freedom: I am therefore a friend before I am an individual.

SUMMARY

Through empirical and theoretical research, in this chapter I have suggested that the relationships between community musicians and music participants can be understood within the ethical structure of the call and welcome. I explained that although collaborative group music making is community music's modus operandi, the interaction between facilitator and the individual participant is paramount to its success. It is here, between the "I" and the "Other," that the ethical experience is found in the form of a questioning of the ego. Any encounter between both community music facilitator and participant always demands, or desires, more than is possible to give.[16] Initiated through an act of hospitality, and conditioned by a silent or weak heteronomy, the face-to-face interactions of community musicians and their participants demand responsibility. In order to "hear" individual and group voices, community music facilitators consciously cultivate environments of trust and respect through emphatic understanding. Although there is desire to eradicate hierarchy, it is in fact essential that demarcations be in place because without them nothing responsible would happen.

Community music relationships are therefore unequal, operating within an asymmetrical structure in which the music facilitator and participant are able to share their world as a gift through intersubjective communication. The face-to-face encounter emerges as a friendship, an open, committed, and respectful relationship. As a friendship of fluctuating inequality, responsibility is the bond within the heteronomous encounter, an encounter that cannot be reduced to comprehension. Located within group connecters that are open and porous, friendships established within community music practice may cut across those mutual and reciprocal structures commonly associated with ordinary conceptions of friendships. Sometimes as invitations and sometimes as visitations, friendships between music facilitators and participants occur as a direct result of hospitality, a welcome that generates conversation and music making along a spectrum of conditionality and unconditionality.

Making good my promise to remain both connected and faithful to community music's inheritances, the next chapter reexamines and resites the notion of cultural democracy within the theoretical frame I have been describing.

CHAPTER 11

Cultural Democracy Revisited

This chapter marks a return to the political imperatives of community music. Building from the discussions in part I, what follows is a resituating of cultural democracy within the philosophical scheme I have been describing in part II. I will be addressing the following question: How can community music's political force manifest within a claim that locates community music as an act of hospitality? As a caveat to this, and from the perspective of addressing an international audience, it would not be possible to assume that one person could, or should, outline community music's political ambitions; they will vary from nation to nation and culture to culture. However, based on my research and experience, I am prepared to say that community music exerts a political force in the following two ways: (1) on a micro level, the relational interaction between individuals (music facilitator and participants) within the workshop environment, and (2) on a macro level, a challenge, and the raising of questions, to those who arbitrate funding for music, music organizations, and institutions that engage people in music making, teaching, and learning. Political relationships encompass nation-states as well as one-on-one individual interactions. It is across these two themes that I explore a cultural democracy to come.

CULTURAL DEMOCRACY TO COME

Those who work in community music seek to redefine, or at least ask questions about, the role of the *musician* in society. There are often attempts to demystify the artistic-doing and undermine discriminatory distinctions between "high" and "low" art. Illustrations of this can be found in the "junk" instrument workshops of Mark Powers (chapter 9), and ensembles such as PickleHerring Theatre Company (chapter 6) and Urban Strawberry Lunch,[1] as well as those grounded in popular culture, for example the work of the Kivsharivka Youth and Community Activity Organization in Ukraine (chapter 6). Inherent within these types of projects lies a challenge toward those organizations and institutions that increased the value of Western art music at the expense of other musics. Instances of this can be found in concert hall programming, music companies, universities, and schools. Like those working in community arts and community cultural development, community musicians are radically opposed to the notion that some humans are born musically talented, and are therefore entitled to be nurtured toward a life in music, and some humans are not, consigned to a life of musical consumerism and tokenistic parts in the school choir, orchestra or band. Believing instead in coauthorship, collaborative problem solving, and in the creative potential of all sections of the community, those who work in, and advocate for, community music attempt to transform attitudes, behaviors, and values toward music making through their practice. This has been exampled through projects such as those with at-risk teenagers as part of the "Jasut ha Noar" project in Israel (chapter 6), the wind band projects in Brazil in areas of high social vulnerability and oppression (chapter 6), the Youth Open Festival in Kumanovo in the former Yugoslav Republic of Macedonia (chapter 6), and the community songwriting workshops held in Northern Australia (chapter 9). Each of these illustrations demonstrates that community music has the potential to provide empowering and transformative experiences and, as such, can be a powerful medium for social and political change.

Although not always explicitly articulated, the notion of *cultural democracy*, rather than the democratization of culture that attempts to establish cultural equality while preserving domination, is paramount in the work of community musicians. A call for both action and appropriate intervention, cultural democracy promotes a system of support and respect for the many cultures and communities across the world while attempting to give voice to those who have been historically excluded from the public domain. With no claim of superiority or special status, cultural democracy advocates that people need to create culture rather than having culture made for them: "Culture isn't something you can *get*. You've already got it" (Graves, 2005, p. 15). When I discussed cultural democracy in chapter 2, I did so against the background of the New Left, who had in turn reworked Marxism into an open, critical, and humanist project. Although one might levy the accusation that through deconstruction, my main strategy for conceptual analysis, there has been a sidestepping away from this line of thought, let us say an apoliticization of community music, the spirit of Marxism continues to haunt all the ideas I have presented. Reflecting on his own enterprise, Derrida (1994) remarks that "deconstruction would have been impossible and unthinkable in a pre-Marxist space" (p. 92). The Marxist critique thus remains urgent and necessary. Resurrecting Marx in a ghostly form, Derrida displaces Marx's ontology and considers it as "hauntology," proclaiming, "Not without Marx, no future without Marx" (p. 13). The "sidestepping" is in fact a stepping to the beat of Marx, albeit a beat that is not always regular but that wanders into impromptu improvised sections, maddening refrains, and risky moments of discord. Like the traces of community music history, the ghost of Marx continues to spook its practice and cannot be eradicated. In fact, it should remind those who work within community music that they have a responsibility toward its memory, a resistance to an all-encompassing capital system that may provide obstacles to active cultural participation and choice.

Democracy can be understood as an ideal or doctrine, a type of behavior toward others, or a certain institutional and legal arrangement (Crick, 2002). As a political system, democracy often starts with the assumption of popular sovereignty, a political community in which there is some form of political equality among the people (Held, 1989). Abraham Lincoln's elegant phrase "Of the people, by the people, for the people" is a succinct declamation of its popular ideals (Graves, 2005, p. 16). The history of this idea is complex and marked with conflicting conceptions and disagreements that are certainly beyond the scope of this book. However, one might say that in a contemporary pluralistic democratic state, power is usually exercised in groups, organizations, or institutions in a complex system of interactions that involves compromises, negotiation, and bargaining. This decision process most often includes four concepts: individualism, liberty, equality, and fraternity.[2] Mindful of this, and with Marx's ghost on his shoulders, Derrida (2005b) suggests that democracy embodies two laws: (1) the *autos* of autonomy, symmetry, and homogeneity and (2) the *other*, the heterogeneity, dissymmetric, and multiplural. Derrida shows that there are internal contradictions inherent within democracy's textual operation and suggests that although we are not able to fully know what *democracy* means, we should not stop using it because its heritage is undeniable, "even if its meaning is still obscured, obfuscated, reserved" (p. 9). I took the same position in chapter 8 when claiming that *hospitality* was a way through which one might understand the *community* in *community music* rather than eradicating or changing the prefix to better reflect the practice.

Examining the old and well-used word *democracy* with contemporary sensibilities, Derrida (1994) responds to the claim of Francis Fukuyama (1992) that the fall of communism had ended the conflict of ideologies that had dominated the modern world since the French Revolution.[3] Finally suggesting that democracy should not be thought of as fully present now, or as an entity entirely embodied in the future-present, Derrida advocates a democracy that is yet to arrive, a democracy to come. Like *community*, the *event*, and the *gift*, *democracy* is connected to an unpredictable future, and the promise of the unforeseeable. It exists within the structure "to come" and as such operates in the realm of *the* impossible, a structure of openness to the future (Derrida, 1997b). Described this way, democracy should not be closed off; its timing should always remain "out of joint" because the moment it becomes fully present, it also becomes insulated from other possibilities. Following this line of thinking, equality of musical opportunity is inscribed in a cultural democracy to come, a "dream" toward that which will never fully finally arrive. Through the face-to-face encounter, there cannot be cultural democracy without respect for the irreducible singular person; however, there cannot be cultural democracy without a community of friends.

In other words, cultural democracy does not assimilate but is respectful toward the singular other and the multitude of diverse communities and groups found across this planet. As Critchley (2007) suggests, the task after Marx is a reactivation of politics through the articulation of new political subjectivities because "the acceleration of capitalism does not lead to the emergence of a unique political subject, but rather to the multiplication of social actors, defined in terms of locality, language, ethnicity, sexuality or whatever" (p. 91). Entwined with the experience of the decision and the "yes," the affirmation of the welcome, cultural democracy must remain open to the event and toward an act of hospitality, an ethical and political response of the other.[4] In this way, the ethics of hospitality underlines it, as does the question of friendship.

Politics is about organizing oneself around a name: for example, and following Critchley (2004), "Marx's name for the political subject is the proletarian, more specifically the proletarian as communist." As a nomination, cultural democracy is community music's situated name through which a politics for resistance can claim a place. One might say that when one calls for cultural democracy to come, nothing can live up to what is implied in that name. As a call, then, the name is, as Caputo (2007b) suggests, "a kind of shelter or temporary housing for the event" (p. 59). This is so because when we speak of something being worthy of the name, it is for the *event* that the name contains—not the name itself. Why? Because events are not names or things but something going on *in* names or things. Subsequently, the form of cultural democracy being described here is not associated with any type of regime or national identity: its name can be given to any kind of experience in which there are people, participation, place, equality of opportunity, and diversity. What this means is that rather than focusing on the *we*, community musicians might focus their interest upon the other that interrupts the *we*. This is an amplification of two previously discussed points: (1) the open welcome that is in excess of any conditional realities community musicians work and (2) the ethical manifestations inherent within any promise of access. As discussed in chapter 10, both points call the facilitator's ego into question. Following this logic, rather than emphasizing a sense of *our community*, community musicians might turn toward the stranger, immigrant, and foreigner. Practical illustrations that underline this have included the Buddy Beat drumming group, which serves to promote socially inclusive mental health recovery (chapter 6), the Virtual Classroom for Students with Disabilities Project (chapter 6), the prison work of Elvera Voth (chapter 8), and those who worked on the community projects I visited in the United Kingdom, United States, and Italy (chapter 10). It is there, through the call of the *friend* (the music participant), that the welcome is evoked, a response for a more porous concept of democracy, a more open-ended, hospitable cultural democracy to come, a society of friends without the dominant concepts of national identity, citizenship, national borders, and immigration laws that seem now to prevail.

Like the one-to-one political negotiations inherent within the face-to-face relationships between facilitator and participant, a democracy to come depends upon asymmetry: "It would therefore be a matter of thinking an alterity without hierarchical difference lying at the root of democracy" (Derrida, 1997c, p. 232). As an aspect of the cultural politics of difference, a position that I suggest is vital to community music practice, the deconstructive gesture aides the dismantling of essentialism and class reductionism, which consequently enables an increase in sites of political antagonism that are directed toward dominant cultural expressions. This movement, according to Jonathon Rutherford (1990), breaks the narrow theoretical parameters of socialist politics, removing the logocentricity[5] that hides cultural diversity and conceals social structures that insist on the preservation of hierarchical relations. Speaking to the practice of community music therapy, Brynjulf Stige and colleagues (2010) make a similar observation: "The collaborative negotiations of talk conveyed a spirit of democratic participation and empowerment—one that afforded possibilities for 'making friends'" (p. 233). As an important political touchstone that aims to promote difference through participation, the (re)visitation of cultural democracy can still be seen as a doctrine of empowerment but one that heeds the dangers of totalization and closure.

In the next section I put forward the proposition that community musicians work through music to present daring ways to imagine the future. They are dreamers at heart who exercise a passion for the impossible.

DREAMERS

Cultural democracy, as described above, is made from the stuff of dreams. However, this is not a dreaming about what will never be, an aimless wander of the mind toward utopian ideals or a place of pure plenitude. This is not a dream of pure nonviolence,[6] which is an impossible dream, but rather "the dream of the emergence of something different, something that disturbs the sleep of the rule of the same" (Caputo, 1997b, p. 23). When the dream of pure plentitude is dispelled, the way is opened toward a new dream, a chance to dream provocative and evocative thoughts. Instead of a frivolous activity, dreaming becomes an affirmative opportunity to exert a passion for the impossible, a lens to see in and between, over and beyond. It may be a truism that people who dream often ask questions that have perhaps not been considered before; they are often optimists constantly asking "why not?" The "why not" is defiant, always challenging those who suggest something cannot or should not be done. Many of the projects used as illustrations throughout this book have been established by asking this type of question. Examples include the Kivsharivka Youth and Community Activity Organization, working against a background of an HIV epidemic, the success of the Filarmônica Ufberê wind band in keeping young people away from drug trafficking and violence, the challenge of creating a computer program that will enable group music making, the performance of the Sidney Lanier students at Carnegie Hall, the strong, cohesive social networks formed through the work of Buddy Beat, and the choirs of the Conductors Without Borders program that bring together groups of difference through music. There lies a deep belief among community musicians that nothing happens until someone invites you to dream. How many of those interviewed for the previous chapter would have declared friendships toward one another if they had not been asked to dream?

Underscored through the traces of community music past, cultural democracy, as inscribed above, is an old name but with a new promise. As a strategy for dreaming, cultural democracy is maneuvered through the call and the welcome, which in turn releases a sense of responsibility between community musicians and the participants. However, because the type of dreaming I am trying to evoke here is an affirmation, both ethically and politically, the transition from blue sky thinking to decision must inevitably be made. This, as I have already discussed, conjures up Kierkegaard's "leap."[7] As a figure taken up by both Derrida (1995a) and Caputo (2000), this is not a wild and blind leap or choice, but a necessity to act inventively, a judgment without guardrail, a movement and decision toward the sphere of community *without* unity, friendship *without* friendship, and of safety *without* safety. It is through a *faith* in a dream, a passion for what I cannot know but might dare to imagine, that a certain political force is ignited enabling a welcome toward those that call. Considered here, *faith* is only faith when there is a longing for what appears unattainable (Derrida, 2005a). Following this, the power of passion becomes a passion of unknowing, a passion not driven so much through knowledge but much more an indeterminate act of affirmation for what presently exceeds our cognitive grasp (Dooley, 2003). This is not to say that there is not a place for passion when we know what we are impassioned about, but that there is also a passion for something that vibrates within us that we cannot quite put our finger on.

Through the approaches of practice and general dispositions toward music making that promotes people, places, participation, equality of opportunity, and diversity, community musicians challenge us to dream of a politics of, and for, a musical future that is marked with active and meaningful participation. This dream is not of a politics of sovereignty, of top-down power, but rather a politics that builds from the bottom up and is marked by impromptu improvisations, maddening refrains, and risky moments of discord. As previously discussed, invention is the breaking in, the incoming of something unforeseeable and, like the journey of music creation, the political aspirations of community music require a faith in the process. It is not a matter of becoming what you are already but rather becoming something new.

SUMMARY

The place of the political in community music can be described as twofold: (1) through the "negotiation" between those who take part in community musicking and those who just might, and (2) a challenge to individuals, organizations, and institutions that have a hand in arbitrating funding for music, music teaching, and musical resources. By folding back through the traces of community music, I have suggested that the notion of cultural democracy remains its most pressing political attribute. Driven by a response to situate injustices and wrongs, community music as a political force comes by way of an unexpected event that shatters our horizon of expectations. As a practice, community music is not perfect or a solution to all things problematic to participatory music making. Why? Because its actions are not in the name of horizons of perfectibility and foreseeable ideals, but rather, it is a response to the urgency of friendship and hospitality. Its political aspirations are rooted in cultural democracy while dreaming of and desiring a cultural democracy to come:

> The democracy to come will be marked by justice beyond the law, by equality and freedom beyond fraternity, by an infinite dissymmetry beyond equality, by a friendship beyond the fraternalism of the canonical concept of friendship that has contracted democracy to something less than it is, by a friendship which can only be measured by the measurelessness of its gift. (Caputo, 2000, p. 63)

This is not a question of utopia, a dream of pure plenitude existing as a sovereign lament; democracy is always a heterogenic relation to the other, a matter of negotiation or compromise between fields of forces, as they currently exist. A cultural democracy to come is constantly readjusting each day in relation to the flux of daily living. Political action, such as the choice to develop and maintain the *International Journal of Community Music*, is therefore considered contextual and strategic. Within the circle of return and through a leap of faith, there is a sense of seizing the madness of the moment, a passion to be possessed but not to possess. Those who are denied music-making opportunities will always be there, but by virtue of the gift, circles can be opened and change can begin to happen through an ever-widening ring of hospitality. What ends up being important is not the term *democracy* but the *to come*, a thinking of the event, the opening of a space that is not grounded in the future-present but situated in the realm of the impossible, meaning something whose possibility one did not and could not foresee. Activating a cultural democracy to come requires interstitial practices, one for which intervention, invention, dreaming, and faith form a backbone through which hospitality and friendship can emerge as a strategic praxis.

CHAPTER 12

Another Opening

Community musicians move in and between many diverse settings. They can be found facilitating local music activities in arts centers, schools, prisons, health settings, places of worship, music festivals, on the streets, and in a wide range of other community contexts. As skilled music facilitators, there is an emphasis on active participation, sensitivity to context, equality of opportunity, and a commitment to diversity. Community musicians seek to create relevant and accessible music-making experiences that integrate activities such as listening, improvising, inventing, and performing. On the whole, they are committed to the idea that everybody has the right and ability to make, create, and enjoy their own music. As such, community musicians seek to enable accessible music-making opportunities for those they are working with, and are consciously encouraging and developing active musical knowing while acknowledging both individual and group ownership of the music that they make. There are of course many musicians and music educators throughout the world who work in these ways. However, what distinguishes community music facilitators is their connection to local, national, and international organizations that support, advocate, and describe their activities under the banner of community music.

Flowing from both personal and professional concerns, I set out to achieve four goals: (1) to describe what community music does rather than what it is, (2) to construct a historic perspective describing the development of community music from the late 1960s to the present day, (3) to present a portrait and celebration of community music projects worldwide, and (4) to articulate a theoretical framework through which community music practices can be analyzed, described, and understood.

Split into two sections, part I, "Inheritances and Pathways," and part II, "Interventions and Counterpaths," the following three areas of research have provided the domains through which my exploration has taken place: (a) historical (re)construction of community music through documentation and autobiographical foreknowledge, (b) illustrations and exemplars of community music in action, (c) community music's key characteristics expressed through the themes of hospitality, the workshop, facilitation, friendship, and cultural democracy. Comparative musical epistemologies such as community music therapy, cultural diversity in music education, and applied ethnomusicology helped to delineate community music's distinction, while ethnographic and case study fieldwork provided the opportunity to witness it firsthand. Through a journey of experience and research, I have arrived at the following conclusions.

HISTORY

Historical perspectives of community music are important because the character of community music is formed in its past. Questioning and exploring the circumstances that led to the growth of community music ensures continuity with its heritage and traditions. A perspective of the past is always oriented toward the future. Turning toward what has been thought and practiced is the only way of turning toward what is still to be thought and practiced. The chain of past events, understood as community music, takes meaning from those given contexts in which it is currently inscribed. This movement makes the appeal to other contexts in which community music will be known. Future community music contexts are therefore transformations of past community music contexts. The promise of the future of community music will open up new contexts, and these openings are still to come. In this way, historical perspectives of community music's traditions, characteristics, and contexts become a liberating link on the horizon of the future of community music practice and theory. As an emancipatory activity within a rhizomatic structure, historical perspectives are to be understood as a key component to the future providing pathways, counterpaths, flight lines, and openings toward events to come.

Destination can never be assured, but thinking as memory is inseparable from thinking the future. The location of community music's past as a cultural response to issues concerning active participation in music making will always haunt community music's present and future. A recognition of a community music history has enabled a certain form of emancipation while preserving the memory of past community music encounters. Movement of this sort demonstrates a healthy respect and disrespect for community music's past encounters, and therefore places the act of transformation within unfolding pathways. The exposé of community music from a historic standpoint provided the bridge through which I was able to progress my ideas. Historical perspectives of community music deserve close attention, and there are many more narratives to be told. Community music's future comes to us from the passivity of the past, a necessity to the very appearance of the present. The possibilities of community music transformations are embedded in an understanding of the collision between past, present, and future.

PRACTICE

Because humans are such social creatures, the need for human connectedness and belonging is strong. Music is primarily a communal activity, and therefore plays an important role in our lives. While it is true that musicians may isolate themselves to create or rehearse music, these behaviors usually lead to sharing within a group. In *The Anthropology of Music*, Alan Merriam (1964) asserted, "Music is clearly indispensable to the proper promulgation of the activities that constitute a society; it is a universal human behavior—without it, it is questionable that man could truly be called man, with all that implies" (p. 227). My illustrations demonstrate that community music as a field of activity can provide a complex and rich experience for personal and societal growth.

Community musicians who lead projects encourage dialogue between themselves and their participants that are built on trust, respect, and responsibility. Although there is a concern for quality musicianship and performance, facilitation enacted through the workshop as event emphasizes and places a higher value on the process that may or may not lead to a sharing or performance. Another distinctive feature of community music practice is that there is a genuine reception for both experienced and inexperienced musicians. It is often the case that many potential music participants have not been given, or have not taken up, the opportunity to play music. Community music facilitators are generally delighted to welcome new participants, offering a greeting that extends beyond those who are already engaged. The act of hospitality becomes significant in these instances.

Although all music-making groups are to some extent context-bound, community music ensembles are particularly conscious of themselves as a community and of their relationship to their local community. For example, members of the Peterborough Community Samba Band celebrate their diverse membership by having parties and consequently creating networks of friends who otherwise would not "hang out" together. Other examples include the weekly movie night sponsored by the Ukrainian Kivsharivka Youth and Community Activity; the outdoor, family-friendly fun generated through the HONK! bands; the social interactions among those involved in the intercultural Discovering Abilities project in New York City; and the "sing when asked to" outreach project of the Canadian Gettin' Higher Choir.

As acts of hospitality, community music projects flourish through accumulative personal interactions, because human interaction is viewed as paramount. Community music practice can lead to new friendships and foster deeper relationships between old acquaintances. Community music groups can open new social doors and a whole new outlook on life as people interact with others outside of their regular social and economic groups. Participating in community music projects is much more than *just* music making—it can have life-changing effects (Coffman and Higgins, 2012).

THEORY

Following a creative turn that has roots in Nietzschean thinking, the concept building throughout this book has an imaginative quality that has unhinged (although not lost) community music's debt to the Marxist critique. This has been important because it has provided a fresh view of what community music is, what it does, and what community music might be. I have developed theoretical ideas through Continental philosophy, a post-Kantian position in which finitude is replaced with contingency and a demand for transformation. By leaning on the shoulders of Jacques Derrida, Emmanuel Levinas, Simon Critchley, and John Caputo, among others, I have had conceptual ideas and philosophical spaces open before me. This has provided access to a language that is removed from the orderly or functional manner from which one most often thinks and acts. Economic imperatives that drive community music practice have historically restricted this type of broader theoretical engagement. This habit still persists, and unless challenged it may leave community music practice conceptually marooned.

If community music is to flourish as a field of practice in the ways its growing number of protagonists proclaim, those who advocate for it must recognize the value of scholarly inquiry. In short, those who support the notion of community music would benefit from a greater understanding of the relationship between theory and practice. Philosophical or theoretical inquiry allows the mind to venture beyond the day-to-day complexities of executing a community music project. Conceptual thinking enables a certain space in which to problematize practice and challenge orthodoxy. Theory is community music's inadequate dimension, and addressing this issue would enable significant steps toward the further development of community music.

IMPLICATIONS AND FUTURE DIRECTIONS
Music Participation

From the perspective of musical learning, community musicians strive to work within flexible facilitation modes and are committed to multiple learning relationships and processes. They aim for excellence in both the processes and products of music making, and these are commonly relative to the individual goals of the participants. In this way, community musicians recognize that the participants' social well-being and personal growth are as important as their musical development, and therefore advocate lifelong musical learning. As a distinctive trait, community musicians are also aware of the need to include disenfranchised and disadvantaged individuals or groups, recognizing the value of music in fostering intersocietal and intercultural acceptance and understanding.

Although community musicians predominantly work outside formal instructional settings, when they do work within an educational setting, their programs are most vibrant and sustainable when both parties—the community music facilitator and the institution—work in partnership. It is through collaboration and a sense of shared purpose that a dynamic relationship can be fostered that enriches the cultural life of the institution and its curriculum. In such cases, community musicians are able to offer rich cross-cultural resources for classroom use (Higgins and Bartleet, 2012).[1]

If, as I have suggested, hospitality, participation, friendship, equality of opportunity, and diversity are intrinsic agents within active and creative music making, then those who teach music, run departments of music, perform, or write cultural policy documents might consider the importance of community music. Although the indelible signatures of the traits of community music, as described above, can be hidden from view, masked, or displaced, they are always present and as such surround any music that is being made or discussed. From this perspective, it would be interesting to consider how these ideas might permeate *all* music programs, from primary through third-level education. This suggestion does not call for the immediate implementation of dozens of community music programs and wholesale changes to music curricula; that would be inappropriate. The point is a philosophic one but with practical implications. Although there is growing interest in community music across conservatories, colleges, universities, and schools, it continues to be a marginalized activity. Situations that perpetuate this are complex and deep, but I believe rest on a lack of understanding of the full dimensions of music making. This situation doubles and doubles again, as each new batch of musicians becomes exposed to a limited version of what music can do or can be. Community music as an act of hospitality challenges our philosophical understandings of music and will, I hope, generate fresh perspectives. Exposing music educators and potential music educators to the wider dimensions of music might enhance teaching and learning possibilities. As a result, students of music might gain a wider grasp of music's materiality and thus be open to greater choice. This does not dilute, reduce, or shun efforts to train and harness specialized musical practices. The point is to open musicians to the question of responsibility before themselves and toward the others with whom they share musical discourse.

As an extension to this, and the discussion in chapter 5 surrounding education, training, and professional preparation, I want to make a few suggestions regarding the broad areas I see as important for establishing a program of study in community music. As I have discussed, community music is context dependent, and as such programs, courses, modules, and units need to be developed with the locality firmly in mind. This will, and should, shape the content, learning goals, assessment strategy, teaching staff, and field opportunities. I would also suggest that working alongside sympathetic community partners would enrich the development and eventual running of any such program. The "course" suggestions below are organized under four headings, "Community Music Perspectives," "Music Project Management," "Creative Processes and Community Music Skills," and "Community Music Project," and are built around four general aims:

1. To enable potential students to develop and articulate a critical conception of community music within current discourse together with an ability to negotiate practice and theory according to the contexts that they encounter.
2. To develop a working knowledge of techniques applicable to the students' own practice, interests, or research in community music.
3. To develop self-direction, creativity, and originality through praxis, together with a practical understanding of how established techniques of research and inquiry are used to create and interpret knowledge within community music.
4. To develop the qualities and transferable skills necessary for employment within the growing sectors that do, or may in the future, provide work opportunities.

Community Music Perspectives

This is the type of course that would ask students to consider the past, present, and future of community music. Drawing upon the social, cultural, political, and economic milieu, including movements in music therapy, music education, and ethnomusicology, this course could offer a possible range of reasons as to the growth and development of community music. Students might be asked to conduct and present a detailed case study derived from primary data collection critically assessing both practice and ethos. Through consideration of a specific manifestation of community music practice, such as criminal justice, health and well-being, lifelong learning, and so on, students may be in a position to articulate a philosophical statement pertaining to the future of community music as practice and as a scholarly pursuit.

Music Project Management

This course would aim to develop or extend students' knowledge and understanding of key concepts relating to initiating and implementing music projects, and to develop their ability to apply these concepts in creating, planning, and delivering their own practical music projects within a broad community setting. Key areas of this course might include working with stakeholders to identify needs; researching a potential project; creating a project definition; conducting a project pitch and/or feasibility study; developing, writing, and implementing a detailed project plan; fundraising; and undertaking a project assessment and evaluation.

Creative Processes and Community Music Skills

This type of course would help students develop both pedagogic strategies and musical skill sets to facilitate and lead participatory music-making activities and projects. As I have discussed, fundamental to the work of the community musician is an ability to generate creative music making through sustainable group building and effective collaboration. Through insight into the dynamics behind the process of teaching and facilitating musical doing plus the skills inherent in the music genres under consideration, this course might concentrate on structures of creative processes—such as group work, planning, delivery, and strategy—while also assessing the content, form, and context of the musical genre in question. This will mean providing students with a flexible set of teaching, workshop, and facilitation skills, and a range of techniques and strategies that enable group creativity so that students develop not only the skills and confidence to effectively plan, deliver, and evaluate creative music-making sessions and programs, but also the capabilities to evaluate creative processes and the framework in which they happen. A course like this should embrace a wide approach to the concept of creative processes and the relationships between particular musical skill sets. It should also be flexible to include a variety of musical styles such as improvisation, songwriting, drumming, singing, and music technology.

Community Music Project

I envisage this type of course offering the student an opportunity to undertake a project in a particular location. This is the chance to bring together the skills obtained throughout the previous three courses. This course should enable students to demonstrate a comprehensive understanding of the chosen area of community music practice, run an effective community music project, secure creative practices, organize and manage personnel's/participants' time in relation to the community music projects, and, importantly, evaluate community music projects. I believe that this course would work well if students and their supervising tutor/professor negotiated a learning contract that would, among other things, determine the appropriate means of assessment.

Scholarship

To get a sense of the research strategies currently in use within community music research, I did a content analysis of scholarly articles and papers that specifically addressed and named community music as its principal concern. Articles and papers were drawn from the *IJCM*; CMA materials, both published and unpublished; and a selection of other writings from music education journals, one-off reports, and project evaluations. In all, there were 257 articles and papers from 1990 to 2011. I reviewed each article to determine the primary research approach driving the investigation. Four areas of inquiry dominated: case study research, project evaluations, project reports, and theoretical explorations. Personal reflection, ethnographic research, philosophical research, historic research, and survey followed in descending order. Other strategies—such as policy research, narrative, biographical research, phenomenological research, and action research—played all but a cameo role.[2] It is worth noting that the inauguration of the *IJCM* has provided a site for presenting scholarly activity and has consequently introduced a wider variety of research approaches and a higher degree of methodological understanding and practice. Many of the later research strategies were introduced in these articles.

Because community music research is an emerging scholarly discipline, the results of the content analysis are not surprising. One might expect a high percentage of reportage, project and case study evaluations, and speculations on what community music means and where it ought to go. Given that this is a growing corpus of work, it might be timely to ask, how effective has this research been at reflecting the practical realities of community music? I would begin answering this question by saying that the body of research has, on the whole, been progressively deepening the insights into practice—this book would not be possible to write if this were not so. Although to date there have been a good number of "insider" views—often through interview, personal reflection, or report— I might like to encourage more community musicians to "study" their practice. My concern is that researchers or thinkers who have little or no connection to the actual practice of community music might misrepresent the practice through both writing and program development. Of course I realize that any field needs a balance of protagonists, and community music benefits from a wide range of views and perspectives. My point is to encourage the practitioner to ask the questions that cannot be addressed sufficiently without firsthand experience of working as a community musician.

Furthering these thoughts, I want to suggest that arts-based research might provide community musicians who wish to investigate community music with an approach that would resonate strongly with the principles embodied in the notion of active music intervention. From a postmodern perspective, arts-based research offers direct challenges to modernity's assumptions about universality of reason, the premise of external reality to be detected through scientific modes of investigation, and rationality that allows humans to agree on what is real, right, just, and humane. As a consequence, arts-based research can destabilize our multidisciplinary reliance on objective, detached, and neutral research inquiry. It can call into dispute our facts about the social world and the disinterested language of representation available to reflect them while stressing that there is contingency, temporality, and situational logic for any definition of "the world out there."

Arts-based research can be defined as

> the systematic use of the artistic process, the actual making of artistic expressions in
> all of the different forms of the arts, as a primary way of understanding and examin-
> ing experience by both researchers and the people that they involve in their studies.
> (McNiff, 2008, p. 29)

To illustrate further, arts activist Susan Finley's (2005) work flows from the inheritances of community music. Finley suggests that arts-based researchers should seek to "construct action oriented processes for inquiry that are useful within the local community where the research originates" (p. 682). Finley (2003) articulates the dispositions of arts-based research, describing them as (1) relational to community—to dialogical, nurturing, caring, and democratic relationships between researchers and participants who share their commit- ments to understanding of social life, (2) to action within community, to engage in research work that is local, usable, and responsive to cultural and political issues and that takes a stand against social injustice, and (3) to visionary critical discourses—to research efforts that examine how things are but also how things could be otherwise. Certainly one of its significant strengths is, as Patricia Leavy (2009) suggests, "to allow research questions to be posed in new ways, entirely new questions to be asked, and new nonacademic audiences to be reached" (p. 12).

As an approach that celebrates the art-making process, arts-based research can put the method of inquiry back into the hands of the community musician. In some instances, this would enable the *scholar-self* and the *community musician-self* to merge. This would blur the distinction between traditionally understood *pro- fessional* and *academic* practices. Although it is possible to say that there are clear demarcations between the sets of expertise of the *scholar* and of the *musician,* many creative musicians with university posts or affiliations also continue artis- tic practices outside academic institutions. I would like to encourage those in positions of research supervision to look for possibilities in which arts-based research might put the scholar/musician in the best position to answer the ques- tions pertaining to community music. I would also like to encourage practitio- ners to consider undertaking arts-based research. This might mean taking a risk, working beyond or outside one's comfort zone. It might also mean challenging our colleagues, the administration, and the various research boards that decide what appropriate research is and what is not. I believe that as community music programs and courses grow more popular, there will be an opportunity from the outset to merge the *scholar-self* and the *community musician-self.* Providing the research tools to enable community musicians to answer challenging questions surrounding practice and theory while continuing dynamic music facilitation seems the most responsible thing to do. This will go some way in ensuring that practice and scholarship do not drift too far apart. It is, I hope, clear why arts-based research might provide an appropriate strategy for community music research.

Employment

As a political manifestation, community musicians have challenged the dominant position of "high" art and its cultural implications such as elitism. This position is often understood within the rubric of Western classical music, but must now traverse the cultural changes that stress music stardom through television programs such as *American Idol* and *The X Factor*. The culture of the celebrity appears to influence young people's choices when thinking about a career in music.[3] This demonstrates a distorted picture of the possibilities of active music making. I have proposed a vision of music making as an act of hospitality, a place to find your "voice" and to make friends. The ramifications of this gesture might result in redressing some of the current perceptions of music and music making, thus allowing potential musicians to make an informed decision about their career path.

Community music projects are on the rise, and so are the training and education provisions to meet the demand. This is good news because musicians are beginning to see alternative role models beyond those traditionally cited, such as the band and orchestra conductors, the classroom music teacher, or the pop star. As musicians engage in a wider variety of music-making environments and contexts, they also engage with a diverse array of music professionals. When musicians can identify the community musician as a distinctive entity, they are far more likely to consider a career path that takes them toward community music employment. As a consequence, musicians would be less likely to perceive the narrow focus of the music business as the pinnacle of musical achievement. Emily's and Joel's stories in chapter 4 illustrate this point.

Demonstrative examples, such as those illustrated throughout this book, affirm music's role in the everyday lives of people. Through such descriptions, the work of the community musician becomes a positive force that suggests that community music is a rewarding and viable employment opportunity. The integration of practice and theory might enable greater access through the educational and political arenas and in turn enable pressure to be exerted in areas that are likely to lever meaningful employment opportunities.

AFTERWORD

I hope that my research will be a catalyst to open the door, leave it ajar, and invite others to walk through. As Levinas (1985) would say, "*Après vous, Monsieur*" (p. 89). As an unprogrammable future, my ideas and vision for community music practice are on the horizon, but this does not make them any less real. As boundary-walkers, community musicians affirm and embrace the margins. Like Hamlet's father parading the castle's battlements, community music practice is a ghostlike figure, a haunting presence that weaves in and out of all musical folds. As a "ghost," Hamlet's father was visible only because of the armor he wore. Acts of hospitality represent the "clothing" of the community musician, and it is this that enables us to experience their distinctive approach toward musical doing.

As an experiential moment linking the past and the future, the 2000 CMA meeting in Toronto enabled this community musician, Lee Higgins, to consider his understanding of community music practice. Beginning with the self-reflexive question, "What has this got to do with the community music I understand?" this research has been a journey that has brought me face to face with my life and my relation to music and music making. As Derrida (1985) suggested, "It is the ear of the other that signs" (p. 51). In other words, the ear of the other, your ear as a reader, constitutes the *autos* of my autoethnographic memory, confirming who I am through the process of engagement. In order for my work to communicate, one must take into account the unrepresentable scenes of the life journey each time one claims to identify with any utterance signed by Lee Higgins. Through the traces of historical (re)construction, autoethnographic memory, fieldwork, philosophical investigation, and professional endeavor, the writing of this book represents another experiential moment. It is the next node that, in an instant, gathers its threads and then releases them through lines of flight beyond the pages of this book and toward a future to come.

NOTES

CHAPTER 1

1. First published in the March 1990, this magazine, later described as a journal, focuses on the United Kingdom but does occasionally feature articles from around the world.
2. The *International Journal of Community Music* published a retrospective in 2010. See issue 3 (3).
3. Published three times a year, this journal, which began publishing online in 2004, was launched with a commercial publisher, Intellect, in 2008. Seen as the premiere international forum for research articles and project reports, the *International Journal of Community Music* includes contributions from music educators, community musicians, and community music advocates from around the globe.
4. This article was reprinted with personal reflections from Cole in 2011. See Cole (2011a; 2011b).
5. Continental philosophy, or modern European philosophy, refers to a set of traditions of nineteenth- and twentieth-century philosophy from mainland Europe and is, as Critchley (2001) rightly suggests, often contested. As a categorizing term, *continental philosophy* originated in the second half of the twentieth century among English-speaking philosophers who found it useful for referring to a range of thinkers and traditions outside the analytic philosophy movement, a wave of thought that dominated academic philosophy departments most notably in Great Britain and the United States.
6. As a term, *deconstruction* has been adapted and translated from the German *destruktion*, or *abbau*, terms Heidegger had used in his reexamination of metaphysics. Stephen Mulhall (1996) suggests that Heideggerian philosophy forms the point of origin for deconstruction, while Barbara Johnson (1981), a translator of Derrida's work, underlines these assumptions, suggesting that, "'de-construction' is closely related not to the word 'destruction' but to the word 'analysis,' which etymologically means to 'to undo'—a virtual synonym for 'to de-construct'" (p. xiv).
7. See Derrida (1997b, pp. 5–6; 1995c, p. 211).
8. A text is not limited to the written word; community music as a set of practices is a text to be read. Derrida (1988) supports this by clarifying that his initial statement might be read as "nothing *exists* outside context" (p. 152).
9. As Christopher Norris (1992) asserts, "On the contrary: what gives deconstruction its critical edge is its address to issues in . . . three main areas—epistemology, ethics, and aesthetic judgement" (p. 32). Deconstruction becomes not a passion for transgression, but rather, a passion for trespassing the horizons of possibility, "a thought, of an absolute heterogeneity that unsettles all the assurances of the same within which we comfortably ensconce ourselves" (Caputo, 1997b, p. 5).

10. Derived from the Latin *alter*, meaning "other," as in "alternative" or "alter ego," alterity constitutes a description for the property of "otherness" and can be broadly thought of here as "difference."

11. Levinas's work was influential throughout continental philosophy: for example, Jacques Derrida (1978b), Luce Irigaray (1993), Maurice Blanchot (1995), and Judith Butler (2005) all built upon his ideas. Derrida (1999) claimed in Levinas's funeral eulogy that the "reverberations of this thought will have changed the course of philosophical reflection of our time" (p. 4). Levinas had his critics though. Paul Ricoeur (1992), Slavoj Žižek (2001), and Alain Badiou (2001) have all interrogated Levinas's ethical vision, challenging its scale, relevance, and detail. B. C. Hutchens (2004) offers an overview to the key aspects of these challenges.

12. Although Derrida and Levinas's thinking has been influential in shaping my ideas, it would be wrong to assume that their philosophic systems were always in harmony: indeed, there are significant divergences between the two philosophers. However, it is also clear that they both influenced each other and had the utmost respect and admiration for each other's work. This can be seen through a chain of dialogical meetings (Derrida, 1978b, 1991a, 1999; Levinas, 1981, 1991). From the perspective of this book, two areas of interest define the crossing of their paths: (1) the ethical responsibility toward the other and (2) the "religious." The thought of Critchley and Caputo represent significant developments in both of these areas.

13. See Caputo and Scanlon (1999, 2005) and Caputo, Dooley, and Scanlon (2001).

CHAPTER 2

1. The Federal Music Project also provided classes in rural areas and urban neighborhoods. See http://www.wwcd.org/policy/US/newdeal.html.

2. Max Kaplan was a professor at the University of Illinois Champaign-Urbana, the same university as Charles Leonard, who wrote *Foundations and Principles of Music Education*, a text that was hugely influential in American music education.

3. For another historic perspective, see Leglar and Smith (2010). Their paper was first published in *The Role of Community Music in a Changing World* (Leglar, 1996).

4. The community arts subcommittee operated for six years, ending in 1979. This was due to the Arts Council restructuring program; the responsibility for funding community arts was devolved to what was then called the Regional Arts Associations (RAB).

5. See also Rowland (1973) and Landry et al. (1985). Although these books do not emphasize the arts, they document the broader struggle that community arts was part of.

6. Dickson (1995) offers "another history" of community arts, locating the work alongside the environmental work of artists such as John Latham, a member of the Artist Placement Group, an organization that emerged in London during the 1960s that actively sought to reposition the role of the artist within a wider social context, including government and commerce.

7. This figure has been adapted from the work of Ihab Hassan. See Hassan (1987).

8. A theater group that was part of a radical socialist theatre movement in Britain known as agitprop. See http://www.redladder.co.uk/.

9. The Theatre Workshop worked alongside the play-worker network on a program of street theater for young people. See Braden (1978, pp. 26–29).

10. Needleworks was a project located in Glasgow, Scotland, and was based around sewing. The project managed to create a community business by selling its merchandise. See Brinson (1992, p. 38).

11. See Kershaw (1992, pp. 152–167).

12. Beechdale Arts Forum was a project that empowered local people and operated on a large postwar council estate on the edge of Walsal, England until 2004. See Herbert (1997).
13. Action Space Mobile is a community arts company that (1) aims to create work that extends the creative potential of the participants, and (2) leaves behind a self-sustaining structure of people who will continue to work together. See http://www.actionspacemobile.org/.
14. Cardboard Citizens is the United Kingdom's only homeless people professional theater company. See http://www.cardboardcitizens.org.uk/.
15. See Coult and Kershaw (1990) and Fox (1992).
16. See Brinson (1992, pp. 36–37).
17. The varieties of community arts are as follows: (1) general urban projects, (2) specialist urban projects, (3) new towns, (4) rural areas and small towns, (5) festivals and short-term projects, (6) young people, (7) work with special groups.
18. Later Merseyside Arts added two further points: (1) work should occur in areas of cultural, social, and financial need, and (2) work should aim to be for lasting effect and to create autonomous and self-managing groups and activities, which can evolve their own direction and priorities (Dickson, 1995, p. 22).
19. The report clarifies that in practice the term "amateur arts" relates to independent societies, such as traditional drama and music societies.
20. From the Portuguese *conscientização*, meaning the deepening of the attitude of awareness characteristic of all emergences, conscientization is the ongoing process by which a learner moves toward critical consciousness.
21. See http://www.actalive.org/.
22. See http://www.amal-hdn.org/.
23. See http://www.blossomtrust.org.in/.
24. See http://www.aptpchicago.org.
25. See http://www.reverbnation.com/b2ds.
26. See http://www.carclew.com.au/About-Us. For a wider picture of the Australian scene, see also http://www.ccd.net/.
27. See http://www.cardboardcitizens.org.uk/.
28. See http://www.performinglifebolivia.org/.
29. For a database of projects, see http://www.icasc.ca/contact_database.
30. For ongoing debates that include all aspects of community arts work within the United Kingdom and internationally, *MailOUT*, a national magazine for participatory arts, is an excellent resource. After eighteen years in print, it has gone digital. See http://mailout.co/.

CHAPTER 3

1. The National Association of Dance and Mime Animateur predates Sound Sense by three years. Currently called Community Dance Foundation, it publishes the quarterly periodical *Animated*. Chapter 5 in *Dance as Education: Towards a National Dance Culture* offers an excellent overview of community dance from the 1970s until the late 1980s (Brinson, 1991).
2. See Braden and Huong (1998).
3. Kershaw (1992) cites John Arden as a key proponent of early community drama and dates this to around 1963. See also Randell and Myhill (1989) and Grant (1993).
4. See Kershaw (1992), Rendle (1968), Taylor (2003), and van Erven (2001).
5. See Herbert (2010).

6. Using a study written by R. Nettel and published in 1944, Everitt (1997) retells the story of a flourishing amateur choral tradition in the nineteenth century that "arose out of a natural urge for some means of expression denied to men in the lives they were leading" (p. 36).

7. Folk clubs in Great Britain became a popular urban phenomenon during the 1960s and 1970s and still continue today. See Brocken (2003).

8. According to Andrew Blake (1997), the amateur performance tradition can be traced with a continuous thread through choirs, brass bands, through to the homemade instruments of skiffle in the 1950s, and punk in the 1970s.

9. Other noticeable composer-educators include Gavin Bryars, Harrison Birtwistles, and David Bedford.

10. See http://www.corearts.co.uk/.

11. See http://www.asiandubfoundation.com/.

12. Although Blacking (1995, p. 9) agreed with the majority of Merriam's thesis, he felt that music went further than "learned behaviour" and ultimately concluded that Merriam had given insufficient attention to "music itself."

13. When I worked as a music animateur for Peterborough Arts Council, I had these semantic difficulties and eventually changed my job title to "music development officer."

14. Community Music Ltd. is now called CM. See http://www.cmsounds.com/.

15. *Search and Reflect* was finally republished in 2007. See Stevens (2007).

16. *Sniffin' Glue* was the name of a monthly fanzine. It was started by Mark Perry in July 1976 and released twelve issues (Perry, 2000).

17. See http://webarchive.nationalarchives.gov.uk/*/www.musicmanifesto.co.uk/.

18. See http://www.youthmusic.org.uk/musicispower/index.html.

CHAPTER 4

1. Documentation was collected from Peterborough Arts Center's archive on April 2, 2004. Because the council had been dissolved, all of its archive material had been boxed up and stored. The archive was due for disposal later that month, so I was able to physically remove the material that was most important to this project. It included the annual reports and the cultural strategies from 1988 to 2003.

2. I interviewed participants during the period of April and May 2004. I also administered questionnaires from March through July 2004.

3. Personal reflections and documentation such as newspaper cuttings, promotional leaflets, posters, and reports spanning the twelve-year period since the band's inception.

4. All direct quotes with participants are taken from personal interviews with the author or from questionnaire responses. See note 2.

5. See http://www.uksamba.org/bandlist.

6. Examples of those active in this work are organizations such as RedZebra, Ecodecor, and Carnival Collective, as well as individuals such as Gavin Lombos, Graham Surtees, Mally, Anthony Watt, Ian Holmes-Lewis, and Mat Clements.

7. See http://www.worldsamba.org.

8. Meaning "the home in the meadows."

9. When the *Bahianas* arrived in Rio as part of the migration following the end of slavery, their relationship with the African continent was immediately reestablished. The "daughters-of-saints," the women of Bahia who had set up the *candomblé* temples, sold sweets in the daytime and at night sponsored *candomblé* sessions and samba parties. These women knew the religion and had "samba in the foot"; they were also addressed respectfully as "aunts" (Guillermoprieto, 1991, p. 52).

10. Eisteddfods are annual festival in Wales in which competitions are held in music, poetry, drama, and fine arts.
11. Following the initial growth of samba bands in the United Kingdom there was a demand for *mestre* leadership training, for example courses run by One Voice Music. Many of the programs and courses reflect the pedagogic environment the participants are use to finding in the regular samba sessions they attend. See http://www.ovm.co.uk.

CHAPTER 5

1. See the following website for a sample of current projects by an organization called NOMUS: http://www.nomus.org/.
2. See also Elliott (2001).
3. See http://apcmn.edublogs.org/2010/10/05/apcmn/.
4. For CMA's vision and mission statements, see http://www.isme.org/index.php?option=com_content&view=article&id=41:community-music-activity-commission-cma&catid=20:cma&Itemid=14.
5. See http://www.cme.org.uk/.
6. See http://www.communitymusicwales.co.uk.
7. See http://www.moremusic.org.uk.
8. See http://www.sounditout.co.uk.
9. See http://www.thesagegateshead.org.
10. http://www.musicleader.net.
11. http://www.rcm.ac.uk.
12. Both Birmingham and Leeds have stopped offering their discrete community music programs.
13. See http://www.gold.ac.uk/pace/cert-workshop-skills-music.
14. http://music.york.ac.uk
15. http://www.chiuni.ac.uk/music/ContemporaryMusicalStudies.cfm.
16. See http://www.music.ed.ac.uk/Postgraduate/musiccommunity.
17. See http://www.irishworldacademy.ie/postraduate-programmes/ma-community-music/.
18. See http://steinhardt.nyu.edu/music/education/.
19. See http://www.onbunso.or.jp.
20. See the extraordinary story of AfroReggae in Neate and Platt (2010). See also http://www.afroreggae.org.br/ and http://www.favelatotheworld.org/.
21. For a full explanation of these categories, see http://www.soundsense.org/metadot/index.pl?id=25842&isa=Category&op=show and http://www.musicleader.net/content.asp?CategoryID=1279.
22. See page 185 note 4.
23. Managed by Palatine and convened by Paul Kleiman, the Higher Education Academy, Subject Centre for Dance, Drama and Music in the United Kingdom.

CHAPTER 6

1. With thanks to Aaron Brantly. For further information, see Eckstrom (2008).
2. With thanks to Graciela Sandbank. For further information, see Sandbank (2006).
3. With thanks to Jane Bentley. For further information, see the website designed and maintained by the group: http://www.thebuddybeat.co.uk.
4. With thanks to Matt Smith. For further information, see Smith (2008).
5. See http://honkfest.org/.

6. With thanks to Joel Barbosa.
7. The Former Yugoslav Republic of Macedonia experienced an armed conflict in 2001. The conflict between the Albanian National Liberation Army and the Macedonian state army ended after six months of military crisis and negotiations.
8. Interculturalism is the philosophy advocating exchanges between cultural groups within a society. It is ultimately about sharing, collaboration, and cooperation. It encourages people to iron out differences and difficulties and to focus on commonalities first. Incorporating Christopher Small's (1998) term *musicking*, a verb describing an activity, something that people do, *intercultural musicking* refers to the musical activities of sharing and learning across cultures. It celebrates things that people have in common over the things that make them different.
9. With thanks to Alexandra Balandina. For further information see Balandina (2010).
10. With thanks to Steve Dillon and Andrew Brown. For further information, see Dillon et al. (2008).
11. The project requires minimal financial investment: only around US$30 for a webcam.
12. With thanks to Donald DeVito. For further information, see http://www.sbac. edu/~lanier/.
13. See http://www.ifcm.net/.
14. With thanks to Andre de Quadros.
15. See http://www.fanstar.co.uk/showscreen.php?site_id=54&screentype=site&screenid=54.
16. A company limited by guarantee is specific to British and Irish company law. In short, it designates an alternative type of corporation used primarily for nonprofit organizations. A guarantee company like More Music does not usually have a share capital or shareholders, but instead has members who act as guarantors.
17. With thanks to Pete Moser. For further information, see Moser (2010).
18. With thanks to Gillian Howell. For further information, see Howell (2010).
19. With thanks to Mary Kennedy. For further information, see Kennedy (2009).
20. See http://www.drmc.org.au/.
21. Vision Australia, a partnership between people who are blind, sighted, or have low vision, is committed to providing access to participation in all aspects of life. See http://www. visionaustralia.org.au/.
22. With thanks to Jane Southcott. For further information, see Southcott (2009).

CHAPTER 7

1. Anthroposophy is a spiritual philosophy, mainly developed by Rudolf Steiner (1861–1925) at the end of the nineteenth and the beginning of the twentieth centuries.
2. The idea of cultural pluralism in America has its roots in the transcendentalist movement and was developed by pragmatist philosophers such as William James and John Dewey, and later thinkers such as Horace Kallen and Randolph Bourne. One of the most famous articulations of cultural pluralistic ideas can be found in Bourne's (1996 [1916]) essay, "Trans-National America."
3. Terese Volk (1998) gives a comprehensive overview of multiculturalism, multicultural education, and multiculturalism in music education. This is particularly from a U.S. perspective, although she does outline situations in other countries.
4. See http://www.ahk.nl/en/conservatorium/study-programmes/bachelor/music-in-education/.
5. See http://www.rmc.dk/en/programmes_of_study/.
6. See http://www.mhm.lu.se/.
7. See http://www.griffith.edu.au/music/queensland-conservatorium.

8. See http://www.wmdc.nl/en.html.
9. See http://webdb.iu.edu/sem/scripts/groups/sections/applied/applied_ ethnomusicology_section.cfm.
10. See http://www.ictmusic.org/group/applied-ethnomusicology.
11. According to its website, "Cultural Co-operation is a London-based arts and education charity with an internationally respected history of innovation and achievement. Its mission is to unite people through high quality engagement with the world's cultural heritage." See http://www.culturalco-operation.org/.
12. See also Pettan (1998).
13. See http://www.128path.org/.
14. U.K.-based Music for Change has an emphasis on empowerment through music and runs projects in the United Kingdom, but also Africa, Asia, and Latin America. See http://www.musicforchange.org/.
15. See the research of Lucy O'Grady and Katrina McFerran (2007).
16. On reflection of thirty-five years of research with the Suya tribe, Anthony Seeger (2008) says, "The most rewarding public projects for an ethnomusicologist will often come from the desires of the community members themselves" (p. 286).

CHAPTER 8

1. For a detailed account of word *community*, see the first chapter in Roberto Esposito's (2010) book *Communitas: The Origin and Destiny of Community.*
2. The notion of *without* is further utilized and explored in later chapters. See chapters 9 and 10.
3. The data for this illustration are a composite of personal observations and interviews during three trips to Rome, coupled with an ethnographic account carried out by the directors and presented at the 2006 ISME community music seminar in Rome (Iadeluca and Sangiorgio, 2008).
4. Helen Phelan (2007) interrogates Derrida's (2000) expression "Let us say yes . . ." with her analysis on Sanctuary, an Irish initiative to promote greater access to education through the pursuit of cultural activities.

CHAPTER 9

1. Here *desire* is to be understood as positive and productive rather than a conception of desire as premised on a sense of "lack." The concept of desire is thus drawn from the philosophical lexicon of Deleuze and Guattari (1984) rather than Sigmund Freud (Gay, 1989).
2. For a broader consideration of the term *workshop*, see Sennett (2008).
3. As Deleuze and Guattari (1988a) state, "A haecceity has neither beginning nor end, neither origin nor destination: it is always in the middle. It is not made of points, but only of lines. It is a rhizome" (p. 263). The word *rhizome*, from the Greek *rhiza*, meaning "root," is an underground rootlike stem bearing both roots and shoots. For an exposition of this idea see Deleuze and Guattari's (1988b).
4. John Dewey (1859–1952) advocated that teachers should create conditions for learning that guide rather than direct or impose. He emphasized cooperative power and valued individual experiences. See Dewey (1997).
5. Maria Montessori (1870–1952) developed child-centered, experiential, multisensory learning and encouraged children to have self-discipline and responsibility for learning. See Montessori (1912).

6. Alexander Sutherland Neill (1883–1973) advocated a libertarian approach to schooling and founded Summerhill in England in 1924. See http://www.summerhillschool.co.uk/pages/index.html.

7. Kurt Hahn (1902–1987), a German-Jewish educator who founded the Outward Bound movement as the antithesis of the authoritarian schools in Germany during the interwar period. See http://www.kurthahn.org/.

8. Malcolm Knowles (1913–1997) worked extensively within adult learning and coined the term "andragogy" (as opposed to *pedagogy*: child learner). According to Knowles, this phrase best described the characteristics of the adult learner who flourishes more successfully with a facilitative approach. See Smith (2002).

9. Edger Schein removed the idea of "expert consultancy" within the doctor-patient model. See Schein (1998).

10. See McNiff and Whitehead (2002).

11. Carl Rogers (1902–1987) popularized the term *facilitator* in the 1970s and 1980s. He proposed that education should maximize the individual's freedom to learn by removing threats, boosting self-esteem, involving students in learning planning and decision making, and using self-evaluation techniques. See Smith (2004) and Rogers (1951).

12. Robert Chambers championed the developmental methodologies approach called participatory rural appraisal (PRA). PRA is defined as a family of approaches and methods that enables rural people to share, enhance, and analyze their knowledge of life and conditions, to plan and act. See Chambers (1983).

13. Paulo Freire (1921–1997) developed the influential idea of *conscientization*, which is the ongoing process by which a learner moves toward critical consciousness. See Freire (2002).

14. Freire (2002) says that in the banking concept of education, "knowledge is a gift bestowed by those who consider themselves knowledgeable upon those whom they consider to know nothing" (p. 72).

15. See http://www.musicalfutures.org.uk/.

16. See Derrida (1978a, p. 369; 1985, p. 69; 1988, pp. 115–116).

17. With some similarities of the Heideggerian strategy of putting words under erasure (*sous rature*), the *without* forces an openness without limits of the foreseeable horizon. See Gayatri Chakravorty Spivak's "Translator's Preface" in *Of Grammatology* for an explanation of Heidegger's conception of Being under erasure (Derrida, 1997a).

18. The word for *poison* in German is *gift*.

CHAPTER 10

1. See http://www.nya.org.uk/index.

2. Heidegger's (2002) analysis of the "they" considers the other person as just one of the crowd or the group: "Everyone is the other, and no one is himself" (p. 165).

3. This has been derived from Critchley's (2007) formulation of approval and demand, which in turn has drawn upon Dieter Henrich's (1994) grammar of practical reason.

4. In philosophical terms, the ethical subject as self binds itself to some conception of the good and shapes its subjectivity in relation to that good (for a full description of this idea, see Levinas, 1969, pp. 197–201). We might say that there is no "sense" of the "good" without an act of welcome, affirmation, or recognition. Although things are not good just by virtue of approbation, the gesture of the welcome brings the good into view.

5. For a full discussion, see Chalier (2002).

6. The idea of giving opportunities and space to "voice" resonates at the core of community music practice. Feminists working within the field of psychology have used the notion of the "voice" as a metaphor extensively because, it is claimed, women ground their epistemological premises in metaphors that suggest speech and listening: for example "speaking out," "not being heard," and "really listening," while men have used visual metaphors such as "the mind's eye," "blind justice," and "veil of ignorance" (Gilligan, 1982; Belenky et al., 1986; Taylor et al., 1995). It has been important to highlight the achievements of feminist psychology because one could say that there is a certain gendered aspect to my argument. Although Simone de Beauvoir (1993) has rightly accused Levinas of presenting a masculine approach to alterity, his ideas have nevertheless influenced feminist thinkers such as Luce Irigaray, Hélène Cixous, and Judith Butler (Bernasconi and Critchley, 1991; Chanter, 2001). One might say that the business of opening up to alterity presents more of a challenge to socially constructed masculinity than femininity. Hearing metaphors are more passive and vulnerable and constitute central themes in Levinas's thought (Plant, 2005).

7. Within a philosophy of the intersubjective relationship, there are clearly similarities between the thought of Levinas and Martin Buber. Buber's (1996) *I and Thou* designates the encounters between subjects with all the freedom of the other's otherness. By placing the relationship with otherness, or the readiness for such an encounter, at the beginning of the experience means that there are some clear parallels. However, there are significant divergences. For example, Levinas (2004) felt that Buber's thought could not account for the radical separation of between the I and the Other: "The principle thing separating us is what I call the asymmetry of the I-Thou relation" (p. 33). Although Levinas's critique appears inconsistent—his main dispute surrounds the notion of reciprocity— Levinas felt that Buber's ethics were in the end subordinated to ontology and thus reduced the ethical difference between the self and the other. For an in-depth discussion and analysis, see *Levinas and Buber: Dialogue and Difference* (Atterton, Calarco, and Friedman, 2004).

8. Emphatic understanding, in the way it is being used here, does not suggest that one can truly understand another's experience. On the contrary, there is an impossibility of being able to experience someone else's experience.

9. Reflecting on a number of community music therapy projects, Brynjulf Stige, Gary Ansdell, Cochavit Elefant, and Mercédès Pavlicevic (2010) note that the processes inherent within this type of work may well nurture friendships between participants and therapists. This, they point out, is a controversial idea, but their research suggests that it does happen. Although there might be concerns with the violations of standard professional norms, the authors point out that there is one norm through which the therapists seem very concerned about not violating: "namely the responsibility to ensure that the processes are safe and beneficial for participants" (p. 289). Friendship is also touched upon in Allsup's (2003a) article "Mutual Learning and Democratic Action in Instrumental Music Education."

10. Nel Noddings and Paul Shore (1984) describe this type of commitment through the idea of educational *caritas*, related to the words *charity*, *caring*, and *cherish*.

11. Although I have frequently encountered young musicians who would actively say that their school music teacher was the best teacher they ever had, and in numerous cases provided the inspiration for a career in music education or performance, many participants I met through the community music projects I visited did not share these sentiments. This negative perspective toward formal music education may reflect that formal music schooling has often disenfranchised young people who choose to attend community music projects. However, it has also been pointed out to me that the issue of

accountability is very different and as such may indeed enable the types of relationships that I have been discussing over those of the music teacher within the school classroom.

12. This sentiment closely reflects Rogers's (1994) notion of realness, trust, respect, and emphatic understanding described above.

13. The following anthologies offer excellent overviews: Badhwar (1993) and Pakaluk (1991). For a concise introduction, see Mark Vernon's *The Philosophy of Friendship* (2007). For a more detailed debate, see *Philosophy and Friendship* by Sandra Lynch (2005).

14. "End" friendships, on the other hand, are relationships in which one loves and cares for the person because of the friend's particular qualities.

15. Aristotle (1938) supports this aspect of friendship when he says that there is "no stable friendship without confidence" (p. 381, VII.2.40).

16. In synergy with the positive and productive use of the term outlined in the previous chapter, *desire* as experienced here becomes that which seeks and that which can never be achieved or consummated. Desire is therefore insatiable, and encounters with things desired only further and deepen the desire. By welcoming the participant, the facilitator is opening pathways rather than offering to provide everything the participant needs. Fueling desire of the sort is positive, but community musicians might acknowledge what they cannot know or cannot give.

CHAPTER 11

1. See http://www.usl.org.uk/.

2. See Keane (2009).

3. Francis Fukuyama (1992) had claimed that there was now only one ideology (or system)—that of the liberal market. In effect, history, as understood by Hegel and Marx (dialectical interplay), had all but ended. Derrida (1994) responded to Fukuyama in the *Specters of Marx*. See also *Derrida and the End of History* (Sim, 1999).

4. As discussed in chapter 10, this is so because in order to say "yes" to any proposition or welcome, one must understand that the decision takes place across a structure that has multiple possibilities. The "yes" therefore inaugurates the future to come, a promise that cannot be guaranteed, and a responsibility that always includes the possibility of turning out otherwise.

5. Stuart Sim (2001) offers a good working definition of *logocentricity*: the assumption that words can unproblematically communicate meanings present in individuals' minds such as how the listener, or reader, receives them in the same way as the speaker/hearer intended. Words and meanings are therefore considered to have some internal stability. This is a standard assumption in Western culture, but one that has come under attack from Derrida, who regards this as an unsustainable position to adopt, on the basis that words always carry traces of previous meanings, and they suggest other words that sound similar to the one being used.

6. This is the same idea discussed in chapter 8 where the unconditional was described as implying a sense of "violence" toward that which is stable, fixed, and comfortable.

7. This is a reference to a leap of faith idea often attributed to Søren Kierkegaard's conception of how an individual would believe in God or how a person would act in love. See Caputo (2007a).

CHAPTER 12

1. For a wide range of practical examples of such partnerships in the United Kingdom, see *Music and the Power of Partnerships* (Coll and Deane, 2008).
2. *Revista*, the Brazilian music education journal, published an earlier version of this research. See Higgins (2010).
3. Martin Milner addresses these issues in the chapter "Bandwork." See Moser and McKay (2005).

REFERENCES

Adams, Don, and Arlene Goldbard. 2001. *Creative Community: The Art of Cultural Development.* New York: Rockefeller Foundation.

———. 2002. *Community, Culture and Globalization.* New York: Rockefeller Foundation.

Adolfo, Antonio. 1996. Rhythmic Music Education in Brazil. In *Rhythmic Music Education: Jazz-Rock-World Music,* edited by J. O. Traasdahl, 30–37. Copenhagen: Danish Music Council.

Adorno, Theodor. 2001. *The Culture Industry.* London: Routledge.

Allsup, Randall Everett. 2003a. Mutual Learning and Democratic Action in Instrumental Music Education. *Journal of Research in Music Education* 51 (1):24–37.

———. 2003b. Praxis and the Possible: Thoughts on the Writing of Maxine Greene and Paulo Freire. *Philosophy of Music Education Review* 11 (2):157–169.

———. 2003c. Transformational Education and Critical Music Pedagogy: Examining the Link between Culture and Learning. *Music Education Research* 5 (1):5–12.

———. 2007. Democracy and One Hundred Years of Music Education. *Music Educators Journal* 93 (5):52–56.

Alperson, Philip 1991. What Should One Expect from a Philosophy of Music Education? *Journal of Aesthetic Education* 25 (3):215–242.

———. 2002. *Diversity and Community: An Interdisciplinary Reader.* Oxford: Blackwell.

Althusser, Louis. 1972. *Lenin and Philosophy and Other Essays.* Translated by B. Brewster. New York: Monthly Review Press.

Amit, Vered, and Nigel Rapport. 2002. *The Trouble with Community: Anthropological Reflections on Movement, Identity and Collectivity.* London: Pluto Press.

Anderson, Benedict. 1991. *Imagined Communities.* New York: Verso.

Angelo, Michael. 1997. *The Sikh Diaspora: Tradition and Change in an Immigrant Community, Asian Americans.* New York: Garland.

Ansdell, Gary. 2002. Community Music Therapy and the Winds of Change. *Voices: A World Forum for Music Therapy* 2 (2). https://normt.uib.no/index.php/voices/article/view/83/65.

Ansdell, Gary, and Mercedes Pavlicevic. 2001. *Begining Research in the Arts Therapies: A Practical Guide.* London: Jessica Kingsley.

Aquinas, Thomas. 1989. *Summa Theologiae: A Concise Translation.* Translated by T. S. McDermott. London: Eyre and Spottiswoode.

Araujo, Samuel 2008. From Neutrality to Praxis: The Shifting Politics of Ethnomusicology in the Contemporary World. *Musicological Annual* 44 (1):13–30.

Archer, Robin. 1989. *Out of Apathy: Voices of the New Left Thirty Years On: Papers Based on the Conference Organized by the Oxford University Socialist Discussion Group.* London and New York: Verso.

Aristotle. 1938. *Eudemian Ethics.* Translated by H. Rackham. London: William Heinemann.

———. 2000. *Nicomachean Ethics.* Translated by E. B. R. Crisp. Cambridge: Cambridge University Press.

Aston, Peter, and John Paynter. 1970. *Sound and Silence.* Cambridge: Cambridge University Press.

Attali, Jacques. 1985. *Noise: The Political Economy of Music.* Translated by B. Massumi. Minneapolis: University of Minnesota Press.

Atterton, Peter, Matthew Calarco, and Maurice Friedman, eds. 2004. *Levinas and Buber: Dialogue and Difference.* Pittsburgh: Duquesne University Press.

Augustine. 1977. *On Christian Doctrine.* Translated by D. W. Robertson. Indianapolis, Ind.: Bobbs-Merrill Educational.

Badhwar, Neera Kapur. 1987. Friends as Ends in Themselves. *Philosophy and Phenomenological Research* 48:1–23.

———. 1993. *Friendship: A Philosophical Reader.* Ithaca, N.Y.: Cornell University Press.

Badiou, Alain. 2001. *Ethics: An Essay on the Understanding of Evil.* Translated by P. Hallward. New York: Verso.

Bailey, Derek. 1993. *Improvisation: Its Nature and Practice in Music.* New York: De Capo Press.

Balandina, Alexandra. 2010. Music and Conflict Transformation in the Post-Yugoslav Era: Empowering Youth to Develop Harmonic Inter-ethnic Relationships in Kumanovo, Macedonia. *International Journal of Community Music* 3 (2):229–244.

Baldry, Harold. 1974. *The Report of the Community Arts Working Party.* London: Arts Council of Great Britain.

Banks, James A. 1992. Multicultural Education: Approaches, Developments and Dimensions. In *Cultural Diversity and the School: Education for Cultural Diversity Convergence and Divergence,* edited by J. Lynch, C. Modgil, and S. Modgil, 83–94. London: Falmer Press.

———. 1996. *Multicultural Education, Transformative Knowledge, and Action: Historical and Contemporary Perspectives, Multicultural Education Series.* New York: Teachers College Press.

Banks, James A., and Cherry A. McGee Banks. 2001. *Multicultural Education: Issues and Perspectives.* 4th ed. New York: John Wiley.

Barber, Benjamin R. 1996. Multiculturalism between Individuality and Community: Chasm or Bridge? In *Liberal Modernism and Democratic Individuality: George Kateb and the Practices of Politics,* edited by A. Sarat and D. R. Villa, 133–146. Princeton, N.J.: Princeton University Press.

Barbosa, Joel. 2008. Music Education Projects and Social Emancipation in Salvador. In *CMA XI: Music Education Projects and Social Emancipation in Salvador, Brazil: Proceedings from the International Society for Music Education 2008 Seminar of the Commission for Community Music Activity,* edited by D. D. Coffman, 95–101. Tel Aviv, Israel: International Society for Music Education.

Bartleet, Brydie-Leigh, Peter Dunbar-Hall, Richard Letts, and Huib Schippers. 2009. *Sound Links: Community Music in Australia.* Brisbane: Queensland Conservatorium Research Centre, Griffith University.

Bartolome, Sarah J, and Patricia S. Campbell. 2009. John Langstaff: Community Musician and Reveller. *International Journal of Community Music* 2 (2&3):157–167.

Bartram, Anthony. 1994a. Pirates Ensure that the Beat Goes On . . . and On. *Evening Telegraph,* January 20.

———. 1994b. Shhh . . . No More Samba. *Evening Telegraph,* January 14.

Barz, Gregory F., and Timothy J Cooley. 1997. *Shadows in the Field: New Perspectives for Fieldwork in Ethnomusicology.* New York: Oxford University Press.

———. 2008. *Shadows in the Field: New Perspectives for Fieldwork in Ethnomusicology.* 2nd ed. Oxford and New York: Oxford University Press.

Bastide, Roger. 1974. *Applied Anthropology*. New York: Harper & Row.

Bataille, Georges. 1988. *Inner Experience*. New York: SUNY Press.

———. 1991. *The Accursed Share: An Essay on General Economy, Volume 1*. Translated by R. Hurley. New York: Zone Books. Original edition, 1967.

Batt-Rawden, Kari, and Tia DeNora. 2005. Music and Informal Learning in Everyday Life. *Music Education Research* 7 (3):289–304.

Beating out the Samba Message. 1995. *Peterborough and Oundle Herald*, July 20.

Bee, Frances, and Roland Bee. 1998. *Facilitation Skills*. London: Institute of Personnel and Development.

Beiner, Ronald. 2002. *Liberalism, Nationalism, Citizenship Essays on the Problem of Political Community*. Vancouver: University of British Columbia.

Belenky, Mary Field, Blythe McVinker Clinchy, Nancy Rule Goldberger, and Jill Mattuck Tarule. 1986. *Women's Ways of Knowing: The Development of Self, Voice, and Mind*. New York: Basic Books.

Bellekom, Tony. 1988. *Planning for the Future: The Development of the National Association of Arts Centres*. London: National Association of Arts Centres.

Benjamin, Walter. 1992. *Illuminations*. London: Fontana Press.

Benson, Jarlath F. 2010. *Working More Creatively with Groups*. 3rd ed. London: Routledge.

Bentley, Jane 2009. Community; Authenticity; Growth: The Role of Musical Participation in the Iona Community's Island Centres. *International Journal of Community Music* 2 (1):71–77.

Berger, Jason. 1981. *A New Deal for the World: Eleanor Roosevelt and American Foreign Policy, Atlantic Studies*. New York: Social Science Monographs; Distributed by Columbia University Press.

Bergethon, Bjornar. 1961. Music Education in Norway, Sweden, and Denmark. *Music Educators Journal* 47 (5):33–36.

Berghaus, Günter. 1995. Happenings in Europe: Trends, Events, and Leading Figures. In *Happenings and Other Acts*, edited by M. R. Sandford, 310–388. New York: Routledge.

Bernasconi, Robert, and Simon Critchley. 1991. *Re-reading Levinas, Studies in Continental Thought*. Bloomington: Indiana University Press.

Bernstein, Daniel. 2002. *Samba Groups: A Snapshot as Part of the National Carnival Policy Consultation Document*. London: Arts Council of England.

Bhabha, Homi K. 1990. *Nation and Narration*. London and New York: Routledge.

Blaazer, David. 1992. *The Popular Front and the Progressive Tradition: Socialists, Liberals, and the Quest for Unity, 1884–1939*. Cambridge and New York: Cambridge University Press.

Blacking, John. 1973. *How Musical Is Man?* London: Faber and Faber.

———. 1995. *Music, Culture and Experience*. Chicago: University of Chicago Press.

Blake, Andrew. 1997. *The Land without Music*. Manchester: Manchester University Press.

Blanchot, Maurice. 1988. *The Unavowable Community*. Translated by P. Joris. New York: Station Hill Press. Original edition, 1983.

———. 1995. *The Writing of the Disaster*. Translated by Ann Smock. Lincoln: University of Nebraska Press.

———. 1997. *Friendship*. Translated by E. Rottenberg. Stanford, Calif.: Stanford University Press.

Block, Peter. 2008. *Community: The Structure of Belonging*. San Francisco: Berrett-Koehler.

Boal, Augusto. 2000. *Theater of the Oppressed*. 2nd ed. London: Pluto Press.

———. 2002. *Games for Actors and Non-actors*. 2nd ed. Translated by A. Jackson. London: Routledge.

Bourdieu, Pierre, and Jean Claude Passeron. 2000. *Reproduction in Education, Society and Culture*. 2nd ed. London: Sage.

Bourne, Randolph S. 1996. Trans-national America. In *Theories of Ethnicity: A Classical Reader*, edited by W. Sollors, 93–108. New York: New York University Press. Original edition, 1916.

Bowles, Chelcy Lynn. 2008. Regional Initiative 1: North American Coalition for Community Music. *International Journal of Community Music* 1 (2):287–288.

Bowles, Samuel, and Herbert Gintis. 1976. *Schooling in Capitalist America: Educational Reform and the Contradictions of Economic Life*. New York: Basic Books.

Bowman, Wayne, 1998. *Philosophical Perspectives on Music*. New York: Oxford University Press.

———. 2001. Music as Ethical Encounter. *Bulletin of the Council for Research in Music Education* (151):11–20.

———. 2002. Educating Musically. In *The New Handbook of Research on Music Teaching and Learning: A Project of the Music Educators National Conference*, edited by R. Colwell and C. P. Richardson, 63–84. Oxford and New York: Oxford University Press.

———. 2009. The Community in Music. *International Journal of Community Music* 2 (2&3): 109–128.

Braden, Su. 1978. *Artist and People*. London: Routledge.

Braden, Su, and Than Thi Thien Huong. 1998. *Video for Development: A Casebook from Vietnam*. London: Oxfam Academic.

Brah, Avtar. 1996. *Cartographies of Diaspora: Contesting Identities*. London: Routledge.

Brandon, David, and John Knight. 2001. *Peterborough Past: The City and the Stoke*. Chichester, West Sussex, U.K.: Philimore.

Brent, Jeremy. 1997. Community without Unity. In *Contested Communities: Experiences, Struggles, Policies*, edited by P. Hoggett. Bristol, U.K.: Policy Press.

Brinson, Peter. 1991. *Dance as Education: Towards a National Dance Culture*. London: Falmer Press.

———, ed. 1992. *Arts and Communities: The Report of the National Enquiry into Arts and Communities*. London: Community Development Foundation.

Brocken, Michael 2003. *The British Folk Revival 1944–2002*. Aldershot, U.K.: Ashgate.

Brooks, Rod. 1988. *Wanted! Community Artists*. London: Calouste Gulbenkian Foundation.

Brown, Allan. 1992. *Groupwork*. 3rd ed. Farnham, Surrey, U.K.: Ashgate.

Buber, Martin. 1996. *I and Thou*. Translated by W. Kaufmann. New York: Touchstone.

Burgess, Sybil. 1995. Professional Development. *Sounding Board* (Summer):9.

Burley, John. 1987. Adult Music Education in the USA. *International Journal of Music Education* 9:33.

Burton, Bryan, J. 2003. Music. In *Encyclopedia of Community: From the Village to the Virtual World*, vol. 2, edited by K. Christensen and D. Levinson, 950–953. Thousand Oaks, Calif.: Sage.

Butler, Judith. 2005. *Giving an Account of Oneself*. New York: Fordham University Press.

Cahill, Anne. 1998. *The Community Music Handbook: A Practical Guide to Developing Music Projects and Organisations*. Sydney: Currency Press.

Campbell, Patricia Shehan. 2003. Ethnomusicology and Music Education: Crossroads for Knowing Music, Education, and Culture. *Research Studies in Music Education* 21:16–30.

Caputo, John D. 1993. *Against Ethics*. Bloomington: Indiana University Press.

———. 1997a. Justice, if Such a Thing Exists. In *Deconstruction in a Nutshell: A Conversation with Jacques Derrida*, edited by J. D. Caputo, 125–155. New York: Fordham University Press.

———. 1997b. *The Prayers and Tears of Jacques Derrida: Religion without Religion*. Indiana: Indiana University Press.

————. 2000. *More Radical Hermeneutics: On Not Knowing Who We Are, Studies in Continental Thought.* Bloomington: Indiana University Press.

————. 2006. *The Weakness of God: A Theology of the Event.* Bloomington: Indiana University Press.

————. 2007a. *How to Read Kierkegaard.* New York: W. W. Norton.

————. 2007b. *What Would Jesus Deconstruct?* Grand Rapids, Mich.: Baker Academic.

Caputo, John D., Mark Dooley, and Michael J. Scanlon. 2001. *Questioning God. Indiana Series in the Philosophy of Religion.* Bloomington: Indiana University Press.

Caputo, John D., and Michael J. Scanlon. 1999. *God, the Gift, and Postmodernism. Indiana Series in the Philosophy of Religion.* Bloomington: Indiana University Press.

————. 2005. *Augustine and Postmodernism: Confessions and Circumfession. Indiana Series in the Philosophy of Religion.* Bloomington: Indiana University Press.

Cardew, Cornelius. 1974. *Scratch Music.* Cambridge, Mass.: MIT Press.

Chalier, Catherine. 2002. *What Ought I to Do? Morality in Kant and Levinas.* Translated by J. M. Todd. Ithaca, N.Y.: Cornell University Press.

Chalmers, David. 1991. *And the Crooked Places Made Straight: The Struggle for Social Change in the 1960s.* London: John Hopkins University Press.

Chalmers, F. Graeme 1996. *Celebrating Pluralism: Art, Education, and Cultural Diversity.* Santa Monica, Calif.: Getty Center for Education in the Arts.

Chambers, Robert. 1983. *Rural Development: Putting the Last First.* Harlow, Essex, U.K.: Longman.

Chang, Heewon. 2008. *Autoethnography as Method, Developing Qualitative Inquiry.* Walnut Creek, Calif.: Left Coast Press.

Chanter, Tina, ed. 2001. *Feminist Interpretations of Emmanuel Levinas.* University Park Pennsylvania State University Press.

Chapman, Duncan. 1992. "Get Connected!" *Sounding Board* (Autumn):19.

Childs, John Brown. 2003. *Transcommunality: From the Politics of Conversion to the Ethics of Respect.* Philadelphia: Temple University Press.

Christo. 1985. *Christo, Surrounded Islands: Biscayne Bay, Greater Miami, Florida, 1980–83.* New York: H. N. Abrams.

Christodoulidis, Emilios A. 1998. *Communitarianism and Citizenship. Avebury Series in Philosophy.* Aldershot, U.K., and Brookfield, Vt.: Ashgate.

Cicero, Marcus Tullius. 1967. *On Old Age, and On Friendship.* Translated by F. O. Copley. Ann Arbor: University of Michigan Press.

Cockcroft, Eva. 1974. Abstract Expressionism, Weapon of the Cold War. *Artforum* 15 (10): 39–41.

Coffman, Don. 2002. Banding Together: New Horizons in Lifelong Music Making. *Journal of Aging & Identity* 7 (2):133–143.

————. 2008a. Survey of New Horizons International Music Association Musicians. *International Journal of Community Music* 1 (3):375–390.

————, ed. 2008b. *CMA XI Projects, Perspectives, and Conversations: Proceedings from the International Society for Music Education 2008 Seminar of the Commission for Community Music Activity.* Tel Aviv, Israel: ISME.

————, ed. 2010. *CMA XII: Harmonizing the Diversity that Is Community Music Activity: Proceedings from the International Society for Music Education 2010 Seminar of the Commission for Community Music Activity.* Hangzhou, China: Open University of China.

————. 2011. "And They Lived Happily Ever After": Community Music and Higher Education. *International Journal of Community Music* 4 (2): 97–104.

Coffman, Don, and Lee Higgins, eds. 2006. *Creating Partnerships, Making Links, and Promoting Change: Proceedings from the 2006 Seminar of the Commission for the Commission for Community Music Activity.* Singapore: ISME.

Coffman, Don, and Lee Higgins. 2012. Community Music Ensembles. In *The Oxford Handbook of Music Education*, edited by G. McPherson and G. F. Welch. New York: Oxford University Press.

Cohen, Anthony P. 1985. *The Symbolic Construction of Community*. New York: Tavistock.

Cohen, Mary L. 2007a. Explorations of Inmate and Volunteer Choral Experiences in a Prison-Based Choir. *Australian Journal of Music Education* (1):61–72.

———. 2007b. Hallelujah!—Prison Choirs: Studying a Unique Phenomenon. *Choral Journal* 48 (5):47–50.

———. 2008. Conductors' Perspectives of Kansas Prison Choirs. *International Journal of Community Music* 1 (3):319–333.

———. 2010. Risk Taker Extraordinaire: An Interview with Elvera Voth. *International Journal of Community Music* 3 (1):151–156.

Cole, Bruce. 1999. Community Music and Higher Education: A Marriage of Convenience. In *Making Music Work*, 139–150. London: Royal College of Music.

———. 2011a. Community Music and Higher Education: A Marriage of Convenience. *International Journal of Community Music* 4 (2):79–89.

———. 2011b. Reflections on Community Music and Higher Education. *International Journal of Community Music* 4 (2):91–95.

Coll, Helen, and Kathryn Deane, eds. 2008. *Music and the Power of Partnerships*. Matlock, Derbyshire, U.K.: National Association of Music Educators.

Collins, Jannette. 2009. Education Techniques for Lifelong Learning Lifelong Learning in the 21st Century and Beyond. *RadioGraphics* 29:613–622.

Corlett, William. 1995. *Community without Unity: A Politics of Derridian Extravagance*. Durham, N.C.: Duke University Press.

Coult, Tony, and Baz Kershaw. 1990. *Engineers of the Imagination: The Welfare State Handbook*. London: Methuen.

Crick, Bernard. 2002. *Democracy: A Very Short Introduction*. Oxford: Oxford University Press.

Critchley, Simon. 1998. The Other's Decision in Me (What Are the Politics of Friendship?). *European Journal of Social Theory* 1 (2):239–279.

———. 1999. *The Ethics of Deconstruction: Derrida and Levinas*. 2nd ed. West Lafayette, Ind.: Purdue University Press.

———. 2001. *Continental Philosophy: A Very Short Introduction*. Oxford: Oxford University Press.

———. 2004. The Problem of Hegemony. *Political Theory Daily Review*. http://www.politicaltheory.info/essays/critchley.htm.

———. 2007. *Infinitely Demanding: Ethics of Commitment, Politics of Resistance*. London: Verso.

———. 2009. Post-Deconstructive Subjectivity. In *Ethics, Politics, Subjectivity: Essays on Derrida, Levinas, and Contemporary French Thought*, edited by S. Critchley, 51–82. New York: Verso.

———. 2010. *How to Stop Living and Start Worrying*. Malden, Mass.: Polity Press.

Critchley, Simon, and Robert Bernasconi, eds. 2002. *The Cambridge Companion to Levinas*. Cambridge: Cambridge University Press.

Crosland, Anthony. 1963. *The Future of Socialism*. Abridged and rev. ed. New York: Schocken Books.

———. 1974. *Socialism Now and Other Essays*. London: Cape.

Dabback, William M. 2008. Identity Formation through Participation in the Rochester New Horizons Band Programme. *International Journal of Community Music* 1 (2):267–286.

Dadson, Philip, and Don McGlashan. 1990. *The From Scratch Rhythm Workbook*. Auckland, N.Z.: Heinemann Educational.

Davis, Christine S., and Carolyn Ellis. 2008. Emergent Methods in Autoethographic Research: Autoethnographic Narrative and the Multiethnographic Turn. In *Handbook of Emergent Methods*, edited by S. N. Hesse-Biber and P. Leavy, 283–302. New York: Guilford Press.

Davis, Martha E. 1992. Alternative Careers, and the Unity between Theory and Practice in Ethnomusicology. *Ethnomusicology* 36 (3):361–387.

de Beauvoir, Simone. 1993. *The Second Sex*. Translated by H. M. Parshley. New York: Alfred A. Knopf.

De Groot, Gerard J. 2008. *The Sixties Unplugged: A Kaleidoscopic History of a Disorderly Decade*. Cambridge, Mass.: Harvard University Press.

Deane, Kathryn. 1995. In Search of Peterborough. *Sounding Board* (Summer):12–15.

———. 1998. *Which Training?* Bury St Edmunds, Suffolk, U.K.: Sound Sense.

———. 1999. Making Change Work, Four-Year Plan, 2000/2001 to 2004/2005. Bury St Edmunds, Suffolk, U.K.: Sound Sense.

———. 2002. Let's Work Together. *Sounding Board* (Summer):15.

Debord, Guy. 1995. *The Society of the Spectacle*. Translated by D. Nicholson-Smith. 3rd ed. New York: Zone Books. Original edition, 1967.

———. 2009. *Correspondence: The Foundation of the Situationist International (June 1957–August 1960)*. Los Angeles, Calif.: Semiotext(e). Distributed by MIT Press.

Delanty, Gerard. 2003. *Community*. London: Routledge.

Deleuze, Gilles, and Félix Guattari. 1984. *Anti-Oedipus: Capitalism and Schizophrenia*. London: Athlone Press.

———. 1988a. 1837: Of the Refrain. In *A Thousand Plateaus: Capitalism and Schizophrenia*, 310–350. London: Continuum.

———. 1988b. Introduction: Rhizome. In *A Thousand Plateaus: Capitalism and Schizophrenia*, 3–25. London: Continuum.

Demaine, Jack, and Harold Entwistle. 1996. *Beyond Communitarianism: Citizenship, Politics, and Education*. New York: St. Martin's Press.

DeNora, Tia. 2000. *Music in Everyday Life*. Cambridge: Cambridge University Press.

Derrida, Jacques. 1973. *Speech and Phenomena and Other Essays on Husserl's Theory of Signs*. Translated by D. B. Allison and N. Garver. Evanston: Northwestern University Press.

———. 1978a. Structure, Sign, and Play in the Discourse of the Human Sciences. In *Writing and Difference*, 351–370. London: Routledge. Original edition, 1963.

———. 1978b. Violence and Metaphysics: An Essay on the Thought of Emmanuel Levinas. In *Writing and Difference*, 97–192. London: Routledge.

———. 1981a. *Dissemination*. Translated by B. Johnson. London: Athlone Press.

———. 1981b. *Positions*. Translated by A. Bass. London: Athlone Press.

———. 1982. Différance. In *Margins of Philosophy*, 1–27. Sussex, U.K.: Harvester Press.

———. 1985. *The Ear of the Other: Otobiography, Transference, Translation*. Translated by P. Kamuf. Edited by C. McDonald. New York: Schocken Books.

———. 1988. Afterwords: Towards An Ethic of Discussion. In *Limited Inc.*, 111–154. Evanston, Ill.: Northwestern University Press.

———. 1989. *Edmund Husserl's "Origin of Geometry": An Introduction by Jacques Derrida*. Translated by J. John P. Leavey. Lincoln: University of Nebraska Press.

———. 1991a. At This Very Moment in This Work Here I Am. In *Re-reading Levinas*, edited by R. Bernasconi and S. Critchley, 11–48. London: Athlone.

———. 1991b. Letter to a Japanese Friend. In *A Derrida Reader: Between the Blinds*, edited by P. Kamuf, 269–276. New York: Columbia University Press.

———. 1992. *Given Time: I. Counterfeit Money.* Translated by P. Kamuf. London: University of Chicago Press.

———. 1994. *Specters of Marx: The State of the Debt, the Work of Mourning, and the New International.* Translated by P. Kamuf. London: Routledge.

———. 1995a. *The Gift of Death.* Translated by D. Wills. London: University of Chicago Press.

———. 1995b. "A 'Madness' Must Watch Over Thinking." In *Points . . . Interviews, 1974–1994*, edited by E. Weber, 327–338. Stanford, Calif.: Stanford University Press.

———. 1995c. There Is No *One* Narcissism: (Autobiophotographies). In *Points . . . Interviews, 1974–1994*, edited by E. Weber, 196–215. Stanford, Calif.: Stanford University Press.

———. 1997a. *Of Grammatology.* Translated by G. C. Spivak. Baltimore: John Hopkins University Press.

———. 1997b. Politics and Friendship: A Discussion with Jacques Derrida. http://hydra.humanities.uci.edu/derrida/pol+fr.html.

———. 1997c. *Politics of Friendship.* Translated by G. Collins. London: Verso.

———. 1997d. The Villanova Roundtable. In *Deconstruction in a Nutshell: A Conversation with Jacques Derrida*, edited by J. D. Caputo, 1–28. New York: Fordham University Press.

———. 1999. *Adieu: To Emmanuel Levinas.* Translated by P.-A. Brault and M. Naas. Stanford, Calif.: Stanford University Press.

———. 2000. *Of Hospitality.* Translated by R. Bowlby. Stanford, Calif.: Stanford University Press.

———. 2001. *On Cosmopolitanism and Forgiveness.* Translated by M. Dooley and M. Hughes. London: Routledge.

———. 2002. Faith and Knowledge: The Two Sources of "Religion" at the Limits of Reason Alone. In *Acts of Religion*, edited by G. Anidjar, 42–101. London: Routledge.

———. 2005a. Epoché and Faith: An Interview with Jacque Derrida. In *Derrida and Religion: Other Testaments*, edited by Y. Sherwood and K. Hart, 27–50. New York: Routledge.

———. 2005b. *Rogues: Two Essays on Reason.* Translated by P.-A. Brault and M. Naas. Stanford, Calif.: Stanford University Press.

———. 2007. *Psyche: Inventions of the Other.* 2 vols. *Meridian, Crossing Aesthetics* (Series). Stanford, Calif.: Stanford University Press.

Dewey, John. 1916. *Democracy and Education: An Introduction to the Philosophy of Education.* New York: Macmillan.

———. 1997. *Experience and Education.* New York: Touchstone. Original edition, 1938.

Dick, Kirby, and Amy Ziering Kofman. 2002. Derrida: The Movie. New York: Jane Doe Films. Distributed by Zeitgeist Video.

Dickson, Malcolm, ed. 1995. *Art with People.* Sunderland, U.K.: AN.

Dillon, Steve, Barbara Adkins, Andrew Brown, and Kathy Hirche. 2008. Communities of Sound: Examining Meaningful Engagement with Generative Music Making and Virtual Ensembles. *International Journal of Community Music* 1 (3):357–374.

Donnan, Hastings, and Thomas M. Wilson. 2001. *Borders: Frontiers of Identity, Nation and State.* Oxford and New York: Berg.

Dooley, Mark, ed. 2003. *A Passion for the Impossible: John D. Caputo in Focus.* Albany: State University of New York.

Douglas, Tom. 2000. *Basic Group Work.* London: Routledge.

Drummond, John. 1991. The Community Musician: Training a New Professional. Paper read at ISME Commission on Community Music Activity, Oslo.

———. 2005. Cultural Diversity in Music Education: Why Bother? In *Cultural Diversity in Music Education: Directions and Challenges for the 21st Century*, edited by P. S. Campbell,

J. Drummond, P. Dunbar-Hall, K. Howard, H. Schippers, and T. Wiggins, 1–11. Brisbane: Australian Academic Press.

Duarte, Eduardo Manuel, and Stacy Smith, eds. 2000. *Foundational Perspectives in Multicultural Education.* New York: Longman.

Duelund, Peter. 2007. Nordic Cultural Policies, a Critical View. http://www.nordiskkulturin stitut.dk/pdf/nordic_cultural_policies_a_critical_view.pdf.

Durkheim, Emile. 1984. *The Division of Labor in Society.* 2nd ed. Translated by W. D. Halls. New York: Free Press.

Dykema, Peter W. 1934. Music in Community Life. *Music Supervisors' Journal* 20 (4): 34–74.

Eckstrom, Erika. 2008. Ukrainian Youth Development: Music and Creativity, a Route to Youth Betterment. *International Journal of Community Music* 1 (1):105–115.

Eilert, Grace O. 1940. The Music Educator and the Community. *Music Educators Journal* 27 (2):17–61.

Elliott, David J. 1989. Key Concepts in Multicultural Music Education. *International Journal of Music Education* 13:11–18.

———. 1995. *Music Matters: A New Philosophy of Music Education.* Oxford: Oxford University Press.

———. 1998. Community Music and Postmodernity. Paper presented at the Commission for Community Music Activity's conference, *Many Musics-One Circle,* chaired by B. Oehrle, Durban, South Africa.

———. 2001. Modernity, Postmodernity and Music Education Philosophy. *Research Studies in Music Education* 17:32–41.

Ellis, C., and A. P. Bochner. 2000. Autoethnography, Personal Narrative, Reflexivity: Researcher as Subject. In *Handbook of Qualitative Research,* edited by N. Denzin and Y. S. Lincoln, 733–768. Thousands Oaks, Calif.: Sage

Elrod, Pamela Gail. 2001. Vocal Music at Hull-House, 1889–1942: An Overview of Choral and Singing Class Events and a Study of the Life and Works of Eleanor Smith, Founder of the Hull-House Music School. Dissertation, University of Illinois at Urbana-Champaign, Illinois.

Emerson, Ralph Waldo. 1841. Friendship: An Essay. Hoboken, N.J.: BiblioBytes. http://www.emersoncentral.com/friendship.htm.

Erb, J. Lawrence. 1926. Music for a Better Community. *Musical Quarterly* 12 (3):441–448.

Ervin, Alexander M. 2004. *Applied Anthropology: Tools and Perspectives for Contemporary Practice.* 2nd ed. Upper Saddle River, N.J.: Pearson.

Eskola, Katarina, and Pauline Hammerton. 1983. *Thinking about Action: The Role of Research in Cultural Development.* Strasbourg: Council of Europe.

Esposito, Robert. 2010. *Communitas: The Origin and Destiny of Community.* Translated by T. Campbell. Stanford, Calif.: Stanford University Press.

Etzioni, Amitai, Drew Volmert, and Elanit Rothschild. 2004. *The Communitarian Reader: Beyond the Essentials.* Lanham, Md.: Rowman & Littlefield.

Everitt, Anthony. 1997. Joining In: An Investigation into Participatory Music. London: Calouste Gulbenkian Foundation.

Falck, Robert, Timothy Rice, and Mieczyslaw Kolinski. 1982. *Cross-Cultural Perspectives on Music.* Toronto and Buffalo: University of Toronto Press.

Fenn, John, ed. 2003. Applied Ethnomusicology. Special issue, *Folklore Forum* 34 (1–2).

Finley, Susan. 2003. Arts-Based Inquiry in QI: Seven Years from Crisis to Guerrilla Warfare. *Qualitative Inquiry* 9 (2):281–296.

———. 2005. Arts-Based Inquiry: Performing Revolutionary Pedagogy. In *The Sage Handbook of Qualitative Research,* edited by N. K. Denzin and Y. S. Lincoln, 681–694. London: Sage.

Finnegan, Ruth. 1989. *The Hidden Musician—Music-Making in an English Town.* Cambridge: Cambridge University Press.

Firth, Raymond William. 1963. *Elements of Social Organization.* 3rd ed. London: Watts.

Fletcher, Samantha 2007. "Good Works" with Benefits: Using Applied Ethnomusicology and Participatory Action Research in Benefit Concert Production at the Unitarian Church of Vancouver. Thesis, Memorial University of Newfoundland, Canada.

Folkestad, Göran. 2005. The Local and the Global in Musical Learning: Considering the Interaction between Formal and Informal Settings. In *Cultural Diversity in Music Education: Directions and Challenges for the 21st Century,* edited by P. S. Campbell, J. Drummond, P. Dunbar-Hall, K. Howard, H. Schippers, and T. Wiggins, 23–28. Brisbane: Australian Academic Press.

———. 2006. Formal and Informal Learning Situations or Practices vs Formal and Informal Ways of Learning. *British Journal of Music Education* 23 (2):135–145.

Ford, Simon. 2005. *The Situationist International: A User's Guide.* London: Black Dog.

Fox, Chistopher. 1999. Introduction to Community Music. In *Making Music Work,* 135–137. London: Royal College of Music.

Fox, John. 1992. *Eyes on Stalks.* London: Methuen Drama.

Freire, Paulo. 1985. *The Politics of Education: Culture, Power, and Liberation.* South Hadley, Mass.: Bergin & Garvey.

———. 2002. *Pedagogy of the Oppressed.* New York: Continuum. Original edition, 1970.

Freire, Paulo, and Antonio Faundez. 1989. *Learning to Question: A Pedagogy of Liberation.* New York: Continuum.

Friedman, Michael. 1972. *The New Left of the Sixties, Independent Socialist Clippingbook,.* Berkeley, Calif.: Independent Socialist Press.

Froehlich, Hildegard. 2008. Music Education and Community: Reflections on "Webs of Interaction" in School Music. *Action, Criticism, and Theory for Music Education* 8 (1).

Fukuyama, Francis 1992. *The End of History and the Last Man.* New York: Avon Books.

Funchess, Lloyd V. 1939. Community Music Project. *Music Educators Journal* 26 (1):36.

Gablik, Suzi. 1992. *The Reenchantment of Art.* London: Thames and Hudson.

Galton, Bridget. 1997. Sizzle to the Sound of the Samba Beat. *Evening Telegraph* (Peterborough, U.K.), October 24.

Gann, Lewis H., and Peter Duignan. 1995. *The New Left and the Cultural Revolution of the 1960's: A Reevaluation.* Stanford, Calif.: Hoover Institution on War, Revolution, and Peace, Stanford University.

Garafalo, Reebee. 2011. Not Your Parents' Marching Band: The History of HONK! Pedagogy and Music Education. *International Journal of Community Music* 4 (3):221–236.

Garratt, Steve. 2001. Cardiff Rap—Ghanaian Beats. *Sounding Board* (Winter):16.

Gay, Peter, ed. 1989. *The Freud Reader.* New York: W. W. Norton.

Gelder, Ken, and Sarah Thorntone, eds. 1997. *The Subcultures Reader.* London: Routledge.

Gerstin, Julian 1998. Reputation in a Musical Scene: The Everyday Context of Connections between Music, Identity and Politics. *Ethnomusicology* 42 (3):385–414.

Gibson, Margaret Alison. 1976. Approaches to Multicultural Education in the United States: Some Concepts and Assumptions. *Anthropology & Education Quarterly* 7 (4):7–18.

Gilbert, Bart-Moore, and John Seed. 1992. *Cultural Revolution? The Challenge of the Arts in the 1960s.* London: Routledge.

Gilbert, Jeremy. 2004. Becoming-Music: The Rhizomatic Moment of Improvisation. In *Deleuze and Music,* edited by I. Buchanan and M. Swiboda, 118–139. Edinburgh: Edinburgh University Press.

Giles, Steve, and Maike Oergel, eds. 2003. *Counter-cultures in Germany and Central Europe: From Sturm und Drang to Baader-Meinhof.* Oxford: Peter Lang.

Gilligan, Carol. 1982. *In a Different Voice: Psychological Theory and Women's Development.* Cambridge, Mass.: Harvard University Press.

Girard, Augustin. 1972. *Développement culturel: expérience et politiques.* Paris: Unesco.

Giroux, Henry A. 1993. *Living Dangerously: Multiculturalism and the Politics of Difference.* New York: P. Lang.

Goldbard, Arlene. 2006. *New Creative Community: The Art of Cultural Development.* Oakland: New Village Press.

Gonzalves, Theodore S. 2010. *The Day the Dancers Stayed: Performing in the Filipino/American Diaspora.* Philadelphia: Temple University Press.

Gosse, Van. 2005. *Rethinking the New Left: An Interpretative History.* New York: Palgrave Macmillan.

Gramsci, Antonio. 1988. *An Antonio Gramsci Reader: Selected Writings, 1916–1935.* Edited by D. Forgacs. New York: Schocken Books.

Grant, Carl A. 1977. Multicultural Education: What Does It Mean to Infuse It into a Discipline? *Multicultural Education: Commitments, Issues, and Applications.* Olympia, Wash.: Association for Supervision and Curriculum Development.

Grant, Carl A., and Christine E. Sleeter. 1992. Discipline-Based Art Education and Cultural Diversity: Seminar Proceedings, August 6–9, 1992, Austin, Texas.

Grant, David. 1993. *Playing the Wild Card: A Survey of Community Drama and Smaller-Scale Theatre from a Community Relation Perspective.* Belfast: Community Relation Council.

Graves, James Bau. 2005. *Cultural Democracy: The Arts, Community, and the Public.* New York: University of Ilinois Press.

Greater Peterborough Arts Council. 1978. *The Way Forward.* Peterborough: Greater Peterborough Arts Council.

Green, Jonathon. 1998. *All Dressed Up: The Sixties and the Counter-culture.* London: Jonathan Cape.

Green, Lucy. 2002. *How Popular Musicians Learn: A Way Ahead for Music Education.* Aldershot, U.K., and Burlington, Vt.: Ashgate.

———. 2008. *Music, Informal Learning and the School: A New Classroom Pedagogy.* Aldershot, U.K.: Ashgate.

———, ed. 2011. *Learning, Teaching, and Musical Identity: Voices across Cultures.* Bloomington: Indiana University Press.

Greene, Maxine. 2000. *Releasing the Imagination: Essays on Education, the Arts, and Social Change.* San Francisco: Jossey-Bass.

Gregory, Christopher A. 1982. *Gifts and Commodities.* London: Academic Press.

Guillermoprieto, Alma. 1991. *Samba.* New York: Departures.

Gutek, Gerald Lee, and Patricia Gutek. 1998. *Visiting Utopian Communities: A Guide to the Shakers, Moravians, and Others.* Columbia: University of South Carolina Press.

Guy, Nancy 1999. Governing the Arts, Governing the State: Peking Opera and Political Authority in Taiwan. *Ethnomusicology* 43 (3):508–526.

Hägglund, Martin. 2008. *Radical Atheism: Derrida and the Time of Life.* Stanford, Calif.: Stanford University Press.

Hallam, Susan, Andrea Creech, Clare Sandford, Tiija Rinta, and Katherine Shave. 2010. Survey of Musical Futures: A Report From Institute of Education, University of London for the Paul Hamlyn Foundation. London: Institute of Education, University of London.

Hamilton, Neil A. 1997. *The 1960s Counterculture in America.* Santa Barbara, Calif.: ABC-CLIO.

Hannerz, Ulf. 1996. *Transnational Connections: Culture, People, Places, Comedia.* London and New York: Routledge.

Hansen, Al. 1965. *A Primer of Happenings and Time/Space Art.* New York: Something Else Press.

Harrison, Gillian. 2010. Community Music in Australia. *International Journal of Community Music* 3 (3):337–342.

Hassan, Ihab. 1987. *The Postmodern Turn: Essays in Postmodern Theory and Culture.* Columbus: Ohio State University Press.

Hawkins, Gay. 1993. *From Nimbin to Mardi Gra: Constructing Community Arts.* St Leonards, N.S.W.: Allen & Unwin.

Heath, Deborah 1994. The Politics of Appropriateness and Appropriation: Recontextualizing Women's Dance in Urban Senegal. *American Ethnologist* 21 (1):88–103.

Hebdige, Dick 1981. *Subculture: The Meaning of Style.* London: Routledge.

Heidegger, Martin. 2002. *Being and Time.* Translated by J. Macquarrie and E. Robinson. Oxford: Blackwell.

Heifetz, Ronald A. 1994. *Leadership without Easy Answers.* Cambridge, Mass.: Belknap Press of Harvard University Press.

Held, David. 1989. *Models of Democracy.* 2nd ed. Stanford, Calif.: Stanford University Press.

Hemetek, Ursula. 2006. Applied Ethnomusicology in the Process of the Political Recognition of a Minority: A Case Study of the Austrian Roma. *Yearbook for Traditional Music* 38:35–57.

Hendricks, Jon, and Arthur Coleman Danto. 2002. *What's Fluxus? What's Not! Why = O que é Fluxus? O que não é! O porquê.* Rio de Janiero, Brazil: Centro Cultural Banco do Brasil; Detroit, Mich.: Gilbert and Lila Silverman Fluxus Collection Foundation.

Hennessy, Sarah. 2005. "Taiko SouthWest": Developing a "New" Musical Tradition in English Schools. *International Journal of Music Education* 23 (3):217–226.

Henrich, Dieter. 1994. The Concept of Moral Insight and Kant's Doctrine of the Fact of Reason. In *The Unity of Reason: Essays on Kant's Philosophy.* Cambridge, Mass.: Harvard Univeristy Press.

Henry, Ian, P. 1993. *The Politics of Leisure Policy.* London: Macmillan Press.

Herbert, Jonathan. 1997. Community Arts and Empowerment on the Beechdale Estate. In *Finding Voices, Making Choices,* edited by M. Webster, 12–17. Nottingham, U.K.: Educational Heretics Press.

Herbert, Trevor, ed. 2010. *The British Brass Band: A Musical and Social History.* London: Oxford University Press.

Hetrick, Harold F. 1941. Good Neighbors through Music. *Music Educators Journal* 27 (5): 30–32.

Higgins, Lee. 1998. Carnival Street Drumming: The Development and Survival of Community Percussion Ensembles in the UK. In *Ubuntu: Music Education for a Humane Society: Conference Proceedings of the 23rd World Conference of the International Society for Music Education, Pretoria, South Africa,* edited by C. Van Niekerk, 251–257. Pretoria, South Africa: ISME.

———. 2007a. Acts of Hospitality: The Community in Community Music. *Music Education Research* 9 (2):281–291.

———. 2007b. *The Impossible* Future. *Action, Criticism, and Theory for Music Education* 6 (3):74–96.

———. 2008. The Creative Music Workshop: Event, Facilitation, Gift. *International Journal of Music Education* 26 (4):326–338.

———, ed. 2000. *Community Music and New Technology: Conference Report and Reflections.* Liverpool: Mimic.

———. 2010. Representação de prática: música na comunidade e pesquisa baseada nas artes. *Revista de Associação Brasileira de Educação Musical* 23 (March):7–14.

Higgins, Lee, and Brydie-Leigh Bartleet. 2012. The Community Musician and School Music Education. In *The Oxford Handbook of Music Education,* edited by G. McPherson and G. F. Welch. New York: Oxford University Press.

Higgins, Lee, and Patricia Shehan Campbell. 2010. *Free to Be Musical: Group Improvisation in Music.* Lanham, Md.: Rowman & Littlefield.

Higham, Ben. 1994. *The Tale of the Tiger. Sounding Board* (Winter):25–26.

———. 1995. Professional Development. *Sounding Board* (Autumn):12.

Hill, Roger. 1993. *You Might Not Call It Singing.* London: Arts Council Print Unit.

Hiltunen, Mirja. 2008. Community-Based Art Education in the North: A Space for Agency? In *Art, Community and Environment: Educational Perspectives,* edited by G. Coutts and T. Jokela, 91–112. Bristol, U.K., and Chicago: Intellect.

Hogan, Christine. 2002. *Understanding Facilitation: Theory and Principles.* London: Kogan Page.

———. 2003. *Practical Facilitation: A Toolkit of Techniques.* London: Kogan Page.

hooks, bell. 1994. *Teaching to Transgress: Education as the Practice of Freedom.* New York: Routledge.

Howell, Gillian. 2010. "Do They Know They're Composing?": Music Making and Understanding among Newly-Arrived Immigrant and Refugee Children. In *CMA XII: Harmonizing the Diversity that Is Community Music Activity Proceedings from the International Society for Music Education 2010 Seminar of the Commission for Community Music Activity,* edited by D. D. Coffman, 35–38. Hangzhou, China: Open University of China.

Huq, Rupa. 2006. *Beyond Subculture: Pop, Youth and Identity in a Postcolonial World.* Abingdon, Oxon, U.K.: Routledge.

Hyde, Lewis. 1979. *The Gift: Imagination and the Erotic Life of Property.* New York: Vintage Books.

Iadeluca, Valentina, and Andrea Sangiorgio. 2008. Bambini al Centro: Music as a Means to Promote Wellbeing: Birth and Configuration of an Experience. *International Journal of Community Music* 1 (3):311–318.

Illich, Ivan. 1983. *Deschooling Society.* New York: Harper and Row. Original edition, 1970.

Impey, Angela. 2006. Culture, Conservation, and Community Reconstruction: Explorations in Advocacy Ethnomusicology and Participatory Action Research in Northern KwaZulu Natal. In *Ethnomusicology: A Contemporary Reader,* edited by J. C. Post, 401–411. New York: Routledge.

International Society for Music Education (ISME). 2002. *Community Music in the Modern Metropolis: Proceedings of the International Society for Music Education 2002 Seminar of the Commission on Community Music Activity.* Rotterdam: CDIME. http://www.cdime-network.com/cma/conference/021230175048483221.

Irigaray, Luce. 1993. The Fecundity of the Caress: A Reading of Levinas, *Totality and Infinity,* "Phenomenology of Eros." In *An Ethics of Sexual Difference,* 185–217. Ithaca, N.Y.: Cornell University Press.

Isserman, Maurice. 1987. *If I Had a Hammer . . .: The Death of the Old Left and the Birth of the New Left.* New York: Basic Books.

Jaffurs, Sherri E. 2004a. Developing Musically: Formal and Informal Practices. *Action, Criticism, and Theory for Music Education* 3 (3):2–17.

———. 2004b. The Impact of Informal Music Learning Practices in the Classroom, or How I Learned How to Teach from a Garage Band. *International Journal of Music Education* (22):189–200.

Johnson, Barbara 1981. Translator's Introduction. In *Dissemination.,* vii–xxxiii. London: Athlone Press.

Jones, Patrick. 2009. Lifewide as Well as Lifelong: Broadening Primary and Secondary School Music Education's Service to Students' Musical Needs. *International Journal of Community Music* 2 (2&3):201–214.

Jones, Stacy Holman. 2005. Autoethnography: Making the Personal Political. In *The Sage Handbook of Qualitative Research*, edited by N. K. Denzin and Y. S. Lincoln, 763–791. London: Sage.

Jorgensen, Estelle R. 1995. Music Education as Community. *Journal of Aesthetic Education* 29 (3):71–84.

Joss, Tim. 1993. A Short History of Community Music. In *The First National Directory of Community Music*, edited by T. Joss and D. Price, 3–8. Bury St Edmonds, Suffolk, U.K.: Sound Sense.

Joss, Tim, and Dave Price, eds. 1993. *The First National Directory of Community Music*. Bury St Edmonds, Suffolk, U.K.: Sound Sense.

Kant, Immanuel. 1964. *Groundwork of the Metaphysic of Morals*. Translated by H. J. Paton. New York: Harper and Row.

———. 1998. *Critique of Pure Reason*. Translated by P. Guyer and A. W. Wood. Cambridge: Cambridge University Press.

Kaplan, Max. 1954. The Social Role of the Amateur. *Music Educators Journal* 40 (4):26–28.

———. 1956. Music, Community and Social Change. *Music Educators Journal* 43 (2):47–49.

———. 1958. *Music in the Community: A Report by the Music in American Life Commission, Music in the Community*. Music Educators' National Conference, Washington, D.C.

Karlsen, Sidsel, and Heidi Westerlund. 2010. Immigrant Students' Development of Musical Agency—Exploring Democracy in Music Education. *British Journal of Music Education* 27 (3):225–239.

Karpf, Juanita. 1999. The Vocal Teacher of Ten Thousand: E. Azalia Hackley as Community Music Educator, 1910–22. *Journal of Research in Music Education* 47 (4):319–330.

———. 2011. For Their Musical Uplift: Emma Azalia Hackley and Voice Culture in African American Communities. *International Journal of Community Music* 4(3): 237–256.

Katsiaficas, George N. 1987. *The Imagination of the New Left: A Global Analysis of 1968*. Boston, Mass.: South End Press.

Kaye, Nick. 2000. *Site-Specific Art: Performance, Place, and Documentation*. London and New York: Routledge.

Keane, John. 2009. *The Life and Death of Democracy*. New York: W. W. Norton.

Keil, Charles 1982. Applied Ethnomusicology and a Rebirth of Music from the Spirit of Tragedy. *Ethnomusicology* 26 (3):407–411.

Keil, Charles, and Steven Feld. 1994. *Music Grooves*. Chicago: University of Chicago Press.

Keith, Mary. 1992. NVQ's and the Community Musician. *Sounding Board* (Autumn):12.

Kelly, Owen. 1984. *Community, Art and the State*. London: Comedia.

Kennedy, Mary C. 2009. The Gettin' Higher Choir: Exploring Culture, Teaching and Learning in a Community Chorus. *International Journal of Community Music* 2 (2&3):183–200.

Kernerman, Gerald P. 2005. *Multicultural Nationalism: Civilizing Difference, Constituting Community*. Vancouver: UBC Press.

Kershaw, Baz. 1992. *The Politics of Performance, Radical Theatre as Cultural Intervention*. London: Routledge.

Kirby, Michael. 1965. *Happenings: An Illustrated Anthology*. New York: E. P. Dutton.

Koopman, Constantijn. 2007. Community Music as Music Education: On the Educational Potential of Community Music. *International Journal of Music Education* 25 (2):151–163.

Kors, Ninja, and Huib Schippers. 2003. Sound Links: From Policy to Practice—Cultural Diversity in Ten Easy Steps. Rotterdam: Academy of Music and Dance.

Kramer, Lawrence. 1995. *Classical Music and Postmodern Knowledge*. London: University of California Press.

Krikun, Andrew. 2010. Community Music during the New Deal: The Contributions of Willem Van de Wall and Max Kaplan. *International Journal of Community Music* 3 (2): 165–174.

Kruse, Nathan. 2009. "An Elusive Bird": Perceptions of Music Learning among Canadian and American Adults. *International Journal of Community Music* 2 (2):215–225.

Kushner, Saville, Barbara Walker, and Jane Tarr. 2001. *Case Studies and Issues in Community Music.* Bristol: University of the West of England.

Kwon, Miwon. 2002. *One Place after Another: Site-Specific Art and Locational Identity.* Cambridge, Mass.: MIT Press.

Lambert, Bruce 1993. Obituaries: Rachel D. DuBois, 101, Educator Who Promoted Value of Diversity. *New York Times,* April 1.

Landry, Charles, David Morley, Russell Southwood, and Patrick Wright. 1985. *What a Way to Run a Railroad: An Analysis of Radical Failure.* Stroud, U.K.: Comedia.

Lane, John. 1978. *Arts Centres: Every Town Should Have One.* London: Paul Elek.

Lave, Jean, and Etienne Wenger. 1991. *Situated Learning: Legitimate Peripheral Participation.* New York: Cambridge University Press.

Laycock, Jolyon. 2005. *A Changing Role for the Composer in Society: A Study of the Historical Background in Current Methodologies of Creative Music-Making.* Oxford: Peter Lang.

Leavy, Patricia, ed. 2009. *Method Meets Art: Arts Based Research Practice.* New York: Guilford Press.

Leglar, Mary A., ed. 1996. The Role of Community Music in a Changing World. *Proceedings of the International Society for Music Education 1994 Seminar of the Commission on Community Music Activity.* Athens: University of Georgia.

Leglar, Mary A., and David S. Smith. 2010. Community Music in the United States: An Overview of Origins and Evolution. *International Journal of Community Music* 3 (3):343–353.

Lehman, Edward W. 2000. *Autonomy and Order: A Communitarian Anthology.* Lanham, Md.: Rowman & Littlefield.

Leppmann, Kevin. 2010. Origins and Evolution of the HONK! Festival. *Harmonic Dissidents* (2). http://www.harmonicdissidents.org/archive/in-issue-2/.

Lévi-Strauss, Claude. 1969. *The Elementary Structures of Kinship.* Boston: Beacon Press.

Levinas, Emmanuel. 1969. *Totality and Infinity: An Essay on Exteriority.* Translated by A. Lingis. Pittsburgh: Duquesne University Press.

———. 1981. *Otherwise than Being or Beyond Essence.* Translated by A. Lingis. The Hague: Martinus Nijhoff.

———. 1984. Dialogue with Emmanuel Levinas. In *Dialogues with Contemporary Continental Thinkers: The Phenomenological Heritage: Paul Ricoeur, Emmanuel Levinas, Herbert Marcuse, Stanislas Breton, Jacques Derrida,* edited by R. Kearney, 47–70. Manchester: Manchester University Press.

———. 1985. *Ethics and Infinity: Conversations with Philippe Nemo.* Translated by R. A. Cohen. Pittsburgh: Duquesne University Press.

———. 1989. Ethics as First Philosophy. In *The Levinas Reader,* edited by S. Hand, 75–87. Oxford: Basil Blackwell.

———. 1991. Wholly Otherwise. In *Re-reading Levinas,* edited by R. Bernasconi and S. Critchley, 3–10. Bloomington and Indianapolis: Indiana University Press.

———. 1996. Transcendence and Height. In *Basic Philosophical Writings,* edited by S. C. Adriaan T. Peperzak, and Robert Bernasconi, 11–31. Bloomington: Indiana University Press. Original edition, 1962.

———. 2001. *Existence and Existents.* Pittsburgh: Duquesne University Press.

———. 2004. On Buber. In *Levinas and Buber: Dialogue and Difference,* edited by P. Atterton, M. Calarco, and M. Friedman. 32–34. Pittsburgh: Duquesne University Press.

———. 2006. *Humanism of the Other*. Translated by N. Poller. Urbana: University of Illinois Press.

Levy, Peter B. 1994. *The New Left and Labor in the 1960s*. Urbana and Chicago: University of Ilinois Press.

Lewis, C. S. 1960. *The Four Loves*. London: G. Bles.

Lombos, Gavin. 1998. Finding the Community in Youth Music Projects. *Sounding Board* (Autumn):12–13.

Long, Priscilla, ed. 1969. *The New Left*. Boston: Extending Horizons Books.

Long, Richard. 1997. *A Walk across England: A Walk of 382 Miles in 11 Days from the West Coast to the East Coast of England*. New York: Thames and Hudson.

Loughran, Maureen E. 2008. Community Powered Resistance: Radio, Music Scenes and Musical Activism in Washington, D.C. Dissertation, Brown University.

Lynch, Sandra. 2005. *Philosophy and Frriendship*. Edinburgh: Edinburgh University Press.

Lyons, Paul. 1996. *New Left, New Right, and the Legacy of the Sixties*. Philadelphia: Temple University Press.

Lyotard, Jean-François. 1988. *The Differend: Phases in Dispute*. Manchester, U.K.: Manchester University Press.

———. 1991. *The Inhuman: Reflections on Time*. Translated by G. Bennington and R. Bowlby. Cambridge, U.K.: Polity Press.

Macdonald, Irene. 1994. Comment. *Sounding Board* (Spring):24.

———. 1995. The Leiston Statement. *Sounding Board* (Spring):29.

Maehl, William H. 2000. *Lifelong Learning at Its Best*. San Francisco: Jossey-Bass.

Malpas, Simon. 2003. *Jean-François Lyotard*. London: Routledge.

Manor, Harold C. 1945. Community Music Program. *Music Educators Journal* 32 (1):40.

Mantie, Roger, and Lynn Tucker. 2008. Closing the Gap: Does Music-Making Have to Stop upon Graduation? *International Journal of Community Music* 1 (2):217–227.

Marcuse, Herbert. 1991. *One-Dimensional Man*. London: Routledge.

Mark, Michael L. 1996. Informal Learning and Adult Music Activities. In *Qualitative Methodologies in Music Education Research Conference II: Selected Papers*. Special issue, Bulletin of the Council for Research in Music Education (130):119–122

Maróthy, János. 1974. *Music and the Bourgeois, Music and the Proletarian*. Budapest: Akadémiai Kiadó.

Marwick, Arthur. 1998. *The Sixties: Cultural Revolution in Britain, France, Italy, and the United States, c. 1958–c. 1974*. Oxford and New York: Oxford University Press.

Masefield, Patrick. 1986. The Arts Ahead: Proposals for the Development of the Arts in Peterborough. Commissioned by Peterborough City Council, Peterborough Development Corporation, Eastern Arts Association.

Matarasso, François. 1994. *Use or Ornament? The Social Impact of Participation*. Stroud, Gloucestershire, U.K.: Comedia.

Matsuoka, Atsuko Karin, and John Sorenson. 2001. *Ghosts and Shadows: Construction of Identity and Community in an African Diaspora*. Toronto: University of Toronto Press.

Mattson, Kevin. 2002. *Intellectuals in Action: The Origins of the New Left and Radical Liberalism, 1945–1970*. University Park: Pennsylvania State University Press.

Mauss, Marcel. 1990. *The Gift*. Translated by W. D. Hall. London: Routledge. Original edition, 1924.

May, Elizabeth. 1983. *Musics of Many Cultures: An Introduction*. Berkeley: University of California Press.

McCance, Dawne. 2009. *Derrida on Religion: Thinker of Differance*. Oakville, Conn.: Equinox.

McCarthy, Marie. 1999. *Passing It On: The Transmission of Music in Irish Culture*. Cork: Cork University Press.

————. 2004. *Toward a Global Community: The International Society for Music Education 1953–2003.* Nedlands, Western Australia: International Society for Music Education.

————. 2008. The Community Music Activity Commission of ISME 1982–2007: A Forum for Global Dialogue and Institutional Formation. *International Journal of Community Music* 1 (1):49–61.

————, ed. 1996. *Cross Currents: Setting an Agenda for Music Education in Community Culture.* College Park: University of Maryland.

McClary, Susan. 2007. *Reading Music: Selected Essays.* Farnham, Surrey, U.K.: Ashgate.

McKay, George. 2005. Improvisation and the Development of Community Music in Britain. In *Community Music: A Handbook,* edited by P. Moser and G. McKay, 61–76. Lyme Regis: Russell House.

McKay, George, and Ben Higham. 2011. *Community Music: History and Current Practice, Its Construction of "Community," Digital Turns and Future Soundings.* Swindon, U.K.: Arts and Humanities Research Council.

McKinzie, Richard D. 1973. *The New Deal for Artists.* Princeton, N.J.: Princeton University Press.

McNiff, Jean, and Jack Whitehead. 2002. *Action Research: Principles and Practice.* 2nd ed. London: Routledge Falmer.

McNiff, Shaun. 2008. Art-Based Research. In *Handbook of the Arts in Qualitative Research,* edited by J. G. Knowles and A. L. Cole, 29–40. London: Sage.

Medhurst, Andy. 1999. What Did I Get? Punk, Memory and Autobiography. In *Punk Rock: So What? The Cultural Legacy of Punk,* edited by R. Sabin, 219–231. London: Routledge.

Mellor, Liz. 2011. What Is "Known" in Community Music in Higher Education? Engagement, Emotional Learning and an Ecology of Ideas from the Student Perspective. *International Journal of Community Music* 4 (3): 257–275.

Merriam, Alan P. 1964. *The Anthropology of Music.* Evanston, Ill.: Northwestern University Press.

Milner, Martin. 2007. Giving People Back to Themselves. *Sounding Board* (Summer): 9

Montaigne, Michel de. 1948. Of Friendship. In *The Complete Works of Montaigne: Essays, Travel Journals, Letters,* 135–144. London: Hamish Hamilton.

Montessori, Maria. 1912. *The Montessori Method.* New York: Frederick A. Stokes. http://digital. library.upenn.edu/women/montessori/method/method.html.

Moran, Nikki, and Gica Loening. 2011. Community Music Knowledge Exchange Research in Scottish Higher Education. *International Journal of Community Music* 4 (2):133–146.

Morris, William. 1962. *Art, Labour, and Socialism: With a Modern Assessment.* London: Socialist Party of Great Britain. Original edition, 1884, 1907.

Moser, Pete. 1994. Approaches to Composition. *Sounding Board* (Spring):15.

———— 2010. Eighteen Years of More Music. In *CMA XII: Harmonizing the Diversity that Is Community Music Activity, Proceedings from the International Society for Music Education 2010 Seminar of the Commission for Community Music Activity,* edited by D. D. Coffman, 71–75. Hangzhou, China: Open University of China.

Moser, Pete, and George McKay. 2005. *Community Music: A Handbook.* Lyme Regis, Dorset, U.K.: Russell House.

Muir, Pauline. 1992. "Get Organised!" *Sounding Board* (Autumn):22.

Mulhall, Stephen. 1996. *Heidegger and Being and Time.* London: Routledge.

Mullen, Bill. 1999. *Popular Fronts: Chicago and African-American Cultural Politics, 1935–46.* Urbana: University of Illinois Press.

Myers, David E. 2008. Freeing Music Education from Schooling: Toward a Lifespan Perspective on Music Learning and Teaching. *International Journal of Community Music* 1 (1):49–61.

Nagle, John 2008. Multiculturalism's Double Bind: Creating Inclusivity, Difference and Cross-Community Alliances with the London-Irish. *Ethnicities* 8 (2):177–198.

Naidus, Beverly. 2009. *Arts for Change: Teaching outside the Frame.* Oakland, Calif.: New Village Press.

Najam, Adil. 2006. *Portrait of a Giving Community: Philanthropy by the Pakistani-American Diaspora, Studies in Global Equity.* Cambridge, Mass.: Global Equity Initiative, Asia Center, Harvard University.

Nancy, Jean-Luc. 1991. *The Inoperative Community.* Edited by P. Conner. Minneapolis: University of Minnesota Press.

Nannucci, Maurizio. 1995. *Fluxus Anthology: A Collection of Music and Sound Events* [sound recording]. Anthology Records, CD 7393.

Neate, Patrick, and Damian Platt. 2010. *Culture Is Our Weapon: Making Music and Changing Lives in Rio de Janeiro.* New York: Penguin.

Nehamas, Alexander. 2008. On Friendship [Podcast]. http://philosophybites.com/2008/10/alexander-neham.html.

Nettl, Bruno. 2002. *Encounters in Ethnomusicology: A Memoir.* Warren, Mich.: Harmonie Park Press.

Neumark, Victoria. 1989. *The Magic Exercise.* Darlington, Durham, U.K.: Parkgate Press.

Nicholls, Derek. 1985. Education in Arts Centres. Darlington, Durham, U.K.: National Association of Arts Centres.

Nicholson, Helen. 2005. *Applied Drama: The Gift of Theatre.* Basingstoke, Hampshire, U.K.: Palgrave MacMillan.

Nietzsche, Friedrich. 1969. *Thus Spoke Zarathustra.* Translated by R. J. Hollingdale. Harmondsworth, U.K.: Penguin Books.

Noddings, Nel. 1992. *The Challenge to Care in Schools: An Alternative Approach to Education, Advances in Contemporary Educational Thought Series.* New York: Teachers College Press.

———. 2002. *Educating Moral People: A Caring Alternative to Character Education.* New York: Teachers College Press.

Noddings, Nel, and Paul J. Shore. 1984. *Awakening the Inner Eye: Intuition in Education.* New York: Teachers College Press.

Nordoff, Paul, and Clive Robbins. 1971. *Therapy in Music for Handicapped Children.* New York: St. Martin's Press.

———. 1977. *Creative Music Therapy: Individualized Treatment for the Handicapped Child.* New York: John Day.

Normann, Theodore F. 1939. Community Projects in Music. *Music Educators Journal* 25 (5): 33–84.

Norris, Christopher. 1992. *Uncritical Theory: Postmodernism, Intellectuals and the Gulf War.* London: Lawrence and Wishart.

Norton, William W. 1931. School Music and Community Culture. *Music Supervisors' Journal* 17 (4):64.

O'Grady, Lucy, and Katrina McFerran. 2007. Uniting the Work of Community Musicians and Music Therapists through the Health-Care Continuum: A Grounded Theory Analysis. *Australian Journal of Music Therapy* 18:62–86.

Olseng, Ingrid, and John Burley. 1987. The Second Chance. *International Journal of Music Education* 9:27–30.

Olsson, Bengt, and Kari Veblen. 2002. Community Music: Toward an International Overview. In *The New Handbook of Research on Music Teaching and Learning,* edited by R. Colwell and C. Richardson, 730–753. New York: Oxford University Press.

Olthuis, James H. 2000. *Towards an Ethics of Community Negotiations of Difference in a Pluralist Society, Comparative Ethics Series 5.* Waterloo, Ont.: Canadian Corporation for Studies in Religion.

Owen, Nick. 1995. An Honours Degree in Community Arts. *Sounding Board* (Spring):16.

Pakaluk, Michael, ed. 1991. *Other Selves: Philosophers on Friendship*. Hackett.

Paton, Rod. 2000. *Living Music: Improvisation Guidelines for Teachers and Community Musicians.* Chichester, West Sussex, U.K.: West Sussex County Council.

———. 2011. Lifemusic: Sounding Out University Community Engagement. *International Journal of Community Music* 4 (2):105–120.

Patton, Paul, and John Protevi, eds. 2003. *Between Deleuze and Derrida*. London: Continuum.

Paynter, John. 1982. *Music in the Secondary School Curriculum*. Cambridge: Cambridge University Press.

———. 1992. *Sound and Structure*. Cambridge: Cambridge University Press.

Peggie, Andrew. 1993. Musicians Go to School. *Sounding Board* (Spring):25.

———. 1997. *Musicians Go to School*. London: London Arts Board.

———. 1998. Getting to the Art. *Sounding Board* (Winter):10–12.

———. 2003. Let's Take the C-word out of Community Music. *Sounding Board* (Autumn):9.

Perry, Laura B. 2005. Education for Democracy: Some Basic Definitions, Concepts, and Clarifications. In *International Handbook on Globalisation, Education and Policy Research*, edited by J. Zajda, 685–692. Dordrecht, The Netherlands: Springer Press.

Perry, Mark. 2000. *Sniffin' Glue and Other Rock 'n' Roll Habits: The Catalogue of Chaos, 1976–1977*. London: Sanctuary.

Pettan, Svanibor. 2010. Applied Ethnomusicology: Bridging Research and Action. *Music and Arts in Action* 2 (2):90–93.

———, ed. 1998. *Music, Politics, and War: Views from Croatia*. Zagreb, Croatia: Institute of Ethnology and Folklore Research.

Pettan, Svanibor, Klisala Harrison, and Eric Usner. 2007. New ICTM Study Group on Applied Ethnomusicology First Meeting: Historical and Emerging Approaches to Applied Ethnomusicology. Ljublijana, Slovenia: International Council for Traditional Music.

Pettersen, Tove. 2008. *Comprehending Care: Problems and Possibilities in the Ethics of Care.* Lanham, Md.: Lexington Books.

Phelan, Helen. 2007. "Let Us Say Yes . . ." Music, the Stranger and Hospitality. *Public Voices* 9 (1):113–124.

Phipps, Alison, and Ronald Barnett. 2007. Academic Hospitality. *Arts and Humanities in Higher Education* 6 (3):237–254.

Pitt, Peter. 1986. *Campaign for a Popular Culture: A Record of Struggle and Achievement; The GLC's Community Arts Programme 1981–1986*. London: Greater London Arts Council.

Pitts, Stephanie. 2000. *A Century of Change in Music Education: Historical Perspectives on Contemporary Practice in British Secondary School Music*. Hampshire, U.K.: Ashgate.

———. 2009. Roots and Routes in Adult Musical Participation: Investigating the Impact of Home and School on Lifelong Musical Interest and Involvement. *British Journal of Music Education* 26 (3):241–256.

Plant, Bob. 2005. *Wittgenstein and Levinas: Ethical and Religious Thought*. New York: Routledge.

Post, Jennifer C. 2006. *Ethnomusicology: A Contemporary Reader*. New York: Routledge.

Powell, Harriet. 2004. A Dream Wedding: From Community Music to Music Therapy with a Community. In *Community Music Therapy*, edited by M. Pavlicevic and G. Ansdell, 167–185. London: Jessica Kingsley.

Pratte, Richard. 1979. *Pluralism in Education: Conflict, Clarity, and Commitment* Springfield, Ill.: Thomas.

Price, David, and Abigail D'Amore. 2007. Musical Futures: From Vision to Practice. London: Paul Hamlyn Foundation.

Procter, Simon. 2001. Empowering and Enabling: Improvisational Music Therapy in Non-medical Mental Health Provision. *Voices: A World Forum for Music Therapy* 1 (2).

————. 2004. Playing Politics: Community Music Therapy and the Therapeutic Redistribution of Musical Captial for Mental Health. In *Community Music Therapy*, edited by M. Pavlicevic and G. Ansdell, 214–230. London: Jessica Kingsley.

Ramnarine, Tina K. 2008. Beyond the Academy. In *The New (Ethno)musicologies*, edited by H. Stobart, 83–94. Lanham, Md.: Scarecrow Press.

Ramsey, Martha, and Ramsey, Duane. 1933. The Settlement Music School. *Music Supervisors' Journal* 19 (5):21–34.

Randell, Nick, and Simon Myhill. 1989. Kaleidoscope: Art Work that Works. Leicester, U.K.: Youth Clubs UK.

Rapport, Nigel, and Joanna Overing. 2000. *Social and Cultural Anthropology: The Key Concepts.* London: Routledge.

Readings, Bill. 1991. *Introducing Lyotard: Art and Politics.* London: Routledge.

Reed-Danahay, Deborah. 2001. Autobiography, Intimacy and Ethnography. In *Handbook of Ethnography*, edited by P. Atkinson, A. Coffey, S. Delamont, J. Lofland, and L. Lofland, 407–425. London: Sage.

Reese, William J. 2001. The Origins of Progressive Education. *History of Education Quarterly* 41 (1):1–24.

Rendle, Adrian. 1968. *Everyman and His Theatre.* London: Pitman.

Renshaw, Peter. 2005. Simply Connect: "Next Practice" in Group Music Making and Musical Leadership. London: Paul Hamlyn Foundation.

Ricoeur, Paul. 1992. *Oneself as Another.* Chicago: University of Chicago Press.

Rigney, Ann, and Douwe Fokkema, eds. 1993. *Cultural Participation: Trends since the Middle Ages.* Amsterdam and Philadelphia: John Benjamins.

Rogers, Carl. R. 1951. *Client-Centered Counseling.* Boston: Houghton-Mifflin.

————. 1994. *Freedom to Learn.* 3rd ed. New York: Macmillan College. Original edition, 1969.

Rousseau, Jean Jacques. 1993. *The Social Contract and Discourses.* London: Everyman.

Rohwer, Debbie. 2011. Community Music as a Part of Higher Education: Decisions from a Department Chair/Researcher. *International Journal of Community Music* 4 (2): 121–131.

Rowher, Debbie, and Mark Rowher. 2009. A Content Analysis of Choral Students' Participation Perceptions: Implications for Lifelong Learning. *International Journal of Community Music* 2 (2&3):255–262.

Rowland, John. 1973. *Community Decay.* Middlesex: Penguin.

Rupp, George. 2006. *Globalization Challenged: Conviction, Conflict, Community, University Seminars/Leonard Hastings Schoff Memorial Lectures.* New York: Columbia University Press.

Russell, Dave. 1987. *Popular Music in England 1840–1914.* Montreal: McGill-Queen's University.

Rutherford, Jonathan, ed. 1990. *Identity: Community, Culture, Difference.* London: Lawrence and Wishart.

Ruud, Even. 2004. Reclaiming Music. In *Community Music Therapy*, edited by M. Pavlicevic and G. Ansdell, 11–14. London: Jessica Kingsley.

————. 2010. *Music Therapy: A Perspectice from the Humanities.* Gilsum, N.H.: Barcelona.

Saal, Ilka. 2007. *New Deal Theater: The Vernacular Tradition in American Political Theater.* New York: Palgrave Macmillan.

Sabin, Roger, ed. 1999. *Punk Rock: So What? The Cultural Legacy of Punk.* London: Routledge.

Sahlins, Marshall David. 1974. *Stone Age Economics.* New York: Aldine.

Sandbank, Graciela. 2006. Community Music in the Rehabilitation of Younsters at Risk. In *ISME: Creating Partnerships, Making Links, and Promoting Change*, edited by D. Coffman and L. Higgins, 122–127. Singapore: International Society for Music Education.

Sandford, Mariellen R., ed. 1995. *Happenings and Other Acts*. New York: Routledge.

Sault, Robert E. 1944. Integrating School Music with Community Life. *Music Educators Journal* 31 (2):20–22.

Saunders, Frances Stonor. 2000. *The Cultural Cold War: The CIA and the World of Arts and Letters*. New York: New Press.

Savage, Jon. 1991. *England's Dreaming: Sex Pistols and Punk Rock*. London: Faber and Faber.

Schafer, R. Murray. 1975. *The Rhinoceros in the Classroom*. Wien, Austria: Universal Edition.

———. 1976. *Creative Music Education: A Handbook for the Modern Music Teacher*. New York: Schirmer Books.

———. 1992. *A Sound Education*. Ontario: Arcana Editions.

Schein, Edgar H. 1998. *Process Consultation Revisited: Building the Helping Relationship*. Boston, Mass.: Addison Wesley.

Schippers, Huib. 2003. SoundLinks. Rotterdam: CDIME.

———. 2009. *Facing the Music: Shaping Music Education from a Global Perspective*. New York: Oxford University Press.

Schrift, Alan D. 1997. *The Logic of the Gift: Toward an Ethic of Generosity*. New York: Routledge.

Seeger, Anthony. 1992. Ethnomusicology and Music Law. *Ethnomusicology* 36 (3):345–359.

———. 2008. Theories Forged in the Crucible of Action: The Joys, Dangers, and Potentials of Advocacy and Fieldwork. In *Shadows in the Field: New Perspectives for Fieldwork in Ethnomusicology*, 2nd ed., edited by G. F. Barz and T. J. Cooley. 271–288. Oxford and New York: Oxford University Press.

Self, George. 1976. *New Sounds in Class: A Contemporary Approach to Music*. London: Universal Editions.

Sennett, Richard. 2008. *The Craftsman*. New Haven, Conn.: Yale University Press.

Sheehy, Daniel. 1992. A Few Notions about Philosophy and Strategy in Applied Ethnomusicology. *Ethnomusicology* 36 (3):323–336.

Shelemay, Kay Kaufman. 2001. *Soundscapes: Exploring Music in a Changing World*. New York: W. W. Norton.

Shelton Trust, the. 1986. *The Manifesto: Another Standard, Culture and Democracy*. Stroud, Gloucestershire, U.K.: Comedia.

Shieh, Eric. 2010. On Punishment and Music Education: Towards a Practice for Prisons and Schools. *International Journal of Community Music* 3 (1):19–32.

Silber, Laya 2005. Bars behind Bars: The Impact of a Women's Prison Choir on Social Harmony. *Music Education Research* 7 (2):251–271.

Sim, Stuart. 1999. *Derrida and the End of History*. Cambridge: Icon Books.

———, ed. 2001. *The Routledge Companion to Postmodernism*. 2nd ed. New York: Routledge.

Sleeter, Christine E. 1996. *Multicultural Education as Social Activism, SUNY Series, the Social Context of Education*. Albany: State University of New York Press.

———. 2005. *Un-standardizing Curriculum: Multicultural Teaching in the Standards-Based Classroom, Multicultural Education Series*. New York: Teacher College Press.

———, ed. 1991. *Empowerment through Multicultural Education*. Albany: State University of New York Press.

Small, Christopher. 1987. *Music of the Common Tongue: Survival and Celebration in Afro-American Music*. London: J. Calder; New York: Riverrun Press.

———. 1996. *Music, Society, Education*. London: Wesleyan University Press. Original edition, 1977.

———. 1998. *Musicking: The Meanings of Performance and Listening*. London: Wesleyan University Press.

Smilde, Rineke. 2008. Lifelong Learners in Music; Research into Musicians' Biographical Learning. *International Journal of Community Music* 1 (2):243–252.

————. 2009. *Musicians as Lifelong Learners: Discovery Through Biography*. Delft, The Netherlands: Eburon Academic.

Smith, Mark K. 2002. *Malcolm Knowles, Informal Adult Education, Self-Direction and Anadragogy*. http://www.infed.org/thinkers/et-knowl.htm.

————. 2004. *Carl Rogers, Core Conditions and Education*. http://www.infed.org/thinkers/et-rogers.htm.

Smith, Matt. 2008. PickleHerring and Marlsite Projects: An Interdisciplinary Approach to Junk Music-Making. *International Journal of Community Music* 1 (2):159–168.

Söderman, Johan, and Göran Folkestad. 2004. How Hip-Hop Musicians Learn: Strategies in Informal Creative Music Making. *Music Education Research* 6 (3):313–326.

Solbu, Einar. 1987. Adults and Musical Involvement. *International Journal of Music Education* 9:23–25.

Sound Sense. 1994. Training Round-Up. *Sounding Board* (Spring):16.

————. 1998. *What Is Community Music?* Bury St Edmonds, Suffolk, U.K.: Sound Sense.

————. 2000. *Making a Difference with Music*. Bury St Edmonds, Suffolk, U.K.: Sound Sense.

Southcott, Jane E. 2009. "And as I Go, I Love to Sing": The Happy Wanderers, Music and Positive Aging. *International Journal of Community Music* 2 (2&3):143–156.

Spafford, Peter. 1997. Beat behind Bars. *Sounding Board* (Summer):14–15.

Spruce, Gary. 2002. Ways of Thinking about Music: Political Dimensions and Educational Consequences. In *Teaching Music in Secondary Schools: A Reader*, 3–24. London: Routledge-Falmer.

Spry, Tami. 2001. Performing Autoethnography: An Embodied Methodological Praxis. *Qualitative Inquiry* 7 (6):706–732.

Stevens, John. 1985. *Search and Reflect*. London: Community Music.

————. 2007. *Search and Reflect*. 2nd ed. London: Rockschool.

Stige, Brynjulf. 2004. Community Music Therapy: Culture, Care and Welfare. In *Community Music Therapy*, edited by M. Pavlicevic and G. Ansdell, 91–113. London: Jessica Kingsley.

Stige, Brynjulf, Gary Ansdell, Cochavit Elefant, and Mercédès Pavlicevic. 2010. *Where Music Helps: Community Music Therapy in Action and Reflection*. Farnham, Surrey, U.K.: Ashgate.

Stock, Jonathan P. J. 2008. New Directions in Ethnomusicology: Seven Themes toward Disciplinary Renewal. In *The New (Ethno)musicologies*, edited by H. Stobart, 188–206. Lanham, Md.: Scarecrow Press.

Stokes, Martin, ed. 1994. *Ethnicity, Identity and Music: The Musical Construction of Place*. Oxford: Berg.

Stone, Brad Lowell. 2000. *Robert Nisbet: Communitarian Traditionalist, Library of Modern Thinkers*. Wilmington, Del.: ISI Books.

Sugarman, Jane C. 1999. Imagining the Homeland: Poetry, Songs, and the Discourses of Albanian Nationalism. *Ethnomusicology* 43 (3):419–458.

Swingler, Tim. 1993. Comment. *Sounding Board* (Autumn):32.

Taylor, Dorothy A. 1987. The Adult Learner and Music: A British Perspective. *International Journal of Music Education* 9 (1):31–32.

Taylor, Jill McLean, Carol Gilligan, and Amy M. Sullivan. 1995. *Between Voice and Silence: Women and Girls, Race and Relationship*. Cambridge, Mass: Harvard University Press.

Taylor, Philip. 2003. *Applied Theatre: Creating Transformative Encounters in the Community*. Portsmouth, N.H.: Heinemann.

Telford Community Arts. 1984. *Telford Community Arts: A Report on the Period May 1983 to April 1984*. Telford, Shropshire, U.K.: Community Arts Telford.

Teodori, Massimo, ed. 1969. *The New Left: A Documentary History*. Indianapolis: Bobbs-Merill.

Titon, Jeff Todd, ed. 1984. *Worlds of Music: An Introduction to the Music of the World's Peoples.* New York: Schirmer Books; London: Collier Macmillan.

———. 1992. Music, the Public Interest, and the Practice of Ethnomusicology. *Ethnomusicology* 36 (3):315–321.

———. 2003. Textual Analysis or Thick Description? In *The Cultural Study of Music,* edited by M. Clayton, T. Herbert, and R. Middleton, 171–180. London: Routledge.

Tönnies, Ferdinand. 2001. *Community and Civil Society.* Edited by J. Harris. *Cambridge Texts in the History of Political Thought.* Cambridge and New York: Cambridge University Press.

Treanor, Brian. 2006. *Aspects of Alterity: Levinas, Marcel, and the Contemporary Debate.* New York: Fordham University Press.

Turner, Victor W. 1969. *The Ritual Process: Structure and Anti-Structure* Chicago: Aldine.

Valøen, Nils. 1987. Adult Music Education in Norway. *International Journal of Music Education* 9:34–36.

van Buren, Kathleen. 2010. Applied Ethnomusicology and HIV and AIDS: Responsibiliy, Ability, and Action. *Ethnomusicology* 54 (2):202–223.

van Buren, Tom. 2003. Working Together: Music Research in Collaboration. *Folklore Forum* 34 (1&2):61–77.

van Erven, Eugene. 2001. *Community Theatre, Global Perspectives.* London: Routledge.

Vattimo, Gianni. 1999. *Belief.* Cambridge: Polity Press.

Veblen, Kari. 2005. Community Music and Praxialism: Narratives and Reflections. In *Praxial Music Education: Reflections and Dialogues,* edited by D. J. Elliott, 308–328. New York: Oxford University Press.

———. 2008a. The Many Ways of Community Music. *International Journal of Community Music* 1 (1):5–21.

———. 2008b. Regional Initiative 2: European Community Music Gathering London, UK 2007. *International Journal of Community Music* 1 (2):288–290.

Veblen, Kari, Stephen J. Messenger, Marissa Silverman, and David J. Elliott, eds. 2012. *Community Music Today.* Landham, Md.: Rowman and Littlefield.

Vernon, Mark. 2007. *The Philosophy of Friendship.* Basingstoke, Hampshire, U.K.: Palgrave MacMillan.

Vickers, George. 1975. *The Formation of the New Left: The Early Years.* Lexington, Mass.: Lexington Books.

Viénet, René. 1992. *Enragés and Situationists in the Occupation Movement, France, May '68.* Brooklyn, N.Y.: Autonomedia; London: Rebel Press.

Vila, Pablo. 2005. *Border Identifications: Narratives of Religion, Gender, and Class on the U.S.– Mexico Border.* Austin: University of Texas Press.

Vincent, Andrew. 2002. *Nationalism and Particularity.* Cambridge and New York: Cambridge University Press.

Volk, Terese M. 1998. *Music, Education, and Multiculturalism: Foundations and Principles.* New York: Oxford University Press.

Vulliamy, Graham, and Edward Lee. 1982. *Pop, Rock and Ethnic Music in School, Resources of Music.* Cambridge and New York: Cambridge University Press.

Watson, Louise. 2003. *Lifelong Learning in Australia.* Canberra: Department of Education, Science and Training.

Weber, Max. 1947. *The Theory of Social and Economic Organization.* New York: Oxford University Press.

———. 1978. *Economy and Society: Vol 1.* Edited by G. Roth and C. Wittich. London: University of California Press.

Webster, Mark, ed. 1997. *Finding Voices, Making Choices.* Bramcote, Nottingham, U.K.: Educational Heretics Press.

Webster, Peter. 1996. Creativity as Creative Thinking. In *Teaching Music,* edited by G. Spruce, 87–97. London: Open University.

Westerlund, Heidi. 2008. Justifying Music Education: A View from Here-and-Now Value Experience. *Philosophy of Music Education Review* 16 (1):79–95.

Whitaker, Dorothy Stock. 2000. *Using Groups to Help People.* London: Routledge.

Wiggins, Trevor. 2005. Cultivating Shadows in Field? Challenges for Traditions in Institutional Contexts. In *Cultural Diversity in Music Education: Directions and Challenges for the 21st Century,* edited by P. S. Campbell, J. Drummond, P. Dunbar-Hall, K. Howard, H. Schippers, and T. Wiggins, 13–22. Brisbane: Australian Academic Press.

Williams, Colin H., and Eleonore Kofman. 1989. *Community Conflict, Partition and Nationalism.* New York: Routledge.

Williams, Raymond. 1985. *Keywords: A Vocabulary of Culture and Society.* Rev. ed. New York: Oxford University Press.

Wilson, Thomas M., and Hastings Donnan. 1998. *Border Identities: Nation and State at International Frontiers.* Cambridge and New York: Cambridge University Press.

Wolheim, Bruno. 1998. *Culture Makes Communities.* York, U.K.: Joseph Rowntree Foundation.

Wood, Stuart, Rachel Verney, and Jessica Atkinson. 2004. From Therapy to Community: Making Music in Neurological Rehabilitation. In *Community Music Therapy,* edited by M. Pavlicevic and G. Ansdell, 48–62. London: Jessica Kingsley.

Woodford, Paul G. 2005. *Democracy and Music Education: Liberalism, Ethics, and the Politics of Practice.* Bloomington: Indiana University Press.

Wortham, Simon Morgan. 2010. *The Derrida Dictionary.* New York: Continuum.

Wright, Ruth, and Panagiotis Kanellopoulos. 2010. Informal Music Learning, Improvisation and Teacher Education. *British Journal of Educational Studies* 27 (1):71–87.

Zanzig, Augustus Delafield. 1930. Richer Uses of Music as Recreation. *Music Supervisors' Journal* 16 (4):27–33.

———. 1932. *Music in American Life: Present and Future.* Edited by N. R. Association. New York: Oxford University Press.

Zilversmit, Arthur.1993. Changing Schools: Progressive Education Thoery and Practice, 1930-1960. Chicago: University of Chicago Press.

Žižek, Slavoj. 2001. *On Belief, Thinking in Action.* London and New York: Routledge.

INDEX

CPSIA information can be obtained
at www.ICGtesting.com
Printed in the USA
BVHW032124031120
592373BV00009B/2